COMMUNICATION AT WORK

Management and the Communication-Intensive Organization

STEPHEN R. AXLEY

Q

QUORUM BOOKS
Westport, Connecticut • London

Library of Congress Cataloging-in-Publication Data

Axley, Stephen R.
 Communication at work : management and the communication-intensive
organization / Stephen R. Axley.
  p. cm.
 Includes bibliographical references (p.   ) and index.
 ISBN 0–89930–913–5 (alk. paper)
 1. Communication in management. I. Title.
 HD30.3.A95 1996
 658.4′5—dc20   95–34540

British Library Cataloguing in Publication Data is available.

Library of Congress Catalog Card Number: 95–34540
ISBN: 0–89930–913–5

First published in 1996

Quorum Books, 88 Post Road West, Westport, CT 06881
An imprint of Greenwood Publishing Group, Inc.

Printed in the United States of America

The paper used in this book complies with the
Permanent Paper Standard issued by the National
Information Standards Organization (Z39.48–1984).

10 9 8 7 6 5 4 3 2 1

Copyright Acknowledgments

The author and publisher gratefully acknowledge permission for use of the following material:

Excerpts from "Sexual Harassment: What to Do," by Anne B. Fisher, from *Fortune*, August 23, 1993.
© 1993 Time Inc. All rights reserved. Reprinted with permission.

"Listening Self-Inventory," by E. Glenn and E. Pood. Reprinted, by permission of publisher, from
Supervisory Management, January/1989. © 1989 American Management Association, New York. All
rights reserved.

To Carmen and our children, Amanda and Jackson, my parents, Jack and Jane, and my brothers, Bob, Jim, David, Don—for love, life, and laughter. To Herb and Elizabeth, for so many kinds of generosity. To Charles, for lessons. And to the poet who showed the way onward.

Contents

Preface

This book explores what it means to "talk about things." Talking about things takes us outside ourselves, stretching the tethers of our consciousness as far as words will take us. Talking about things brings others nearer so that they may share some of our hopes, our laughter, our fears, our dreams, our *selves*—as near as words can bring them. In an important sense, talking about things, in one form or another, is the only way that we humans can accomplish *anything* of lasting value. Talking about things, in this sense, is *the* thing. Everything. All we have.

Things are the way they are, and what they are, because of the way we talk about them. This includes the subject and practice of human communication. An important thesis in this book is that the very act of opening our mouths on the subject of communication can embed subtle yet compelling "lessons" about communicating that seriously reduce our effectiveness as communicators. An additional important thesis is that many of today's most pressing organizational and management challenges—leadership, empowerment, shaping organizational culture, building effective teams, and managing change—hinge on communication activities, and can best be understood and met in terms of communication and communicating. Overarching the entire discussion is the premise that most people and most managers seriously underestimate just how much *hard work* it is to communicate effectively, and that that perspective keeps them from being effective communicators—which, for managers, means that they'll consequently be ineffective at leadership, empowerment, shaping organizational culture, building effective teams, and managing change.

All of this stems in large part from the way we "talk about things," especially communication. This book approaches communication in ways that will challenge many of the most taken-for-granted—and mistaken—assumptions that people hold about the subject. When we're done, I hope you'll look at the power of words—of "talking about things"—differently than before.

Acknowledgments

This book would not have been possible without the patient and unflagging support of my wife, Carmen, and our children, Amanda and Jackson. I am forever intellectually and professionally indebted to the late W. Charles Redding, whose brilliance illuminated and inspired so many lives—and will continue to do so, I am sure. And I thank two colleagues, both seasoned managers, who critiqued early drafts of the manuscript: Paul R. Craig, whose ongoing intellectual "boosts" have always come at just the right time; who truly knows what it means to "talk about things," and can, about almost anything, with great sensitivity, insight, and humor. And James D. Elmer, whose patient listening as a sounding board and candid observations as a critic helped me to stay centered around the needs of managers. I must also thank Don Burks, who long ago introduced me to someone whose thinking we both so admire. And finally, my parents, Jack and Jane Axley, and brothers Bob, Jim, David, and Don, have always supported and amazed me by their words and deeds—and inspired so many of mine. The people mentioned here have only helped me, but sad to say, they could only do so much. Any flaws in my thinking and character evident in this book were assuredly impervious to their good attentions, and, I'm afraid, are probably beyond redemption.

Now—let's talk about things.

Chapter 1

Management and Communication

> Communication is the most important skill in life.
>
> Stephen R. Covey

COMMUNICATION, PEOPLE, WATER, FISH

The setting is an organizational training facility. About 30 managers are present for the first of a series of seminars on "Managerial Communication." After introductions, the very first thing the trainer does is proclaim to the group, "Communication is to people as water is to fish!" Accompanying that statement, he places a transparency with the exact same words, typed in big, bold, all-capitalized letters, on an overhead projector for everyone to see:

COMMUNICATION IS TO PEOPLE AS WATER IS TO FISH!

He stands there scanning the group in silence for a few seconds, and then points to the statement, asking: "What do you think about that—in the next 30 seconds, would you jot down your first reaction?" (If you were there, what would your first reaction be?) Among the participants, there are a few nods of heads, some quizzical looks, a few furrowed brows, and several smiles and chuckles at the request. Despite the press of time—they really do get only 30 seconds—everyone writes something. After that, the trainer collects and then reads the anonymous reactions aloud to the group. They basically verbalize some of those facial expressions and actions observed as the assignment was made. There's acknowledgment and support: "We can learn something about communication by looking at the relation of water to fish." There's puzzlement and confusion: "Worded like a law of nature, but what's it mean?" There's concern and maybe impatience: "Communication, people, water, fish—strange way of starting out." And there's amusement and maybe satire: "Some icebreaker!" Most of the written comments echo these themes.

I've been the trainer in this example many, many times. The reactions that managers have to my opening "pronouncement" and subsequent request always provide a useful point of departure for several fundamental ideas about human communication. In fact, their reactions invariably "demonstrate" a number of qualities of human communication that, no doubt, many of us recognize, but that very many of us seriously underestimate the importance of to our working and personal lives. Three of these qualities of communication are:

1. We actively *make sense* out of "what" people say. The people demonstrating this take the main ideas of the opening statement and start right in working on them, looking to learn something about communication from the relation of water to fish ("We can learn something about communication . . .").
2. We actively *make sense* out of "how" people say something. The people demonstrating this seem to attend mostly to the forceful and certain "tone" of the oral statement, reinforced by the big, bold, all-capitalized lettering on the transparency ("Worded like a law of nature . . .").
3. We actively *make sense* out of "acts" themselves in various contexts, as much as what people say and how they say it. The people demonstrating this evaluate the "act" itself of making such a statement, maybe coupled with the request, in the context of the very first event of a training session ("Strange way of starting out" and "Some icebreaker!").

There are several larger points to be made in all of this. The common element in the three preceding qualities of communication, and one important purpose behind describing that recurrent training episode, was to suggest that people constantly and actively assign message value to, or make sense of, an incredible number of things: what we say, how we say it, merely the fact that we say something, the context of what we say, anything we do (behaviors) or don't do, any activities, events, objects, and situational elements (space, time, etc.) in our sphere of awareness, etc. Quite literally, we all spend a sizable amount of our time striving to make sense of the things around us. What's more, the "sense making" is more or less unique to the specific individuals involved. Please notice the connotation here: "making sense" is an active term—we determine and create what has message value for us individually, and as *perceivers*, we determine and create actual messages. No doubt to many people, this won't seem all that novel or complicated an idea at first glance. But fully appreciating its ramifications for communication and communicating is much harder and more complex than most people realize. It's also one of the keys to becoming a more effective communicator. This book explores those ramifications and sensitizes people to their importance.

That opening training episode provides us a useful beginning for other reasons, too. Throughout this book, numerous cases, anecdotes, brief exercises, and "stories" are drawn upon not only to introduce certain topics or raise questions, but also to demonstrate something at issue on the subject of communication. Many cases and stories from my professional years as a trainer are included for their relevance and value to understanding communication. More often than not, the approach taken will be "inductive," because my experience as an educator and an organizational consultant shows me that the right kind of "particulars" can reveal important and lasting insights of general applicability. The "communication, people, water, fish" episode has the potential to do exactly this, in revealing those three qualities of human communication mentioned above—which, not incidentally, play prominently in the remainder of this book, as they already have. But it's the nature of communication that you'll be the one to determine what each case or exercise *really* means. Although direction will be given, sometimes it will be left entirely to you and the relevant chapter to interpret or create the most important "lessons" from certain stories.

There is one more "layer" of purpose to that opening training episode to discuss because it concerns much of the rest of this book. It pertains to the sentence that started it all: "Communication is to people as water is to fish." Truthfully, that sentence holds a number of valuable insights about communication. One is indirect and subtle, having more to do with the *type* of statement that it is, than with the specific words or subjects of the statement itself. In general, this type of statement is representative of a family of linguistic forms—technically, "tropes"—which basically attempt to acquaint us with one subject by referring to another. The idea here is that we can learn about the relationship of communication to people by looking carefully at other relationships. And although we'll leave "water and fish" behind momentarily, in this book we'll see that the general form of this type of thinking—understanding "A" in terms of "B"—is not just a way of gaining perspective on something, but actually a pervasive, subtle, and compelling determinant of how we come to develop our individual working definitions of "communication" and other important concepts.

But before we abandon that opening sentence, let's look at a brief demonstration of the idea introduced above. Just what kind of perspective can we get on "communication and people" by looking at "water and fish?" How are the two relationships similar? Here are a few basic qualities about the world of water and fish that can illuminate the world of communication and people.

Temperature. Water temperature can be warm, cold, and in between. And as any successful fisherman knows, water temperature affects fish behavior in a number of ways, including aggressiveness, appetite and feeding patterns, physical depth positioning, metabolism, even reproductive cycles. Can "temperature" apply to communication? Can communication be "warm"? What qualities make it that way? Can it be "cold"? What qualities make it that way? How does the "temperature" of communication affect people and relationships? How do people react to warm and cold communication? Have you ever experienced someone's "icy stare" or a "warm manner"?   How did the "temperature" of that communication affect you? Let's try another.

Clarity. Water can be murky, crystal clear, or somewhere in between. What accounts for murkiness or clarity in water? What is the value of each condition to fish? Does it depend on whether we're talking about "predator" fish, "bottom feeders," or "bait" fish? Does murky water benefit some fish more than others? Is clear water the ideal environment? How does clarity affect survival? "Clarity" obviously applies easily to communication, but in extending the water imagery, we still might get some novel but useful questions. What accounts for murkiness or clarity in communication? Does murkiness serve the interests of some people or professions more than others? Does clarity? Is clear communication always the ideal? Does communication clarity have survival value? Have you ever experienced someone's "muddy thinking" or "clear-headedness"? How did the "clarity" of that communication affect you?

Content. There's more to water than just hydrogen and oxygen. Water contains all sorts of other stuff: nutrients, minerals, various chemicals, pollutants, and the like, that fish don't necessarily see, but that nevertheless affect them profoundly. About the content of water we might ask, what's the quality of the water? Is it basically life-supportive or destructive? What are the long-term effects of living in it and ingesting it? Which qualities make the water beneficial for fish? Which make it harmful? What about the "content" of communication? Can communication be toxic? What are the long-term effects of living in such an environment? Can communication be life-supportive or destructive? What qualities of communication make it beneficial for people? Harmful?

Containment. The water that fish live in is contained by all manner of natural and artificial "containers." Some are as deep, as diverse in underwater topography, and as spread out as ocean beds, and others, as shallow, uniform, and localized as a basic goldfish bowl. How does the depth and expanse of water affect fish? Do fish use the depths and the shallows for different purposes? Which are more hazardous, the depths or the shallows? And what about the container? Besides depth and expanse, can't the container itself affect such things as water content, clarity, and temperature? Can communication be "deep," "shallow," "narrow," "broad"? What do we use to "channel" or "contain" communication? Which channels allow depth of communication? Breadth? Which ones promote shallow communication? Is shallow communication safer than deep communication? Does the channel limit or affect communication content, clarity, and how warm or cold the communication is?

That's the basic idea: we can alter and shape our perspective on something by examining it as though it were something else. In the next chapter, we're going to exploit the power and versatility of this tool to get some perspective on the subject of communication as well as several other topics. But we're not done here just yet. Throughout this section on communication, people, water, and fish, we've had mainly one objective in sight. It concerns one feature of the fish's watery world that, when extended to communication, has some extremely far-reaching and serious implications. It is so obvious and so simple, yet its implications are exceedingly subtle and complex.

Environment. At the risk of making the early going here seem more like a "statement" about fish and water than about people and communication, I am yet reminded of something once heard on the subject of fish behavior: "the last thing a fish discovers is water." This statement has great relevance here, and is in keeping with the notion of actively *making sense* of the world.

In terms of just the sensing processes involved, it figures that water itself would be low on the list of attention-getters for fish. Objects in the water? Yes, obvious and immediate survival value there. But the water itself as an object of attention? Not likely, partly for the same reason that right now you're not worrying much about whatever it is that comprises the space between this page and your eyes. Water is like that for the fish: its constancy, immediacy, and sheer "everywhereness" render it virtually imperceptible, simply a "given" of existence. The other reason is that there's no "something else"—no comparison environment—to make the watery nature of the fish's own environment stand out.

A homegrown example can easily show this last point. When you were a kid, do you remember "discovering" that your family had "ways" of doing things that differed from the customs of your friends' families? Take mealtimes, for instance. At one friend's house, meals were a free-for-all of noisy but serious discussion of any subject under the sun, and included both children and grown-ups. At another's, chit-chat was the main discourse for adults, and children were better seen than heard. Or as another example, do you remember discovering how families celebrated the same religious holiday differently? For some, religious and family themes and traditions dominated these times. For others, the most visible themes were basically leisure- and consumption-oriented. Nearly everyone has had these eye-opening experiences. In each case our experiences with another environment gave us perspective and greater understanding of— helped us discover—our own. Does this sound familiar? We're back to "understanding A in terms of B." The fish isn't likely to pay much attention to water because water is contextual, and because there's no frame of reference other than water for the fish. Simply put, it's very easy for fish to take water for granted, even though their existence depends on it.

And how does this relate to communication? *"Communication is to people as water is to fish."* We've seen how certain qualities of water such as "temperature," "clarity," "content," and "containment" can help us begin asking questions about communication that, first, we might not ask otherwise and, second, might stimulate useful insights about communication. None of these comparisons, however, carries more serious implications than the "environmental" nature of water to fish and communication to people.

Like water to the fish, we live our lives in an environment of communication events, where sense-making and our attempts to share the sense we make are necessary and constant. On a daily basis, communication plays an essential role in most people's lives. Whether we're giving directions to a passing motorist or to a "911" dispatcher, whether we're listening to our child talk about how she got an "owie" or to a friend explain why his marriage is ending, whether we're asking for a refund on a defective toaster or for more responsibility in our job, whether we're griping to the boss about our subordinates or to our subordinates about the boss, whether we're ordering the filet medium rare or our kids to clean their rooms, whether we're recognizing our children's accomplishments or only their shortcomings, whether we're explaining our absence from somewhere we should have been or our presence at somewhere we shouldn't, whether we're attentive to what's going on in our kids' lives or to what's going on with the couple next door, whether we're struggling with the "some assembly required" instructions or with understanding a troubled teenager, whether we're seen as hard working or as hardly working—all of these fundamentally involve communication. In fact, communication is so much a commonplace and part of the context of our lives that, like water to the fish, it loses its attention-getting value for most people. Until, that is, something happens to call attention to it, as everyone has experienced—like misunderstandings that cost time, money, emotions, misspent energy, or worse; or unintended "messages" that others somehow get from the things we say, do, don't say, or don't do, and so on; or home and work relationships that aren't what they need to be. Then we're reminded of most people's dependence on communication in some way, hour to hour, day to day.

The exquisite irony of all of this needs to be made explicit: the human world is made up largely of communication-oriented activities and events. In purely practical terms, we literally could not survive, let alone get that promotion, steal the sign from the third-base coach, say "I love you," or order Chinese take-out without communication. Even our very "humanness"—that which distinguishes us from other life forms—is defined importantly by our advanced ability to create and manipulate symbols (natural "spoken" languages, mathematical languages, computer languages, musical languages, behavioral languages, etc.), enabling us to create the human world as we know it. And we "know" it, of course, only because of communication. So communication is definitely a very big deal in the course of human history, accomplishment, and just everyday living.

So why, then, aren't we any better at it than we are? Why do problems stemming ultimately from communication practices cost organizations millions of dollars annually? Why aren't we better at anticipating the potential for communication screw-ups in our organizations and in our relationships? Why are we so easily and frequently "surprised" when an "autopsy" of an organizational, relational, or personal problem reveals that communication did the victim in (*if* we even attempt an explanation)? Why does the pepperoni and mushroom pizza we asked for arrive looking very much like black olives and anchovies?

My personal and professional experiences have shown that human communication is probably the most taken-for-granted, misunderstood, underdeveloped, and misused attribute that we humans have. Over the course of this book I hope to show why this is the case, what its consequences are, and what we can do about it.

COMMUNICATION IN ORGANIZATIONS

Among all the noteworthy developments and advances of the twentieth century, possibly none is as important yet underrecognized as the rise of the modern organization. Consider the scope and depth of our dependencies, direct and indirect, past and present, personal and professional, on organizations: How are we delivered into this world? Out of it? In between, how are we schooled? How do we provide for ourselves? How many hours of each day do we spend in the employ of some organization, or interacting with organizations? What are the sources of our automobiles, stereos, TVs, microwave ovens, washing machines, personal computers, telephones, medications, food, clothing, newspapers, news, books, furniture, houses, buildings, airplanes, airports, and cities? Organizations. It's no exaggeration to say that the world stripped of the artifacts and influences of our organizations would be incomprehensibly different.

Most people rely utterly on organizations for their livelihood and for the goods and services that organizations provide. Nowhere is dependence on communication more visible, essential, and consequential than in today's organizations. The very notion of "organization" as the coordinated activities of people toward the accomplishment of goals implies the essentiality of communication to the "practice" of organization.

So much of what's important in organizations has an essential dependence on communication activities and processes. As you read the following seven short cases, consider where communication plays a role and evaluate its influence in what goes on.

A DIFFERENT KIND OF MANAGER

In an article entitled "An Easygoing Boss—And a Master Motivator," Ann Therese Palmer (1993) profiles a man named Sam Rivera, who, upon becoming an assistant foreman for a successful auto parts supplier, decided "that I was going to be a different kind of manager" (p. 84).

And indeed, a different kind of manager is what he's apparently become: "Instead of acting dictatorially, Rivera tries to place himself in his employees' shoes. He gives his workers plenty of flexibility and discretion. 'As long as the job gets done, that's the bottom line,' he says. And 95% of the time, according to Rivera and the company, Rivera's unit exceeds its objectives" (p. 84).

According to Palmer, Rivera's workers say that his approach to management motivates them "to go the extra mile" (p. 84). One of them, whom Rivera had helped with a family crisis, expressed his gratitude in ideas adopted for improving performance and safety, and puts it this way: "People work harder in the department because of the way Sam is," and, "He makes you feel comfortable on the job." (Palmer, 1993, p. 84)

Where does communication fit into this case? How does Sam Rivera "do" the management style portrayed? How do others recognize it, "make sense" of it, and respond to it? Does it have message value for them? What seem to be the consequences of his management style? How does it benefit his organization and the people who report to him?

THE NEW VINYL

Jim and Sally Anderson were replacing the floor vinyl in their kitchen. On the day the vinyl was to be installed, a two-person crew showed up to do the job: Mike, a man of about 30 or so, accompanied by a boy who appeared to be somewhere between 12 and 13 years old. The job of laying the vinyl was physically challenging. There were two 30- by 6-foot runs of heavy vinyl to handle, each as one piece, with each one requiring cutting to fit it around doors, corners, kitchen cabinets, and into closets and a pantry. While the job was in progress, the Andersons noticed that the boy who came along with Mike was given full responsibility to lay his share of the vinyl. In other words, he wasn't just helping Mike do the job, but was doing the same things Mike was doing.

Later, after the vinyl had been laid and the installers were gone, the Andersons discovered several tears and small punctures in the vinyl. Two tears were especially obvious, although only one was in a high-traffic location where it was likely to be seen. That one had been glued makeshift and raggedly in an apparent attempt to repair it, but it was still quite visible from some distance.

Jim Anderson called Bob, the owner of the store where the vinyl had been purchased, to describe what they had found. Somewhere in the conversation, Jim wondered if other customers ever had any "surprise" at such a young boy doing a job like this. Bob said that the boy was actually 15, but very small for his age. Although the boy's real age was some consolation, circumstances surrounding the tears were still troubling. Bob said that they could relatively easily replace the torn or punctured spots with patches and that the Andersons would never know the difference. Jim wondered out loud whether anyone would have ever disclosed the tears and punctures if he hadn't called about them, because it seemed that the Andersons had to "discover" them before the proper repairs were even offered. (All names are disguised. Printed by permission of the author, whose name has been withheld by request.)

Besides the obvious communication taking place between the customer and the store owner, are there other dimensions of communication at work here? If you were in the customers' shoes, would the "young boy" installer have had message value for you? In view of the job he was performing and the cost of more than $2000, would his presence "mean" anything special to the customers? And what about the customers' discovery of the tears, knowing that someone was aware of at least one of them—having glued it—and that nothing about the proper repairs was brought up until *the customer* raised the issue? Does that have message value? There's more on this case.

REPAIRING THE NEW VINYL

Mike came back to repair the vinyl, this time with a burly 19- to 20-year-old helper. After patching all but one of the flaws, Mike went to work on some carpet elsewhere in the house, leaving his helper to "fix" the last spot, a small puncture in a high-traffic area of the floor. The young helper explained to the Andersons that instead of replacing the square with a new patch of vinyl, he was going to fill the hole with a putty-like substance, and that the putty would bond with the vinyl, dry as hard as cement, and wear like it too. He said that that would probably work as a permanent solution, but that if the customers weren't satisfied later, to call and a patch would be put in instead. The Andersons accepted that explanation.

The next morning Jim was looking closely at the spot that had been puttied. With just a little bit of rubbing, and hardly any pressure or abrasion from his hand, most of the dried putty popped right out of the hole it had filled.

He called Bob the store owner and recounted what he had been told about the putty probably being a permanent "fix," and how it had popped out without ever seeing any foot traffic at all. He told Bob that the repair was only cosmetic, disguising rather than fixing the real problem. Bob listened, and told Jim that they would be back out to fix the spot. Jim expressed disappointment and frustration that all of this had taken up so much of everyone's time and energy when it could have been done so differently from the beginning.

Later that day Jim Anderson got a call from Mike, the installer. Mike had just been verbally blasted by the store owner as a result of Jim's call. Mike, in turn, had just done the same to his helper.

This latest episode was a product of the communication and several assumptions that took place between Mike and his helper, and between them and the Andersons, when the installers were making the repairs: Before Mike's helper repaired the last spot, Mike told him that it was just a temporary measure to seal the hole until it could be repaired with a patch on another day (it was late afternoon and they were needed for an emergency job elsewhere, and there wasn't enough time to make and fit the last patch). Mike assumed that that's what his helper conveyed to the Andersons. For whatever reason, however, the helper told the customers that the putty would probably work permanently, with no mention that Mike was coming back to patch the spot. The customers assumed that the helper spoke for Mike, and that the putty-as-permanent repair carried Mike's "endorsement," which made it all the more maddening when the putty popped so easily out of the hole the very next day. And thinking that the Andersons knew the putty was temporary, Mike was all the more surprised by Jim's call to the owner complaining that the installers were trying to conceal rather than fix the problem.

What happened here? What role did communication play in the mistaken assumptions that helped create this frustrating situation? If you were in the customers' position, would the putty popping out so easily the very next day have had any message value for you?

THE MAN IN THE ICE CREAM STORE

Dan loved ice cream. A shopping center that he frequented was getting a new retail outlet for a nationally known gourmet ice cream brand. With great anticipation, Dan looked forward to the opening of the store. Finally a day arrived when, on his almost-daily reconnaissance of the site, he saw three or four passenger cars rather than the usual contractor trucks parked outside the store. That there still was window paper preventing passers-by from actually looking into the store was hardly a deterrent. It looked very much to Dan like they were either open or about to open. He wanted to see, firsthand.

He tried the door. Locked. But as he turned to leave, a casually dressed silver-haired man opened the door and invited him in. Inside, there were two or three trainees receiving serving instructions from a couple of people in street clothes. The man who opened the door explained that indeed the store wasn't open yet, but that that didn't matter—he wanted his visitor to taste the product. Under the glass counter were ten or twelve different ice creams, sherbets, and sorbets, and the man insisted that Dan try servings of any of them, free of charge.

For the next half-hour or so, Dan sampled any number of frozen yummies, while the nice man grilled him on his opinion of this flavor, that flavor, the texture of this flavor, the appearance of that one, prices the store would be asking, its layout, colors and appearance, location, whether Dan liked the major local competitor's products, how these products stacked up against them, and so on. Up to this point Dan still didn't know who the man was, but assumed he was either the store manager or a company marketing guy, there to oversee the opening of the store. But Dan liked the man's generosity, all those questions notwithstanding.

When Dan finished, the man escorted him out to the parking lot, where their conversation continued. With zero fanfare, the man pulled out a business card that gave his name and the company name, along with his title—*CEO*. To Dan's questioning about his presence at the store, the CEO replied that he liked to personally see what each new store was like, and to use such occasions to do some one-on-one intelligence gathering. He said further that, because not all that many employees at stores around the country knew what he looked like, quite often he "dropped in" on existing stores anonymously, as just another customer, to examine the service, product quality, store cleanliness, and other customers firsthand. He said he felt it was a great way to stay in touch with the marketplace for his firm's products. (All names disguised.)

Being in touch with the marketplace is a matter of communication. The CEO probably had all of the usual formal, sterile reporting mechanisms to "inform" him, from a distance, about the field level of his organization. But he also had firsthand observations and actual contacts with customers and employees to enhance the picture. He created opportunities for his customers and employees to interact directly with him, without intermediaries, and many times without them even knowing who he was.

In their immensely popular book, *In Search of Excellence*, Peters and Waterman (1982) describe two hallmarks of managerial excellence as staying "close to the customer" and using "managing by wandering around." The former orientation manifests itself in the wide variety of methods organizations will use to know and continually monitor their customers' needs, tastes, feelings about the product, and dealings with the firm. The latter is one important way of getting and staying close to what's going on with both employees and customers. The man—the CEO—in the ice cream store was good at getting close to his customers and his employees. He did it by wandering around. He did it with communication.

I'M GOING TO BE FIRED AND C.Y.A.

Not long ago I worked with a small team of managers as a third-party consultant to a long-running and destructive conflict taking place between two of the team members. The situation had deteriorated to the point where it was likely that one or both managers would resign if the conflict wasn't resolved. I was called in by the top-level manager, to whom both of the disputants reported. He told me that the organization couldn't afford to lose either of them.

After interviewing all three affected managers, I facilitated a dialogue between the two disputants, with the top manager present as an observer and a resource person. The dialogue was structured so as to give each disputant uninterrupted opportunities to "air" what behaviors she appreciated, disliked, and wanted to see change in the other person. And before being allowed to criticize the other, each disputant was required to talk about behaviors of her own that might be causing the other some distress. As it turned out, the conflict centered around mutually perceived threats to power and around personal style incompatibilities.

But in the course of the dialogue, it also surfaced that each of the disputants had some issues with the top manager present, and that played an important role in the ongoing conflict. For instance, as her response to the escalating conflict, one of the disputants had practically withdrawn into a shell, keeping very much to herself and hardly talking with anyone else, much less her main antagonist and her manager. Over time she had built, in the absence of face-to-face communication and evidence to the contrary, an elaborate scenario in her head in which her manager had either overtly or covertly thrown all of his support behind the other disputant's position in the conflict. She even assumed that soon she was actually going to lose her job, and so had begun quietly but actively looking for work elsewhere. When her manager heard this "read" of his actions and other events, he emphatically stated that she was a valuable member of the team and that she was assuredly not going to lose her job over the conflict, but that he wanted a solution that served everyone's interests. He concluded by saying that it was the lack of face-to-face communication between himself and her that had allowed such distorted perceptions to flourish. He was right.

The other disputant had an important gripe with the top manager as well, which came out in the dialogue. Several months earlier in the conflict, she had wanted to resign due to a particularly explosive and ugly (and public) confrontation that had taken place with her counterpart. This woman possessed specialized knowledge that was invaluable and almost indispensable in serving the organization's customers. Also, the top level manager had learned from several powerful customers just how happy they were with her abilities. He was understandably loathe to let her get away, and had to work very hard to finally persuade her to stay with the organization (which, of course, helped "convince" the other disputant of his alliance with the enemy camp) in the hope that a satisfactory solution to the conflict could be reached.

During the dialogue this woman revealed that she was left with some bitterness over her decision to stay because she felt that her manager was only interested in "saving his own ass," rather than retaining a valuable contributor to the team. Something he had done or said when she wanted to resign had left her with that impression (or "message"), and it had colored her perceptions of his words and deeds ever since. At hearing her say this in the dialogue, the senior manager was visibly shaken, and took the opportunity to try to clarify his intentions and to affirm her importance as a contributing team member in less self-serving terms. She needed to hear him tell her that.

Most of what went on in this case, including the eventual successful resolution of a very serious conflict, hinged on communication. Perceptions had been formed on the basis of things said, done, not said, and not done. Communication allowed interests to seem threatened. Defenses were raised communicatively. The offensive tactics of each disputant were implemented largely through communication, or through attempts *not* to communicate (which, of course, had considerable message value!). The key to resolving their conflict took various forms of communication, such as my interviewing the participants separately, the structured and candid interaction among all three principals that brought to the surface the real issues causing problems, and communicating openly what each needed from the other to make the working relationships functional again.

The next short case is quoted entirely from an excellent article by Anne B. Fisher (1993), entitled "Sexual Harassment: What to Do."

COMMUNICATION ABUSE

No headline-making subject in recent memory has stirred so much confusion. No doubt you've read your company's policy statement and, from just under its surface, you feel the legal eagles' gimlet stare. But what does sexual harassment really mean? Managers of both sexes are sifting through the past and fretting about next week. Was it okay to say I liked her dress? Is it okay to ask him out to lunch to talk about that project? Should I just stop touching anybody, even if it's only a congratulatory pat on the back? For that big client meeting in Houston, wouldn't it be less risky to fly out with Frank than with Francine? Or, for female managers, vice versa?

. . . 90% of Fortune 500 companies have dealt with sexual harassment complaints. More than a third have been sued at least once, and about a quarter have been sued over and over again. . . . The problem costs the average large corporation $6.7 million a year. . . . Sexual harassment could be tomorrow's asbestos, costing American business $1 billion in fees and damages in the next five years.

Both sexes sometimes feel they're stumbling around in a minefield, lost in enemy territory without a helicopter. What makes the terrain so treacherous is that people have an inconvenient way of seeing the same behavior quite differently.

Consultants who design sexual harassment workshops, and managers who have attended them, agree on one thing: The best training gives participants a chance to talk to each other, instead of just listening to a lecture or watching a film. In classes where men and women are asked to compare their impressions of the same hypothetical situation, real revelations can occur. (Fisher, 1993, pp. 84–86; used by permission)

Sexual harassment is an explosive subject these days, and many, many organizations are moving to educate employees about it and to prevent or eliminate it. It has been rightly labeled as primarily an abuse of power. Equally important, however, are the communication dimensions of the problem. Communication is central to the problem of sexual harassment as well as to its prevention and remedy. As much as it is an abuse of power, sexual harassment is also an abuse of communication. It requires some form(s) of communication to sexually harass another. The victim's response—even if it is "no response"—involves communication. And as shown above, the best training preventatives incorporate direct communication between the sexes about alternative ways of "making sense" of the same situation or behavior.

THE RUNAWAY TRAIN

Recently I consulted to a top-level team of managers on a team building project. As part of a diagnostic phase of the effort, I interviewed all ten members of the team about their perceptions of the team's functioning. In discussing "barriers" to the team being more effective, eight of the ten group members mentioned the behavior of one group member as especially troublesome. They described it this way:

"It's difficult to work with him. He shuts down if there's dissent. He won't admit mistakes. Some other personalities play off of his."

"He's one of the barriers. He has his own way of doing things and doesn't care who he walks over to get things done. This runs him into conflict with others and even in his own group."

"He's an idea man, but pursues ideas beyond their usefulness sometimes. He has trouble letting go of ideas that clash with others. If it's not his idea, he doesn't buy in."

"He's one who has hidden agendas. You and I would write two sentences and if he wasn't part of it, he wouldn't agree. I can give you example after example of difficulty achieving consensus or agreement with him."

"He's a runaway train. Can't stay out of other people's business."

"He's unreasonable. He never, ever gives up an issue until he gets closure with what he wants. That pisses people off. You think you've got closure until he comes back in."

"He's a renegade. Will do things his own way. It irritates people. It's very important to him for his ideas to win out. We all get tired of fighting the battles against him."

"I'm not going to trust him until he gives me reason to."

The idea is clear. Here's an individual who, according to his team mates, single-handedly impaired the functioning of the top-most management team of a large organization. How did he do it? The things he said and did led his team members to characterize him as a "barrier," a "renegade," a "runaway train," "unreasonable,", and "difficult to work with." By what means did he evoke perceptions of such "endearing" qualities in the eyes of his team mates? And frankly, how did he get away with it for so long? He wasn't the boss or even a senior ranking team member. Communication, pure and simple. His communicative actions bugged people and caused problems. But also the communicative actions of his team mates enabled him to influence the group's effectiveness in the ways described above.

If the foregoing seven cases aren't enough, consider this headline of an article appearing in a recent *Wall Street Journal*: "Studies Conclude Doctors' Manner, Not Ability, Results in More Lawsuits" (Bishop, 1994, p. B6). The author goes on to summarize two Vanderbilt University studies, concluding: "The main difference between doctors who get sued a lot and those who don't isn't the quality of their medicine, it's their manner of dealing with patients" (p. B6). "Manner" in this instance refers specifically to "problems communicating and establishing rapport with their patients" (p. B6).

But there's much more that could be said about the pervasive and consequential role of communication in our organizations: missions are formulated and articulated through communication; decision making is informed (or uninformed) through communication; innovations are disseminated through communication; people are hired, oriented, trained, evaluated, promoted, passed over, transferred, developed, and fired through communication; instructions are given through communication; leaders lead through communication; performance is monitored through communication; activities are coordinated through communication;

authority is expressed (and challenged) through communication; people are empowered through communication; departmental and divisional conflicts are waged through communication; friendships are nurtured through communication; and so on. Communication is indeed an essential part of the activities that go into "organization." If we can accept that organizations play a critical role in industrialized societies, and further, that organizational functioning depends on communication, then it is certainly no understatement to conclude that our lives are affected, directly, indirectly, and profoundly, by the quality of the communication processes within our organizations.

Communication and Management

It should be evident in all of the foregoing that our organizations' managers depend crucially on communication. Over the last ten to fifteen years, through management training with more than 60 organizations, large and small, from both the public and private sectors, I've had the opportunity to ask several hundred managers and supervisors about their communication experiences. A question I always ask groups to discuss is, "what percentage of your job activities involves 'communicating' and/or 'communication' of some sort, however you define those two terms?"

Two things about their answers have always been interesting. First, only very rarely has *anyone* reported *less* than a majority of their job activities as involving communication. In other words, the results have been virtually unanimous with managers and supervisors reporting that the *majority* of their work activities involves communication. What's more, easily the largest part of this group reports not just more than half, but a sizable majority of their job activities—75%, 85%, 90%, 100%—connected to communication. The vast majority of the hundreds of managers and supervisors I've worked with agree that most, if not nearly all, of their job activities involve communication in some way. That's strong testimony to its importance among managers and supervisors.

But there's something else that has always been intriguing about their answers. In further talking about what these managers and supervisors mean by the terms "communication" and "communicating," I've been struck by how remarkably narrow the working definitions of the terms are for many people. That is, most often "communication" and "communicating" are found to be associated almost exclusively with whatever kind of speaking and writing is done or received in the course of a job. Communication: message sending, message receiving, spoken or written. Period.

A major premise of this book is that such narrow definitions of communication—even viewing communication in such terms as "sending" and "receiving"—are part of the reason we're not as good at managing communication as we could be. They're also part of the reason we're not as good at communication and communicating as we think we are. The next chapter includes a full explanation of the preceding statements. But the point to be made here is not small: in spite of unrealistically narrow and exclusionary working definitions of "communication" and "communicating," the vast majority of managers and supervisors questioned feel that communication activities pervade their jobs. In the course of this book I hope to show that the percentage of managerial activities having communication dimensions should be much larger than most managers believe, and that the implications of broadening our appreciation of communication in this way are serious.

If it's harder or more precise data we need on the question of communication's role in managerial effectiveness, consider a nationwide survey I recently conducted of more than 300 managers. First a few demographics: 20% of these managers worked in the marketing function of their organizations, 17% in accounting, 13% in operations, 11% in finance, 4% in human resources, with 35% representing some combination of functions. The average number of people reporting to each manager was 13, the average length of time since they themselves had finished their undergraduate degrees (all were college graduates) was 12 years, and the average tenure with their present organization was 6 years.

The survey sought these managers' perceptions about certain knowledge and skill proficiencies they've observed in recent (last five years) business school graduates, as well as the need for those knowledge and skill proficiencies in their own organizations. Some of the results are quite relevant here.

Table 1.1 shows how these managers rate recent business school graduates' proficiencies in ten skill areas. Of the ten skills listed, three are quite clearly mainstream traditional components of communication: oral communication skills, written communication skills, and interpersonal skills. Unimpressively enough, recent business school graduates don't stack up very favorably for these managers on the traditional communication skills. Forty-seven percent of the managers felt that business school graduates are either deficient or severely deficient in their oral communication skills. And it's worse for written communication skills, where 69% saw recent graduates as deficient or severely deficient. Interpersonal skills fared only somewhat better, where 36% of the managers felt that recent business graduates were deficient or severely deficient.

What do these results mean? Not much that's good, as far as these managers and the purposes of this book are concerned. Put most simply, recent business school graduates are viewed as lacking in communication skills by a sizable percentage of firing line managers. But do you suppose it makes any difference?

Almost certainly. Table 1.2 shows how the managers rated the need for those ten skills in their organizations. This isn't good news for those seen as deficient in communication skills. Notably, the three skills most closely associated with traditional communication skills finished first, second, and third in order of importance on the list of needs. Oral communication skills topped the list, with 75% of the managers saying that they're *critically important*—with the remaining 25% indicating that oral communication skills are important in their organizations. Next was interpersonal skills, with 70% of the managers viewing them as critically important. And close behind was written communication skills,

Table 1.1
Managers' Ratings of Recent Business School Graduates' Skill Proficiencies

Skill proficiency
(percentages)

Highly profic.	Satis- fact.	Defi- cient	Severely deficient	Skills (ranked)
11%	59	26	5	Computer literacy skills
6	60	30	3	Analytical skills
4	60	31	5	Interpersonal skills
5	58	32	5	Conceptual skills
6	49	37	8	Problem solving skills
4	50	39	8	Oral communication skills
4	44	42	10	Creative thinking skills
3	40	45	11	Leadership skills
3	36	52	10	Managing skills
2	30	51	18	Written communication skills

This research was supported by a grant from the College of Business, with assistance from the Center for Business and Economic Research, Western Illinois University.

Table 1.2
Managers' Ratings of Skill Proficiency Needs in Their Organizations

Skill proficiency needs
(percentages)

Critical need	Impor- tant	Somewhat import.	No need	Skills (ranked)
75%	25	0	0	Oral communication skills
70	27	2	0	Interpersonal skills
66	32	1	0	Written communication skills
61	37	2	0	Problem solving skills
42	50	9	0	Creative thinking skills
38	55	7	0	Analytical skills
42	45	12	0	Computer literacy skills
39	52	8	1	Leadership skills
35	53	11	1	Managing skills
32	57	11	0	Conceptual skills

with 66% indicating them as critically important.

As part of the same survey, managers were also given an opportunity to comment open-endedly about what they most liked or disliked concerning the proficiencies of recent business school graduates. Far and away, more managers

(63%) used this as a chance to complain or to suggest needed improvements than to praise the products of business schools or the educational processes that produced them (4%). Here's mainly how the comments ran overall, quoting from some of the more experienced managers:

From an Operations Manager, 18 years experience: The most critical shortcoming of the grads I have worked with is their inability to communicate well, either orally or in writing. They generally have poor grammar, create poor sentences and paragraphs, and I often receive calls from clients questioning their abilities (after talking with them) because they cannot express their thoughts in a logical, coherent manner.

From an Accounting Manager, 22 years experience: Graduates are usually very weak in written (including grammar) and oral communication. We fired one new hire with a 3.5+ Grade Point Average who passed the CPA exam in May of his senior year because we and our clients couldn't stand his personality.

From an Operations Manager, 13 years experience: The guys and gals coming in are sharp. Their written communication skills ruin the rest of the package.

From a Project Manager, 16 years experience: From experience with the new hires, their background is light in written communication skills. They can produce reams of spreadsheets, know lots of neat new buzzwords, but can't reduce the facts and figures into a coherent paragraph.

From a Human Resources Manager, 11 years experience: Develop a class in aggression. Timidity has no place in business today. The grads that mix communication skills, initiative, and analytical skills are the ones that show the most promise.

From a Marketing Manager, 17 years experience: As time goes on, the primary deficiency afflicting B-school graduates is poor oral/written communication skills. This means persuasiveness and negotiating skills are lacking.

Not a very happy picture. With the need for communication skills so strong and so widespread, the observed deficiencies of recent business school graduates in these areas spells trouble—for the individuals themselves, for those working with and depending on them, and for their employing organizations.

To be sure, communication has bottom line implications for managers and for organizations. Top executives estimate that miscommunication costs their organizations from 25 to 40% of budget annually, as it affects customer confidence, grievances, absenteeism, turnover, strikes, production retardation, and the like (Haney, 1986, p. 6). In their extensive review of research to date, Downs, Clampitt, and Pfeiffer (1988) document the links between organizational communication practices and such important outcomes as productivity and job satisfaction. Although the relationships are not simple, communication clearly affects productivity and job satisfaction, which of course have obvious benefits and costs connected with them.

THE COMMUNICATION-INTENSIVE ORGANIZATION

These are interesting times. There are revolutions taking place right on our doorsteps. Advances in medical research and technologies have dramatically altered our ability to either prevent altogether or diagnose and treat certain debilitating or fatal diseases and conditions. We're living longer and healthier. Advances in information technologies have put powerful personal computers, vast information databases and networks, and sophisticated software at the fingertips of John and Jane Q. Public.

Revolutions are about change. And nowhere are the currents of change swirling faster and more forcefully than in the environment of our organizations. Several of these currents are clearly discernible.

Globalization. As more and more countries embrace capitalistic economies, and as the economies of industrialized nations have become interlocked, the competition in most industries has become much more global and, therefore, intense.

Technological advances. Advances in manufacturing and information technologies are revolutionizing the way organizations do and make things, as well as the skills required of employees.

Rate of change. The quickening rate of change, in addition to change itself, is pushing organizations to their adaptive limits. This is fueled both by globalization and by technological advances.

Employee expectations. No longer is a job just a paycheck. Today's and tomorrow's employees want personal satisfaction, meaningful responsibilities, literal and psychic ownership of work, as well as a strong voice in important decisions, beyond the simple financial rewards of their jobs.

Customer expectations. Customers are demanding quality and service like never before in the products they purchase from organizations. Furthermore, globalization has increased the choices available to consumers, intensifying the competition for customers among many organizations.

These environmental currents add up to a stretch of organizational "white water" extending into the foreseeable future, and the tricky thing is, every organization has to shoot these rapids. Those organizations that recognize the currents and respond accordingly are the ones likely to remain mostly dry and afloat. And those that don't? They will be much less in control of their own fates.

So how are organizations preparing themselves to shoot the rapids? Pick up just about any business magazine these days and you'll see terms such as "empowerment," "total quality management" (TQM), "organization reengineering," and "self-managed work teams" thrown around. Each of these management trends is an attempt to negotiate—counteract or exploit—one or more of the environmental currents pulling and pushing relentlessly at our organizations. Organizational processes are being "reengineered" from scratch to produce greater abilities to compete globally on such key factors as cost, quality, service, and time. Work is being designed to address people's needs and demands for meaningful, challenging jobs. Decision authority is becoming more widely shared. Flexible project teams are supplanting the linear, sequenced, discrete design and production processes of tradition. "Quality" programs are proliferating in every kind of organization, private and public, large and small, manufacturing and service. Organizational leaders are striving to craft supporting "cultures" that champion values such as constant innovation, quality, everyone-a-leader, information power, developing and utilizing human potentialities, and shared decision making, among others.

Bottom-line: the "white water" will require organizations to rely on several critical qualities for survival, no matter which managerial approaches they embrace. Organizations will have to be *externally aware*, constantly "listening" to key stakeholders, "reading" key forces in their environment, and responding as fast as necessary to further their interests. They will have to be *self-examining*, with numerous mechanisms both for accurately determining "what's going on" inside the organization at any time, and for self-assessing strengths and weaknesses. They will have to be *fast-adapting*, with systems that provide timely external and internal information to anyone needing it, structures that enable those nearest a problem to solve it, and processes that promote commitment, innovativeness, and high-quality, fast decisions and implementation. And finally, to successfully shoot the rapids, organizations will have to be *focused*, with everyone aboard understanding their role, having an ownership stake in accomplishing the purposes of the organization, and pulling in essentially the same direction.

Each of the management trends mentioned above—organization reengineering, TQM, empowerment/participation initiatives, shaping culture, and so on—seeks to produce organizations that are more externally aware, self-examining, fast-adapting, and focused. But to facilitate the full realization of these qualities, organizational leaders must first appreciate the central role of communication processes in all of them. Organizations, in order to be externally aware, self-examining, fast-adapting, and focused in the ways described, must be communication-intensive.

Communication-intensive organizations evolve from a particular "state of mind" that the people in them, particularly leaders, hold with regard to "communication," its nature, and its usefulness to organizations, coupled with the actions deriving from a full appreciation of the implications of that orientation. In communication-intensive organizations, managers understand what communication is, how it *really* "works," the multitude of forms it can take, and what its potential for good and harm can be. They know that communication pervades their activities as well as their organization's. They recognize communication as the most powerful and versatile tool a manager has. And they know that effectively harnessing the power of the tool takes great skill, hard work, and keen, constant vigilance.

How this "mindset" can be developed, and why it should be, are the subjects of the next two chapters. Beyond that, the remaining chapters in the book each deal with an extension of the communication orientation developed here, to areas of management *action* that can be especially instrumental in creating the communication-intensive organization: communicating for accuracy and for strong relationships, leading through communication, empowering others through communication, creating culture through communication, building teams through communication, and managing change through communication.

Communication is hard work. Are you rested and ready?

Chapter 2

Communication: What It Isn't

Man is an animal suspended in webs of significance he himself has
spun.

Clifford Geertz

A world ends when its metaphor has died.

Archibald MacLeish

It ain't the things we don't know that hurt us. It's the things we do
know that ain't so.

Artemus Ward

DEFINITIONS

The statements in Table 2.1 on page 23 all have to do with different views on
the subjects of communication and communicating. What do you think? Take
a look at them and determine, from your point of view, how accurately each one
describes communication and what happens when people communicate. Please
do this now, before continuing.

We'll return to the statements of Table 2.1 later in the chapter. Before that,
however, we need to talk about definitions, first generally, then specifically
definitions of communication. Why definitions? Because definitions are at the
very center of why we do the things we do. An example will help. Please try
as best you can to imagine yourself in this situation:

You are attending a conference in New York City. You're an "out-of-towner," having
visited the city only once or twice before. You've been to a late dinner at a restaurant
that is quite a distance from your hotel, accompanied by several other conferees. After
dinner, several in your party, yourself included, decide to see some of the city sights on
foot. As the evening wanes, all but two of your group hail cabs to return to the
conference hotel. You and a colleague who, though not a native New Yorker, knows the

city much better than you do, remain. By the time you've finally had enough night life, it's late. Your colleague suggests that the two of you take the subway back to the hotel. Having never been on a subway and feeling up for one more adventure, you assent.

The subway platform is nearly deserted at that hour, with only a handful of people waiting. When your train arrives, just the *three* of you get into an empty subway car: you, your colleague, and then a man who steps on just before the doors close. He positions himself on the same side as the two of you, but way in the back corner of the car, where a couple of burned-out bulbs dim the overhead lighting. In an uncomfortably long glance over your shoulder you see that he's young, well over six feet tall, heavy-set and obviously stocky, with a few days' growth of beard, and is wearing tattered blue jeans, sneakers, an old army coat with one of his hands stuck in its pocket, a sock cap, and a frown—as he meets your gaze with a stare. It will be a number of minutes before the first stop on your ride. Almost immediately after the train leaves the platform, in turning your head a little to the side, the man is no longer in your peripheral vision at the back of the car. You turn your head a little farther until you realize that he's now moved up to sit only about six or seven feet off to your side.

You are there—it's real. Take a moment right now, before reading on, and, *as a rider on that train*, define what this situation means to you. What's going on? What sensations and thoughts are going through your mind?

That's how definitions are at the very center of why we do the things we do. Will your definition of this situation affect your thoughts and actions on that train? Almost unquestionably. How would your definition change if, instead of the young man, the person who gets on the subway car with you is a uniformed policeman? Or a woman wearing a nun's habit? Or three such young men together, instead of one? (By the way, this really was my first subway ride, many years ago.)

Definitions and Perception

Essentially, "defining" is the "sense making" referred to in the first chapter. It's the "order," the "organization," the "meaning" that we make of what's going on in and around us, and part of the larger process of perception that governs how we act and react toward the world. Because there are many excellent descriptions of the intricacies of the larger perceptual process (e.g., Haney, 1986), I will offer only a cursory statement about it here, leaving the detailed treatment of the subject to those sources.

At any given time there are innumerable perceivable "events" or possibilities both in and around us. Where you are right now, there are myriad things you could select for attention—motions, colors, smells, sounds, tastes, lighting, surface textures and hardness, temperature, objects, spatial relations, physical sensations, time, the feel of your clothes, the comfort of your shoes, your most recent meal, the length of your fingernails, real estate prices, the stock market, the value of the dollar, bananas, anything. But we register only a tiny bit of what's possible, much of it without conscious interpretation. And an even smaller number of events or things engage our definitional attentions at any time.

Table 2.1
Communication Views

Use the following key to indicate, from your perspective, how *accurately* you feel each of statements 1-7 describes what happens when people communicate.

YES!   This description of communication is *absolutely accurate* in *every* respect.

Yes   This description of communication is *accurate* in *most* significant respects.

Y/N   This description of communication is *accurate* in *some* significant respects, and *inaccurate* in *some* others.

No   This description of communication is *inaccurate* in *most* significant respects.

NO!   This description of communication is *absolutely inaccurate* in *every* respect.

For each statement, please choose the one response that best represents your views. Circle your choice after each statement:

1.   Successful communication essentially involves transferring your ideas, thoughts, feelings, etc., to the minds of receivers.
     YES!   Yes   Y/N   No   **NO!**

2.   In spoken and written communication, people take their ideas, thoughts, feelings, etc., and put them into words.
     YES!   Yes   Y/N   No   **NO!**

3.   In spoken and written communication, words are like packages in that they deliver the communicator's ideas, thoughts, feelings, etc.
     YES!   Yes   Y/N   No   **NO!**

4.   One factor affecting the success of spoken and written communication is whether the communicator selects words that contain just the right meanings.
     YES!   Yes   Y/N   No   **NO!**

5.   In spoken and written communication, the communicator's meanings can be taken out of the words he or she uses.
     YES!   Yes   Y/N   No   **NO!**

6.   Basically, success in communication depends more on "message sending" skills than on "message receiving" skills.
     YES!   Yes   Y/N   No   **NO!**

7.   In communication, perfectly clear communication or understanding is the normal state of affairs, and miscommunication or misunderstanding the exception.
     YES!   Yes   Y/N   No   **NO!**

Where the perceptual process makes the human condition so interesting is in the fact that it idiosyncratically distorts and limits each person's view of everything. Sure, there is something we could call "objective reality." But you and I never deal in it perceptually—"objective" and "perception" are mutually exclusive terms. Both "what" we perceive and the sense, or definitions, we make of it result from the inevitably unique blend of many individual biases, stemming from differences in (among others things): our sensory equipment (e.g., some of us see or hear, etc., more accurately or differently than others); our backgrounds (e.g., family experiences, schooling, religious training, etc.); our physical and psychological needs (e.g., food, water; some of us need affection, social contact, independence, etc., more than others); our personal values and goals (e.g., honesty, status, achievement, pleasure, service, making money, etc.); and our cognitive functioning (e.g., various personality dispositions, so-called left- versus right-brain thinking; information processing capacities, etc.).

Definitions and Language

But something else intervenes between ourselves and an unvarnished view of the world. Something as subtle as your next breath, but just as important in determining the "realities" of your world. Language. In using language, we *represent* the world with symbols. We *create* reality using symbols. That's the closest we can get to it.

If this last point—that language profoundly affects perception—seems a bit overstated, here's something to help bring it into perspective. Below are four questions that I would like you to first look at and then just think about. For the "thinking" part, there is one stipulation, however; do your thinking *without* using language. Can you?

1. You're back in that subway car described earlier: What's your gut feeling at the end of the story, where you realize that the young man has moved up right beside you? (Remember, no language.)
2. What would you do differently in your life if you could? (Remember, no language.)
3. How might your life have been different with the changes in question 2? (Remember, no language.)
4. How difficult is it to keep words out of your head, even when you consciously try to? (Remember, no language.)

Call it what you want—conceptualizing, imagining, envisioning, cogitating, just plain old garden-variety thinking, or whatever—it requires language. We know our world through the terms of, because of, language. Richard Mitchell, a student of language and eloquent spokesman of its power, puts it this way in his instructive and entertaining book, *Less Than Words Can Say*:

The world in which we live is very tiny. . . . That world can only be the world of immediate sensory experience, the world we can perceive in whatever way we can in this moment, which is now gone. The world of sensory experience is so tiny and so brief that, in a sense, we can't *do* anything in it; we can only *be* in it. The world that *was* before this moment is immeasurably big, and so too the world that will be, to say nothing of the world that might have been or the world that may yet be or, the root of morality, the world that someone thinks *should* be. It is the main business of language to evoke such worlds. (Mitchell, 1979, p. 29; emphasis in the original)

And Mitchell's is hardly a solitary view. In characterizing man as the "symbol-using animal," Kenneth Burke, another keen observer of people and of language, wonders, "can we bring ourselves to realize just what that formula implies, just how much of what we mean by 'reality' has been built up for us through nothing but our symbol systems?" (Burke, 1966, p. 5). Likewise, George Lakoff and Mark Johnson (1980), a linguist and a philosopher, respectively, document the ways in which language forms the basis of human concepts. And probably the most succinct expression of it all comes from Joseph Pearce (1971, p. 2): "We *represent* the world to ourselves and *respond* to our representations" (emphasis in the original). As I said earlier, definitions are at the center of why we do the things we do. And definitions are always language-made.

A look in any direction reveals the truth of Pearce's claim. For instance, up to this point in the book I've used a number of short cases to demonstrate certain things. In "The New Vinyl," for example, it was assuredly a definition that angered two customers: "They send a 'kid' to install $2000 worth of vinyl, and then purposely make us discover 'botches' they know about before offering a remedy." In "The Man in the Ice Cream Store," all that free sampling of ice cream and of one customer's opinions almost certainly produced a definition like this: "The top executive of a large corporation cares enough about his customers and what they like to ask them personally." In "I'm Going To Be Fired and CYA" the first part of the title itself was one disputant's definition of her fate in a conflict with another manager. So she put herself through considerable mental and physical anguish, not to mention the troubles of a full-blown, make-time search for employment elsewhere. And the second part of the title was the other disputant's definition of the "real" reason her manager wanted to keep her on the management team. Likewise, "The Runaway Train" characterized a management team's definition of one member who was seen to obstruct the group's effectiveness. They responded to this definition with distrust, anger and frustration, tuning him out at meetings, and end-running him as necessary.

And finally, what of that "subway" adventure that we took earlier? About your definitions, were they mainly fearful? "Why did this guy move up directly beside us? He's going to pull something out of that coat pocket." My response was to get up out of the seat and move across the car to sit, facing both him and my colleague. From there, at least his next move would be visible, but I wasn't sure of what would come next. He then took my options away before I could even think about them. As I perched there in dry-mouthed, coiled anticipation (to do what, I didn't know), out came that fearsome hand from his coat pocket—packing a paperback copy of *Catch-22*, which he proceeded to open at a dog-ear and read in the bright lighting of his new seat. He didn't even notice when we sprinted from the train several minutes later at our stop.

Symbolic Reality

Symbolically created reality. Every day, everywhere. History shows us some of the most vivid examples of it. One of the more astonishing instances occurred on Sunday night, October 30, 1938, Halloween Eve. From a studio in New York City, Orson Welles and the Mercury Theater broadcast, on the Columbia Broadcasting System's coast-to-coast radio network, their live enactment of H. G. Wells's science fiction classic, *War of the Worlds*, the plot of which centers around an invasion of the United States by Martian space ships. The drama was so realistically staged that, despite regular and frequent radio station announcements acknowledging the "reality" behind the ruse, along with police and wire service messages claiming no cause for alarm, literally thousands of people across the nation took to the streets in panic to defend themselves against the onslaught of invaders, while thousands more jammed phone lines or took other, even drastic, measures, believing apparently that the end was at hand. A Princeton University study reveals that of the approximately six million listeners that night, at least one million two hundred thousand people took the program literally and acted accordingly. Additionally, the study indicates that an undetermined, but very large number, of citizens who did not hear the broadcast were nevertheless caught up in the mass hysteria that ensued (Cantril, 1982; Koch, 1970). Clearly, in this instance, language created a "reality" that, for millions of listeners that night, was horrifyingly compelling.

In a broader sweep of time, successful propaganda and political campaigns or movements—which are not much different in form—are also classic illustrations of symbolically mediated reality. The election campaigns of any political figure, Hitler's *Mein Kampf* (1942) scapegoating of Jews and his rantings about a master race, Lincoln's Gettysburg Address, the "dream" that Martin Luther King spoke of that day in Washington, D.C., and media campaigns on the moral and constitutional issues of abortion, are all efforts to create a certain kind of world with symbols.

Speaking most generally, we live in a "semantic world," a world of meanings and definitions, just as surely as we live in a physical one. For instance, below are a number of symbolic expressions from the 1970s, 1980s, or 1990s, and which, for one reason or another, have become capable of evoking a rich variety of "meanings" and definitions in many people. To help with this point, try this exercise: Looking at the list below, which expressions conjure images or "stories" for you? As you review them, what specific meanings, definitions, or words come to mind?

1. The Ford Pinto
2. Cyberspace
3. Union Carbide in Bhopal, India
4. Tylenol
5. The Exxon Valdez
6. HIV
7. The Federal Building in Oklahoma City
8. Vietnam
9. The Dalkon Shield

10. Drive-By
11. David Koresh and the Branch Davidians in Waco, Texas
12. Space Shuttle Challenger
13. Bosnia
14. Pro-Life
15. Smokers' Rights

Each of these expressions can provoke a flood of symbolic associations in people, no two of which will be identical. And the influences of these and associated symbols on thought and action have been as "real" and compelling as any forces in the physical world, although usually in far subtler ways.

Anthropologist Benjamin Whorf demonstrated the influence of language on thought and action as vividly as can be done many years ago (Whorf, 1941). At one time Whorf worked as an analyst for a fire insurance company. His duties included analyzing hundreds of reports on insurance claims so as to help determine how the fires of claimants had started. Besides a number of standard physical causes accounting for many fires, Whorf noticed a peculiar but common source: words. Or more precisely, he found that how people named or defined situations often played decisive roles in the origins of many fires. For instance, people's behavior in situations involving "gasoline drums" was shown to be much more cautious than their behavior around "empty gasoline drums," even though the latter are more vaporous and hence, more explosive. According to Whorf, the notion of "empty" apparently translated to "lack of hazard" (the "hazard" being gasoline) for unfortunate victims—just before their seemingly innocuous fireplay (such as striking matches, smoking cigarettes, etc.) around the "empty" drums blew everything to kingdom come.

In similar fashion, Whorf recounts a number of different episodes where, in essence, "words" or definitions led to behaviors that, in turn, led to the start of fires: In a wood distillation plant, composition insulating materials were called "spun limestone." Consequently, there was little concern about exposing them to excessive heat and flame, evidently based on the definition that "stone" doesn't burn. In another industrial fire, a little-used electric wall heater was defined as a "coat hanger" by one workman, while the heater's wall-mounted switch was defined as "light switch" for a night watchman who, flipping it "on" and seeing no light come on, subsequently defined the bulb as "burned out." He left the switch "on" and the workman's coat hanging over the wall heater eventually ignited, setting fire to the building. As a third example, a tannery fire was started when an outdoor "pool of water" ignited from a lighted match thrown into it by a workman. Water won't burn, but *this* water was emitting gases from decomposing animal matter, which were trapped by a partial wooden cover over the pool. The gases flared, setting fire to the roof and adjoining building. And finally, in a lead-reclaiming operation, a pile of "scrap lead" caught fire next to—instead of "in," where it would have been contained—a coal-fired melting pot because the lead consisted of the lead sheets from old radio condensers, with highly flammable paraffin paper between them. The resulting fire burned half of the roof off the building.

Definitions. They simultaneously frame a part of the world for our attention and action while they exclude or obscure the rest. For example, on our earlier subway adventure, if you originally defined that young man as a "bad guy" or as having "intent to harm," you pretty well ruled out just then that he was instead armed with a paperback and the determination to read it almost anywhere. Or that he was an undercover policeman there to watch over you. Or anything else about him imaginable. In defining our world with language, as we must inevitably do in perceiving and sense making, we're not just framing things "in," but also "out." It's rather like a photograph: the picture shows us one view of what's going on, while concealing or excluding everything else. The problem is, it's very easy to forget that there is always infinitely more excluded than included by our definitional framing.

At this point the hope is that the foregoing discussion of perception, definitions, and language has introduced a fair measure of discomfort into your thinking about human communication. Here's partly why I hope you feel uneasy about it: The nature of perception, including the many built-in physical and psychological biases to the perceptual process, combined with our propensity and need to symbolize our world, in effect forever isolate every perceiver from every other perceiver. Because of perception, you and I can never have the *same* appreciation or understanding of anything.

Now that last statement is really a statement about communication, and it's deadly serious in its implications. Very often, although not always, it is safe to assume that people attempting to communicate with others have the simple objective of wanting, via communication, to achieve sameness, or at least very close similarity, of understandings. We want to perceive and understand the "real" intentions, instructions, wishes, behavior, and so forth (i.e., "meanings") of others, and to have our own intentions, instructions, wishes, behavior, and so on ("meanings") accurately perceived and understood by others. If what has been said here about perception and understanding is true, then the simple communication objective of sameness or even close similarity in "understanding others" and "being understood by others" is going to be thwarted virtually all of the time. And if this is the case, then an obvious key question is, How important is it that the "understandings" you and I take from a communicative transaction match up *identically*? That question is examined more thoroughly in later chapters, so I won't dwell on it at length here. But everyone knows of work and personal situations where *your* perception of my intentions, instructions, and the like, needs to match *my* perception of my intentions, instructions, and so on, which I have tried to communicate to you, or vice versa. The trouble is, the perception process and symbolization guarantee that this isn't going to happen—ever, really. Sometimes it won't matter much. But sometimes it will.

Language, Metaphor, Communication

In conversations with different managers and supervisors, I have heard these expressions used to describe various organizational experiences: "He's climbing the corporate ladder." "That guy's a snake." "She walks on water." "You've got to beat them to the punch." "It's a jungle here." "You have to get back on the horse that threw you." "She's got the inside track on the promotion." "This place is a zoo." "He definitely keeps a personal score on these things." "The culture in that organization is sick." "I want to call the shots in my own shop." "The troops in this firm are very capable." "We have to get this project up to speed in a hurry." "We'll hit the ground running with this." "The board meeting was a donnybrook." "She's the sparkplug of the group." "That was the straw that broke the camel's back." "She's in the opposition's camp." "Here's our plan of attack." "It doesn't take a rocket scientist to figure it out."

Colorful stuff, these expressions; and I would add that they're pretty ordinary examples of the colorful way people use language when they talk about their organizations and the people and things in them. Look again at the imagery in what these people said. They were describing—and understanding—something about their organizations or about people, *in terms of something else*: ladders, snakes, water, jungles, fights, score-keeping, shots, troops, health, and the like. In other words, they were telling something about "A" (a man, a woman, employees, an organization, a meeting, etc.) in terms of "B" (a snake, a sparkplug, military troops, a zoo, a brawl, etc., respectively). This should sound familiar. The book began this way.

To give it a name, the feature that makes these expressions vivid or "interesting" for most people is their *metaphorical* quality. Essentially, metaphor involves "understanding and experiencing one kind of thing in terms of another" (Lakoff & Johnson, 1980, p. 5). It entails the symbolic *re-presentation* of "something *in terms* of something else," bringing out "the thisness of a that, or the thatness of a this" (Burke, 1945, p. 503; emphasis in the original).

Undeniably, metaphors make language interesting and entertaining. But they are more than just some kind of "seasoning" we use to spice up our linguistic fare. Three much more serious applications of metaphors have been illustrated variously by the work of cognitive and developmental psychologists, linguists and psycholinguists, philosophers and philosophers of science, and cultural anthropologists.

First, it is the metaphorical nature of language that underlies the elaboration and formal advance of ideas, notably science. Such authors as myself (Axley, 1984), Brown (1977), and Morgan (1986) document this claim thoroughly, but Burke (1954) crystallizes it most eloquently:

Indeed as the documents of science pile up, are we not coming to see that whole works of scientific research, even entire schools, are hardly more than the patient repetition, in all its ramifications, of a fertile metaphor? Thus we have at different eras in history, considered man as the son of God, as an animal, as a political and economic brick, as a machine, each metaphor, and a hundred others, serving as the cue for an unending line of data and generalizations. (Burke, 1954, p. 95)

Second, and related to the generation of ideas and knowledge, is metaphor's essential connection to human thought and concepts. Earlier in this chapter the work of linguist George Lakoff and philosopher Mark Johnson was mentioned as showing the ways in which language forms the basis of human concepts. In their provocative book, *Metaphors We Live By* (1980), they trace in painstaking detail a wealth of our most ordinary concepts about the world to metaphorical origins. As the authors say,

> Metaphor is typically viewed as characteristic of language alone, a matter of words rather than thought or action. For this reason, most people think they can get along perfectly well without metaphor. We have found, on the contrary, that metaphor is pervasive in everyday life, not just in language but in thought and action. Our ordinary conceptual system, in terms of which we both think and act, is fundamentally metaphorical in nature. . . . The way we think, what we experience, and what we do every day is very much a matter of metaphor. (Lakoff & Johnson, 1980, p. 3)

Third, and implicit in both of the first two applications of metaphor, is metaphor's *performative* role in human affairs. From what both Burke and Lakoff and Johnson say about metaphor, we can see that metaphor has day-to-day "performative" implications, providing what cultural anthropologist James Fernandez calls "images in relation to which the organization of behavior can take place" (1972, p. 42). Hastings sharpens the idea of behavioral performance stemming from metaphor: "Metaphors have assumptions at their roots. These assumptions specify the way we are to respond to the world. They are not assumptions as to how the world is, though they may be phrased that way, but assumptions as to how we are to respond" (1970, p. 188). To understand Hastings's point, just think of the different performative implications in two very common metaphors, "organization as military" and "organization as jungle."

In "organization as military," hierarchy and formality in relationships and roles predominate. Such organizations are populated by "troops" and "officers." "Tactics" and "strategies" are "offensive" and "defensive." There are known "adversaries" or "enemies" of the organization, against which "battles," "wars," "espionage," and other "covert operations" are waged. Internal and external "security" is critical to fulfilling the organization's mission. And a whole universe of related terms, each with action implications, comes into play when viewing an organization as the military.

An "organization as jungle" differs from the military metaphor, with different behavioral implications, including: Jungles are populated by a wide variety of animals, some ordinary and some exotic, some passive and some aggressive, some predators and some prey, some warm- and some cold-blooded. Some can coexist and others can't. Some even have symbiotic relationships with others. "Eat and be eaten" applies to all: there is a definite "food chain," and everyone occupies some place in it. "Survival of the fittest" is everyone's ultimate goal. Behaviors are survival-driven, value-neutral, and so forth. We could "elaborate" and extend the metaphor of "organization as jungle" with certain "performances" or behaviors logically implied by the metaphor.

The performative implications of metaphors are critical, particularly in view of those metaphors that shape the concepts we rely on every day. And if ever there was an "everyday" concept in the human sphere of experience, in the sense of "ordinary" that Lakoff and Johnson described earlier, "communication" would have to be it. As argued in Chapter 1, the practice and the idea of "communication" is so pervasive that communication and communicating are exceedingly easy to take for granted. Michael Reddy (1979) gives us an intriguing example of how this most mundane of concepts is structured metaphorically. We need to understand Reddy's work thoroughly, because it has an important bearing on the rest of this book.

"Communication As . . . ?" Reddy, a linguist, has spent a sizable part of his professional career analyzing the metaphors that English speakers use to characterize "communication." The question guiding his efforts has been, "When people talk or write about 'communication,' what metaphors do they use in describing it?" Or put a little differently to capture the way that metaphor shapes thought, "What metaphors inform people's understanding of communication?" It's really no different from showing you a little earlier that those managers and supervisors understood their organizations and other people through such concepts as ladders, snakes, jungles, fights, health, and the like. Reddy just wanted to see what concepts people use to understand "communication."

Before we look at Reddy's findings, let's do something to "work" our way into them. Here are some expressions you might hear (or see) when people talk (or write) about communication. They are numbered for reasons that will be clear momentarily.

1. I hope I'm not having trouble getting my ideas in this book across to you.
2. As I write this I sometimes wish I was better at putting my thoughts into words.
3. Does my writing contain any useful insights?
4. Are you getting any good ideas from what I've said so far?

There's really nothing strange or remarkable in these statements, wouldn't you say? Don't they look (or sound, if you read them aloud) like expressions you've seen, heard, or used lots of times? I've used numerous expressions in this book that are very similar *metaphorically* to the four above. Here's a sample of four quotations from Chapter 1 (numbers below correspond to those above).

1. The people demonstrating this take the main ideas of my opening statement and start right in working on them.
2. In the next 30 seconds, would you jot down your first reaction?
3. In all truth, that sentence holds a number of valuable insights about communication for us.
4. The other disputant had an important gripe with the top manager as well, which came out in the dialogue.

Again, is there anything odd or noteworthy in the phrasing? (The immediately preceding question, by the way, is metaphorically similar to both numbers 2 above.) If you're like many—even most—English speakers, the metaphorical structure of these preceding eight statements probably doesn't stand out, partly because the metaphor is more "imbedded" than the "he's-a-snake" or "this-is-a-jungle" type of metaphors, and consequently, is more difficult to spot. But another—and probably more important—reason the metaphor might not have jumped out at you is that chances are you've seen it so often in one form or another that it simply has become an essential and customary part of the way we talk about communication. And don't forget that the way we *talk* about something, so cognitive psychologists, psycholinguists, this book, and common sense tells us, shapes the way we *act* about it.

Reddy's extensive research indicates that at least 70% of the "communication about communication" that takes place via English has a semantic and metaphorical structure like these preceding eight statements, with almost endless variations. And so what is this metaphorical viewpoint that informs so much of the way English speakers talk about communication?

It is a *conduit* or *pipeline*. Reddy's work shows that we most often talk about human communication as though it were some kind of conduit or pipeline, capable of physically transporting meanings back and forth from person to person through the vehicles of words. Take a closer look at the pairs of statements numbered 1 to 4. Notice the imagery in certain key phrases. Respectively, the four expressions—their metaphorical images highlighted—exemplify what Reddy calls the *"major framework of the conduit metaphor"* (p. 290). When reading the parenthetical examples of the expressions, focus on the highlighted parts—they operationalize the metaphorical expression. The core expressions, actually assumptions, imply that:

1. Language transfers thoughts and feelings from person to person ("I'm not having trouble *getting my ideas* in this book *across to you*"; "The *people* demonstrating this *take* the main *ideas of* my opening *statement* and start right in . . .").
2. Speakers and writers insert thoughts and feelings in words ("I wish I was better at *putting my thoughts into words*"; "In the next 30 seconds, would you *jot down your* first *reaction*?").
3. Words contain the thoughts and feelings ("Does *my writing contain* any useful *insights*?"; "In all truth, that *sentence holds* a number of valuable *insights* about communication for us.").
4. Listeners or readers extract the thoughts and feelings from the words ("Are you *getting* any good *ideas from what* I've *said* so far?"; "The other disputant had an important *gripe* with the top manager as well, which *came out in the dialogue*.").

Layering complexity and pervasiveness onto what most people would agree is already a subtle metaphor, Reddy documents more than 140 variations of the conduit metaphor in English usage, each one representing an entire class of expressions about communication and communicating. In fact, he states that it is very nearly impossible to avoid talking about communication in terms other than those of the conduit metaphor: "Practically speaking, if you try to avoid all obvious conduit metaphor expressions in your usage, you are nearly struck dumb when communication becomes the topic" (p. 299). More to the point here, Reddy flatly states that "no speaker of English . . . has discarded the conduit metaphor" from his or her speaking and writing (p. 297). So if Reddy's estimate is true—that minimally, 70% of our English language expressions about communication are variations of the conduit metaphor—then can't we suppose, in view of the idea that metaphor structures perspective and action, that the conduit view of communication is quite popular among English-speaking people? And if it is, so what? Lets take these two questions up in turn.

COMMUNICATION, PERSONALLY SPEAKING

I've been asking people—literally hundreds of them, in management training seminars, workshops, consultations, MBA, and undergraduate college classes that I've taught over the last several years—this: "Tell me what *communication* means to you. Define it in your own words." (That last sentence, by the way, is an expression of conduit core assumption 2.) A sample of the resulting personal "definitions of communication" are shown in Table 2.2 on the next page. The definitions in this table are very similar to hundreds more I have collected, and represent a sizable majority of all that I've acquired. Looking at them, is there anything special you see?

They are, each and every one, verbal expressions of one or more of the four core assumptions of the conduit metaphor. Especially common are variations on the first premise, that "language [and therefore communication] transfers thoughts and feelings from person to person."

My late colleague, W. Charles Redding, provided me additional data on the question of the conduit metaphor's pervasiveness. Across a distinguished consulting career spanning almost four decades, Redding put this specific question to thousands of organizational members in workshops and seminars: "When Person X 'communicates' with Person Y, basically what is happening is that X is transferring meanings from his/her mind to the mind of Y" (W. C. Redding, personal communication, 1981). This, of course, is almost a word-for-word statement of the first assumption of the conduit metaphor, developed and employed in such fashion, however, quite independent of Reddy's work with the concept. Redding says that never did he have less than a majority of respondents agree with the statement, with occasional unanimous agreement in groups. My training experiences with essentially the same question or adaptations of it have been just like Charles Redding's: very widespread and sometimes unanimous agreement that communication involves the transfer of meanings from one person's mind to another's.

Which brings us full circle, back to how we started this chapter, with those statements describing communication, what happens when people communicate, and your views about it (see Table 2.1). By now the purpose with the short ques-

Table 2.2
Personal Definitions of "Communication"

1. Exchange of meaning between people.
2. Transmitting meanings to another person.
3. The transference of an idea from one person to another.
4. Transferring ideas to someone else.
5. Getting your thoughts across to someone.
6. Transferring ideas to another person or people.
7. Process of transferring ideas from one person to another.
8. When two people can transfer meaning back and forth.
9. Conveying your ideas to others.
10. Giving what you mean to the other person.
11. Process of transferring ideas from one individual to another.
12. Process of transferring information and ideas between people.
13. Putting your meaning into words and giving them to someone else.
14. Passing your thoughts and feelings to other people.
15. Using words and actions to convey what you mean.
16. The process of sharing meanings between people.
17. The transfer of thoughts or ideas from one person to another.
18. Transferring one's thoughts or ideas to other interested people.
19. The transfer of ideas between individuals.
20. The moving of an idea of one's mind to another person.
21. Taking ideas, thoughts, and emotions and transmitting them to others with words.
22. Transfer meaning from one person to another.
23. Transferring ideas and feelings between two or more persons.
24. Process of transferring thoughts or emotions through speaking or actions.
25. Transferring meaning with language.
26. The exchange of information, intentions, and meanings between two or more people.
27. The exchange of ideas through the use of words.
28. Passing ideas or meaning to another person.
29. Transferring of information, ideas, or thoughts.
30. Relaying your thoughts clearly to another individual or individuals.
31. A way of transporting thought between people.
32. Sharing thoughts and ideas through words.
33. An exchange of meaning through either words or expression between two people.
34. Sharing meanings.
35. Transmitting ideas so that understanding is shared.

---

tionnaire should be transparent. Items 1, 2, 3, 4, and 5 match up with conduit assumptions 1, 2, 3, 3, and 4, respectively. (Items 6 and 7 are explained a little later.)

So what did you think? Conservatively, only the two "Yes" alternatives indicate agreement with the item in question, and thus with an assumption of the conduit view of communication. More liberally, even the "Y/N" and the milder form of "No" could be taken as possibly some degree of acceptance of the assumption in question. But let's not split hairs.

A slightly longer version of this questionnaire has been given to the same hundreds of people who gave their personal definitions of communication (always after they "defined" communication, so as not to bias their wording). The overwhelming majority of them agree that statements 1–5 are accurate depictions of what happens when people communicate (with all five statements showing, minimally, 75% "Yes"/"**YES!**" responses). So even if you are dubious, many people accept the view that communication works like a conduit or pipeline.

Trouble In Paradise

Before we look at the action implications of such popularity, we need to first examine the accuracy of the metaphor itself, that communication functions like a conduit. One way of doing this is to simply scrutinize the core assumptions that Reddy identifies. When we ask about them in seriousness, do they square with what happens when people communicate?

Language transfers thoughts and feelings from person to person. Does it really? Is it actual "meanings"—thoughts, feelings, ideas, and the like—that are transferred or exchanged between people? No. The only things literally transferred from me to you and you to me—and only then assuming you accurately hear or read my words—are the *signals* or the physical *symbols* that we select to represent our messages. Right now, I am transferring these signals—words—to you. Beyond that, nothing else is being transferred from my mind to yours.

Speakers and writers insert thoughts and feelings into words. Is it possible to actually "put" or "insert" anything "into" the signals we exchange? No. As I assemble these words, I'm selecting and ordering ones that I think do the best job, within the limits of my vocabulary and technical writing skills, of representing what's in my head. But what's in my head stays there. It doesn't somehow get put into the words I choose when we communicate.

Words contain the thoughts and feelings. Are words "containers" that somehow "hold" and "transport" meanings from person to person? No. As stated above, there's really nothing except the signals—words—themselves that are transportable or transferrable from one mind to another. The only "containers" of meanings in any communicative exchange are people.

Listeners or readers extract the thoughts and feelings from the words. In light of what has been said about the first three assumptions, refuting this one is just a formality. If meanings can't be transferred, and they can't be put into symbols, and symbols themselves don't contain anything, then is there anything inside words to be extracted or otherwise gotten out? Not if you accept the validity of the challenges to the first three assumptions.

Over the last several years I've expended considerable time and effort challenging the core assumptions of the conduit metaphor—mostly in front of managers who have just written a conduit-oriented "personal definition" of communication, and/or who have agreed that those assumptions of Table 2.1 accurately describe what happens when people communicate. Reactions to the challenges usually fall into one of two categories.

"That's right": After a word-for-word reconsideration of the core assumptions of the conduit metaphor, quite a few people seem to see the absurdity—really, the impossibility—of the expressions.

"That's wrong": But a surprisingly large number of people who "buy" the conduit assumptions, at least on paper, don't buy any "No-it-doesn't" and "No-we-don't" challenges to the expressions at face value. One would think the world had been described as rectangular, judging from the level of amazement. Countervailing arguments usually center around either "Then how do you explain this situation?" type claims, or a kind of "Is this for real?" disclaimer that the conduit expressions are just convenient—if ubiquitous—figures of speech, and therefore something that no one really takes literally or seriously.

Whatever form the disagreement takes, the tenacity with which it is expressed is reminiscent of what Donald Schön (1979) calls "frame conflict." The frames in question are metaphorical frames of reference or perspectives on the world and the things in it—an idea not much different from how metaphor is treated here. However, Schön's application of "frame" is unique in that he relates it to how "problems" are framed or "set" metaphorically. Problems, so he argues, aren't handed to us. Rather, we "set" or define them, often metaphorically. In support of his claim, Schön reviews a number of technological problems and social policy problems that he believes have been, at their roots, metaphorically set or defined. And in a manner not unlike the earlier discussion of definitions influencing actions, Schön shows us how technological and social policy problem solving has been hostage to the metaphorical framing of the particular problems.

The "conflict" part of "frame conflict" essentially involves metaphors that offer incompatible explanations or definitions of the same thing, whether it's a problem, a person, a person's behavior, an organization, whatever. According to Schön (p. 256), the real difficulty in "conflicting frames, generated by different and conflicting metaphors," is that "such conflicts are often not resolvable by recourse to the facts." When a person is committed to a particular metaphorical "problem frame," Schön (p. 269) claims, "it is almost always possible to reject facts, to question data (usually fuzzy in any case), or to patch up one's story so as to take account of new data without fundamental alteration of the story." Conflicting frames "are attentive to different features of reality and are able to assimilate new versions of the facts" (p. 269).

Quite probably frame conflict is behind those instances when I've been unable to reveal to others the inaccuracies, the dysfunctional "lessons," and the consequent perils of the conduit metaphor. Reddy himself acknowledges the challenge of "speaking across the chasm of frame conflict" (p. 286) this way: "I want to suggest at the outset that the discussion that follows is a marvelous opportunity for one of those failures to communicate which we are concerned to prevent. . . . If I am right in what I believe about frames, then it may well be difficult to convince you, because the frames I am talking about exist in you and will resist the change" (p. 286).

In the pages preceding I have argued that language both allows and forces us to cast and define our experiences in a multitude of frames, images, and concepts that are, fundamentally, metaphors. Metaphors shape how we think, and their performative implications, how we act. The dominant metaphor used by many people to frame their understanding of human communication and communicative actions is the conduit metaphor.   What little evidence there is on the subject—Reddy's linguistic analyses, Redding's survey question, my "personal definitions" and questionnaire inquiries—supports this belief. As stated above, despite its seemingly tremendous popularity, the conduit perspective on human communication just plain doesn't square with what happens when people communicate.

But the fact that it's inaccurate isn't all of the problem. Reddy's description of "English" as "its own worst enemy" (p. 286), with the potential to create a kind of "semantic pathology" (p. 297), steers us into deeper, more ominous waters.   The more serious issues lie both in the conduit metaphor as "an entrenched system of . . . attitudes and assumptions" (p. 298), learned over a lifetime of language use, which opposes alternative—but more realistic—models of communication, and especially in the performative implications of the conduit metaphor.   In part, the pervasiveness, the resilience, and the performative implications of the conduit metaphor help explain why "communication" of one form or another always ranks near the top of the survey lists of "problems" plaguing our organizations and our relationships.   Next is a more detailed rationale for that belief.

What Communication Isn't

Ultimately, by extension, the assumptions of the conduit metaphor make human communication out to be a simple, tidy process. As a communication "sender" (which, not coincidentally, is a conduit-oriented label used in most popular published models of communication), what could be cleaner, easier, than just putting your thoughts and feelings into words, or finding the words that mean just what you want to say, and sending them along to another?   And as a communication "receiver" (which enjoys the same distinction and popularity as the "sender" label), what's simpler than hearing or reading another's words, and getting their message from those words?

The nice thing about communication in terms of the conduit metaphor is, well, that it's so nice to us. It helps us feel sure of ourselves, our abilities, and of our communication as "senders" and "receivers." And better yet, it helps us take personal credit for the good things that happen in connection with our communication efforts, and blame others for the bad things. If metaphors were organizations, the conduit metaphor would have an almost irresistibly attractive benefits package, psychologically. And not very many people would want to give it up for less security in another metaphor.

If we assume that somehow communication involves the transfer of meanings from person to person, several logical—although probably unconscious, and therefore all the more compelling—premises follow. The most important concerns the fidelity between messages as "sent" and messages as "received." When something gets "transferred," neither the concept nor the term implies that the thing itself changes in the process. For most people, "transfer" is a very simple idea. What once was "here" is now "there," or vice versa: transferred ownership, transferred money, transferred employees, transferred objects, transferred loyalty, and the like. And our language doesn't help any. Describing the experience of "transfer" seems to "freeze" whatever object it is that is transferred: "He transferred ownership of his '86 Chevy S-10 to me." (Nobody believes that it might become a Ferrari or a Yugo in the process. It just becomes my S-10 instead of his.) "She transferred to the Cleveland office from Oklahoma City." (No one believes she'll become someone different from herself. She'll just be in Cleveland instead of Oklahoma City.)

It's natural and easy to believe that "transferred" things are the same after the transfer as they were before it. The "transfer of meaning" is a comfortable thought: what gets sent, gets received. As a "sender" this means that I can put whatever is in *my* head in *your* head. As a "receiver" it means I can put whatever is in *your* head in *my* head. We both have every reason to be happy about this, because it lets us believe that in any communication exchange, the likelihood of either of us misunderstanding the other is very small. Perfect fidelity between "sent" and "received" meanings is the rule, and imperfect communication, the exception.

And equally nice is the comfort each of us can take in blaming the other—or "something else"—on those rare and unexpected occasions when our meanings don't match up. My responsibilities as "sender" are straightforward enough: I select and send words that convey what I mean. When I feel I've done that, but what you got isn't what I meant, whose fault is it? I can pretty easily absolve myself: "I did my job. I said what I meant. Something happened to the words after I sent them, either on their way to you, or as a result of something you did after receiving them." Often faulty "reception" is the suspected problem: "You read too much into what I said." "Don't you see what I'm saying?" "Do you see what I mean?" "Did you catch my drift?" "Do you get me?" These are common, soft-touch ways of saying, "It's not my fault if you don't get my meaning," with an implicit "It's yours" often thrown in.

On the other hand, my responsibilities as "receiver" are just as self-centered and narrowly defined as the sender's: I get your meaning from the words you use. When I feel I've done that, but it turns out that what I got isn't what you meant, whose fault is it? Again, it's more than likely not me: "I know what I saw. I know what I heard. Something happened to the words before I got them, either on their way to me, or as a result of something you did before sending them." Often faulty "wording" or, more generally, "sending," is the suspected problem: "Why didn't you just say what you meant?" "Why didn't you say so in the first place?" "Say what you mean." "What did you mean to say?" "You said it, so you must have meant it." "If you didn't mean it, then why did you say it?" These are commonly used ways to tell you, "It's not my fault if I don't get your meaning," with "It's yours" often implied.

The really great thing about the conduit metaphor is that it teaches us that we can have communication success without much effort (Reddy, 1979). The world is a place where "I know what you mean" and "You know what I mean" (how many times have you heard and used those expressions?) all of the time, because of our assumptions that meanings are expressible in language that we can easily trade back and forth with one another, like packages. Successful communication becomes mainly an exercise in appropriate packaging and delivery of messages.

Do you remember that the little questionnaire from Table 2.1 had a couple of items (6 and 7) in addition to the conduit statements (1–5)? Item 6 said that "Basically, success in communication depends more on 'message sending' skills than on 'message receiving' skills." Item 7 said that "In communication, perfectly clear communication or understanding is the normal state of affairs, and miscommunication or misunderstanding the exception." There is a third item that should be included but wasn't because some of my earlier statements about communication being "hard work" might have biased your response. However, this item was included in the larger version of the questionnaire that was given to all those people who provided me "personal definitions" of communication. The item is: "All in all, successful communication between people is easy." These three items relate to the conduit statements of the questionnaire as seen by others who have completed them all.

Among the questionnaire respondents, "sending skills" and "receiving skills" differ in importance, relative to how strongly one subscribes to the conduit statements of the questionnaire. People who tended to agree with the conduit statements tended also to agree with item 6 of Table 2.1 (with correlation coefficients of .40 and higher). Or stated another way, people who tended to disagree with the conduit statements tended also to disagree that communication depends more on sending than on receiving skills. Within a conduit framework, this relation between acceptance of conduit views and "sender appreciation" (or "receiver depreciation," as the case may be) makes sense, because the transfer of meaning depends foremost on message "sending," or more particularly, someone "sending" a message. Meanings don't just materialize spontaneously. They are transferred—sent—*from* somewhere *to* somewhere else. The receiver's role in communication is logically devalued because, in an interpersonal exchange, what you in your receiver role learn of my views will hinge largely on what I tell you—what I "send." And as for me in the role of receiver, exactly the same thing applies to what I learn of your views—it will depend on what you "send." So within the conduit view, it seems sensible that the sending side of communication should rightfully enjoy more attention than the receiving side.

A few paragraphs back, we discussed the logical connection between conduit views and assumptions about the fidelity between "sent" and "received" messages.

The previously discussed questionnaire supports this thinking, although again the results are only correlational. Specifically, people who tended to agree with conduit statements tended also to agree that "In communication, perfectly clear communication or understanding is the normal state of affairs, and miscommunication or misunderstanding the exception." (With correlation coefficients of .30 and higher.) And those who disagreed with conduit statements tended to disagree that perfectly clear communication is normal. Without retracing the rationale behind this connection, it suggests there are some pretty confident and comfortable communicators out there—related, apparently, to acceptance of the conduit metaphor.

The item omitted from your questionnaire concerned the perceived ease of "successful communication." Again, what looks to be a logical relationship between conduit views and this view was outlined a few paragraphs earlier. The questionnaire results also support this connection. People tending to agree with conduit views also tended to agree with the statement, "All in all, successful communication between people is easy." (With correlation coefficients of .31 and higher.) Or stated another way, those disagreeing with conduit views tended to disagree that "communication is easy."

So What?

Communication has been discussed so far mostly in terms of what it isn't. This is because a sizable number of English speakers (possibly even a large majority) appear to believe that communication works in a way that, objectively, it really doesn't—like a conduit or pipeline. And the difference that it makes, whether one subscribes to the assumptions of the conduit metaphor, may be the same difference as my believing that that young man on the subway car at the beginning of this chapter was a thug and not someone less dangerous. Definitions shape actions, and the assumptions of the conduit metaphor can lead to corollary beliefs and actions that are anything but benign in furthering the purposes of human communication.

"Sender"/"sending" orientation. The conduit metaphor functions, in Schön's (1979) terminology, as a "problem-setting" metaphor. It points us in certain directions in defining what should receive our attention as communicators, and in anticipating or diagnosing communication problems. The conduit metaphor elevates the status of "sending" and neglects or at least downplays that of "receiving." Fundamentally, meaning is regarded as largely "sender" controlled, because the sender's meanings are assumed to be transferred. So both personally and organizationally, the most sensible preventative and remedial measures to "improve communication"—my own or my organization's—should center around improving "sending skills": vocabulary, message creation techniques of speaking and writing, how to send messages using such communication channels as computer networks, voice mail, electronic bulletin boards, and the like. The "receiving" side of communication will automatically benefit if the "sending" side improves, so the thinking goes. Consequently, "receiving" needs—and will

probably get—little formal attention.

Confidence, complacency. The conduit metaphor describes a communicative world where "sent" and "received" messages are most often the same, a natural corollary of sender control over the transfer of meaning. This of course also presumes "intentional" meanings to be the most common and relevant result of communication. "Unintended" communication—you know, where you say "A," but for some reason it's taken as "Q"—is more or less dismissed as improbable or simply irrelevant, or both. In any event, the message that "counts," within the conduit framework, is the one "sent" by the sender. And the one sent is assumed to be the one that gets there—whether it does or not. The conduit framework instills an effortless confidence about the fidelity of sent and received meanings. This kind of confidence helps us congratulate ourselves, no doubt. But it's no different from the misplaced self-congratulation of the man who, in the expression, "was born on third base and grew up thinking he hit a triple." The bigger problem is not so much the arrogance of the conduit view, but the complacency that so often comes with assuming "easy success." Ultimately it justifies investing minimal effort in communication responsibilities, personal and organizational. And the perverse beauty of it is, we think we're doing all that's necessary.

A limited vocabulary. The conduit metaphor has given us an entire vocabulary with which to talk about communication between people and in organizations. As suggested earlier, some of the old "stand-by" terms in published discussions of communication are pretty clear expressions of the conduit metaphor. In a 1984 article I reviewed more than 20 popular management textbooks used in business schools, looking specifically at metaphorical imagery in the books' treatments of organizational and managerial communication (Axley, 1984). Altogether, almost certainly thousands of these books have been sold. The published discussions of communication used in "educating" many present and future managers are grounded in the conceptual vocabulary of the conduit metaphor. We hear about "senders" of meaning and messages on one end and "receivers" of same on the other, connected by "channels." Virtually every published model of interpersonal or organizational communication there is relies on these terms. And a whole *network* of related terms reinforces the pipeline imagery, and thus the core assumptions. One of the most ubiquitous expressions of the conduit metaphor (right up there with "network") is "flow." Try to find a published discussion of organizational communication that does not somewhere employ at least some of the following "flow-connected" expressions: "communication flow," "information flow," "information leaks," "flow of messages," "downward communication flow," "upward communication flow," "horizontal communication flow," "filtering of information," "bottlenecks in communication," "communication barriers," "communication blockage," "free flow of communication," "grapevine," "flow of feedback," "open communication," "gatekeeper," and many others.

The conduit metaphor influences our thinking about communication through a vocabulary of expressions that supports its core assumptions. Its objectification of "meaning" not only allows us to speak, straight-faced, of endless varieties of "communication flow," but also to actually quantify the exact amount of "meaning" moving through the pipeline:

"Research indicates that facial expression and tone of voice account for 90 percent of the communication between people" (Bateman & Zeithaml, 1993, p. 510).
"When people communicate in person, as much as 60 percent of the content of the message is transmitted through facial expressions and body movement" (Hellriegel & Slocum, 1992, p. 509).
"Studies often conclude that over 50 percent of the impact of communication comes through facial expressions, another 30 percent from inflection and tone of voice, and less than 10 percent from the content of the message" (Aldag & Stearns, 1991, p. 487).

There is hardly a published discussion of organizational or interpersonal communication that does not throw around numbers like these. The numbers themselves are unimportant. What is important, however, is the point of view purveyed, allowing otherwise thoughtful people to think and speak in earnest about the creation and totality of "human meaning" as though it can be more or less "semantically engineered." Can we assemble and disassemble "meanings" like we might cars, or toasters—with such precision, objectivity, and control implied by our vocabulary of expressions? Or do the expressions deceive us—and help us deceive ourselves?

Gaining Perspective

This chapter has examined how definitions shape our lives by determining our actions. Definitions are language-made, and one of the most important ways we use language in defining things is with metaphors. It has been suggested that the conduit metaphor is a very popular view of communication, and understandably so: it's simple, helps us feel sure about ourselves and our communication, makes communication seem easy, but lets us duck the blame when we discover it isn't. And maybe most important, our language helps us constantly, if unwittingly, reinforce the perspective.

But of course perspective is, by definition, a relative term. Perspective implies a view *from* somewhere. We've been looking at communication from the point of view of the conduit metaphor. And, we've been trying to look at the conduit metaphor itself more or less from the inside, through its assumptions, linguistic expressions, and so forth. However, to really reveal the limitations of the conduit perspective, it is best to view it from a different perch, a perspective that more realistically accommodates the idiosyncracies of perception and that portrays both how communication works, and how communication *is* work. That's the subject of the next chapter.

Chapter 3

Communication: What It Is

The great enemy of communication is the illusion of it.

William H. Whyte, Jr.

You can't have the fruits without the roots.

Stephen R. Covey

Revolutions begin with an assault on awareness.

Richard Pascale

TWO ILLUSTRATIONS

Let's address what communication *is* by first looking at two common instances of what communication *does*. Examples like the following are legion.

THE FOUR-POUND PINBALL

Superior Steel Works (SSW) is a supplier to the oil exploration industry. It manufactures heavy equipment used on off-shore drilling platforms, including various sized tanks or "bottles" for huge gas compressors, and gigantic "skids" on which the compressors themselves are mounted. Much of what is made is done with cutting torches, arc-welders, and finished with grinders, sand-blasters, and paint.

Ed was a welder's helper, newly graduated from high school, working a summer job at SSW before beginning college. He assisted Sam—a very skillful welder and his boss—with whatever Sam needed to fabricate the skids and bottles to certain specifications.

It was a blisteringly hot Friday afternoon in July. A large bottle that Sam had welded together was ready for finishing, inside and out. The tank was cylindrical like a railroad tank car, with rounded ends, was 15 feet long, large enough around for a man to stoop in, and had two round "portals," each about 2 feet or so in diameter, on opposite sides near one end. Ed had polished the weld seams on the inside of the tank with a hand grinder, and afterward, other workers had sprayed the whole inside of the tank with primer to protect it from rust. Finally, before the bottle was sent elsewhere in the plant, Ed needed to remove the "gussets" from the inside. Gussets were pieces of metal that had been "spot-welded" across the seams of the steel plates to hold the plates in place until the seams could be completely welded. Then, their purpose served, the gussets were to be removed before the product was shipped.

It was Ed's first experience "in a bottle" and with gussets. There were two conversations that took place between Sam and Ed. The first one went like this:

SAM: Once you get in that tank to knock those gussets off, work fast or the primer fumes will get you.

ED: Okay.

SAM: They've just been spot-welded in there, but you'll have to knock hell out of 'em with a hammer to bust 'em off. You got it?

ED: Okay. Gotcha.

And off Sam went, to do other things, confident, as was Ed, that Ed had "got it." As it turned out, Ed "got it" alright. He and Sam had another conversation a little later—at the plant's first aid station:

ED: You told me to "knock hell out of 'em with a hammer" . . . I guess I did, huh?

SAM: Yeah, but I meant, "give her a tap with a 16-ounce hammer," *NOT* "swing from the floor with a *sledgehammer*!"

ED: Oh. I guess I didn't duck fast enough when the gusset ricocheted off the wall?

SAM: Nope . . . about eight stitches too slow.

(All names are disguised. Printed by permission of the author, whose name has been withheld by request.)

What Ed got from Sam's instructions (which, by the way, expresses assumption number four of the conduit metaphor—"extracting meanings from words") was a "surprise." Both men thought Ed knew what Sam meant by, "knock hell out of 'em with a hammer." The trouble was, Sam meant one thing, Ed meant something different, but both thought they meant the same thing. Ed chose a hammer that, to his inexperienced hand, was worthy of "knocking hell out of" those gussets. On his first swing a gusset shot off its spot-welds and became, in effect, a four-pound pinball—with lots of irregular, sharp edges—ricocheting all over the inside of the tank until it hit Ed's head. Eight stitches in his right eyebrow, a monster headache, a king-sized shiner that lasted for weeks, some lost work time, and embarrassment that something so preventable hadn't been. And it could have been worse.

SMOKIN' MOE

Moe Davies was a foreman of electricians for a large construction contractor. He was openly known by company regulars as "Smokin' Moe," partly in acknowledgement of the unfiltered Camels he smoked one after another, but mostly in tribute to how his visible "energy" level resembled the fighting style of once heavyweight boxing champ, "Smokin' Joe Frazier." Smokin' Moe the foreman was, like Smokin' Joe the fighter, a buzzsaw of a man. It was said that in his days before becoming a foreman, he would routinely accomplish, working alone, what two or three other skilled people might do in the same amount of time. Smokin' Moe got things done.

On a personal level Smokin' Moe got along with his crews okay. He enjoyed organizational "storytelling," and every now and then would join his crews at break or lunch time, to just sit and talk about anything under the sun.

On a supervisory level, however, there were some quirks of his style that bugged most of the people who worked for him. The main one was a sometime "inconsistency" between what he would *say* about certain jobs versus what he would then *do* regarding those jobs. Here are two examples.

The crews consisted of two or three people: a journeyman electrician or lead man and apprentice(s). Often crews were combined on large jobs. They worked only on industrial, commercial, and institutional jobs, not private residential ones. When a job was assigned, the crew working on it was given a blueprint with the relevant specifications. The blueprint showed the "what" of the job—what the final product should look like. Customarily, the crews involved were responsible for the "how" of the job—planning how the job would be done, coordinating with other building crafts, determining what materials would be needed, the approximate time frame for completion, executing the plans, and so on. This allowed crew members to invest themselves in their jobs—which was very satisfying for most of them.

Except that Smokin' Moe sometimes "surprised" crews. Basically this took the following form: In the earliest stages of a job, he almost always made it a point to leave the responsibility for planning the job with the crew, even saying explicitly that that's "your baby." But from planning to execution, Moe's "hands-off" approach could change unpredictably. His apparent initial confidence would evaporate. Sometimes this occurred a little at a time throughout the course of the job: He might wonder, about a part of the job that had been completed, "why'd you do it *that* way?" followed by something like, "I think maybe I'd have done it *this* way," and then just leave it at that. Other times, though, his confidence—and virtually all latitude—dried up instantaneously: "Jeez, why'd you do it *that* way? *We'll* have to re-do it *this* way," followed by detailed instructions as to how it was to be re-done, and probably even his own physical labor in re-doing it.

These weren't violations of electrical code. About that there would never be an argument. These were different personal preferences about how something should be done, and the need to have things *his* way. But more than that, was the problem of "saying" one thing, while in other ways saying something contradictory. Crews were routinely given lots of "rope" initially, sometimes to be "hung" with it by Smokin' Moe later. Both the "affirmation" and any eventual "negation" meant something to Moe's people. But one message was a whisper, and the other, a shout.

The second example of this style could be seen on a more one-to-one level. There were many times when Moe would give his "it's-your-baby" endorsement of a very specific job, even relatively "harmless" ones, such as bending and mounting a run of electrical conduit, but then would "hover" practically right on top of the worker—whether a journeyman or an apprentice—watching every move with a running commentary "suggesting" alternate ways of doing the work. In case you've never experienced this kind of "under-the-microscope" observation, it frequently makes the "observed" *very* self-conscious, sometimes even to the point of blundering in exactly the ways that the observer is so hell-bent on avoiding. Sometimes people made mistakes—including getting "bitten" by live wires—mainly because of their "Oh-____-he's-watching-me!" preoccupation with avoiding those mistakes under the omnipresent and critical eye of Smokin' Moe. (All names are disguised.)

Lessons Learned

The lessons learned are (1) communication is more complicated than people realize; (2) communication is more consequential than people realize; (3) a great deal of misery, frustration, anger, destructive relationships, wasted time, money, and energy could be spared if people understood how communication works and how it *requires* work; and (4) a great deal of human productivity and fulfillment in organizations and relationships could be gained if people understood how communication works and how it requires work. These are just four of the more important "lessons" of "The Four-Pound Pinball" and of "Smokin' Moe." And each lesson has subtle and serious implications. The remainder of this chapter shows what it is that so complicates communication and previews the *real work* needed to communicate effectively. Chapter 4 then goes into the practical details of this work.

A SNEAKY METAPHOR

The last chapter introduced the ideas that our language not only does things *for* us, but also *to* us. The same hammer that drives the nail busts our thumbs. In his inimitable style, Richard Mitchell (1979) warns us of consequences of language, which may be less dramatic and sudden than smashed thumbs, but which are ultimately much more serious in our lives: "When our forebears had no language and no knowledge, the best they could do was sniff the lion in the long grass," he says (p. 34). And of course, the development of language changed all of that, allowing us to learn from and share narrow escapes from lions in the past so as to maybe anticipate and avoid the lions altogether in the future. Unless we don't get our language right. Mitchell updates us: "Nowadays, we notice that there is very little danger of being eaten by lions. Nevertheless, the destiny that waits in the long grass for the silly boob who can't get his language straight is not a good one, although, of course, it does last longer than the business of being eaten by a lion. It's more like being eaten by a worm, slowly" (Mitchell, 1979, p. 35).

Mitchell's book, *Less Than Words Can Say* (1979), is still the cleanest, one-swing knockout of wrong-headed language around. And although his concern is more with language and its grammar as a whole than mine, our common purpose is to heighten awareness of the power of language to shape human destinies, for better and worse. That's a necessary first step toward betterment.

Mitchell's eye for "abusers" and the abuse of language is as keen as any eagle's, but with his disposition of offenders a little more malevolent—maybe as merciful as the shrike. But *this* book is not really about "abusers" and "abuse" as it concerns language and what I've portrayed as our nemesis, the conduit metaphor. It's not as though the linguistic structures which more or less make us talk and write about communication in terms of the conduit metaphor somehow pervert good grammar or mark their users as ignoramuses or sloppy thinkers. Rather, it is more the built-in biasing features of our language about communication that limit our thinking, than the other way around.

It's neither reasonable, nor probably even possible, to eradicate the conduit metaphor from our language, and many people probably wonder what all the fuss is about. Along the lines of "frame conflict" discussed in chapter 2, you might not be convinced. But even if you have been, there's the question of, "for how long?" As Michael Reddy (1979) lamented, it's certainly possible, for purposes of discussion, to shift metaphorical frames from the conduit metaphor to something more realistic but less comfortable. But there's every reason to expect the shift to be fleeting and fragmentary, as any contending perspective must challenge, for many, a deeply insinuated and psychologically rewarding habit of mind and of language.

No, the antidote for the conduit metaphor is not a one-shot dose of prose exposing its limits and its unfortunate by-products. The conduit metaphor is less like an infection that can be treated once and for all with a blast of antibiotics, and more like a chronic affliction that never really leaves, but rather moves in and out of dormancy. Our language will ensure that it's never far from our consciousness, or more likely, our subconscious. The goal concerning the conduit metaphor shouldn't be eradication, but rather *mindfulness* and *vigilance*: Mindfulness of alternative views of communication; mindfulness of the conduit metaphor's subtlety in our expressions ("subtlety in our expressions" expresses assumption three of the conduit metaphor—"words contain . . ."); mindfulness of just how frequently our ordinary thinking and talking about communication is filled with expressions of the conduit metaphor ("thinking and talking . . . is filled with expressions" expresses assumptions two and three of the conduit metaphor—"people insert thoughts and feelings in words" and "words contain the thoughts . . ."); mindfulness of its consequences; and mindfulness of what's needed to counteract its destructive effects. Mindfulness of this sort can enable the vigilance necessary for self-control of its consequences.

The conduit metaphor is a formidable adversary of effective communication. Its main advantages are stealth and pervasiveness, and its main appeal is psychological comfort. Let's compare it to a view of communication that squares more with the realities of communicating, and that I hope will help make us all *less* comfortable and certain about what we're doing when we try to communicate.

DEFINING COMMUNICATION

The conduit metaphor is essentially an informal model of communication—an "in-the-head" model. There are literally scores of other, formal, published "communication models." These are often more "in-the-book" than "in-the-head." A communication scholar friend of mine once critiqued the discipline's work, only partly facetiously, as "boxology run amuck"—a search for the ultimate configuration of "boxes" in a model, with interconnecting vectors ("sending," "receiving," and "feedback," of course), and just the right labels on everything, to reveal, finally, what communication is and what happens when people communicate. But of course, like all symbols, any "map" of a given "territory" can only describe a minuscule portion of, never *all* of—and often not even the most interesting parts of—the territory. In *The Log from the Sea of Cortez*, John Steinbeck demonstrates this idea beautifully, in writing about, of all things, fishing:

> The Mexican Sierra has 17 plus 15 plus 9 spines in the dorsal fin. These can easily be counted. But if the sierra strikes hard on the line so that our hands are burned, if the fish sounds and nearly escapes and finally comes in over the rail, his colors pulsing and his tail beating the air, a whole new relational externality has come into being—an entity which is more than the sum of the fish plus the fisherman. The only way to count the spines of the sierra unaffected by this second relational reality is to sit in a laboratory, open an evil-smelling jar, remove a stiff colorless fish from the formalin solution, count the spines, and write the truth. . . . There you have recorded a reality which cannot be assailed—probably the least important reality concerning either the fish or yourself.
>
> It is good to know what you are doing. The man with his pickled fish has set down one truth and recorded in his experience many lies. The fish is not that color, that texture, that dead, nor does he smell that way. (Steinbeck, 1941, p. 2)

Symbols frame things "in" and frame things "out." But let's talk about what we do know of communication in use, of what happens and doesn't happen when we communicate. This will help provide some lessons that contrast with those of the conduit metaphor.

How Communication "Works"

Just as there are communication models everywhere, there are also abundant definitions of communication. The most instructive and *con*structive definition comes from W. Charles Redding (1972). "Communication," says Redding, consists of "those behaviors of human beings, or . . . those artifacts created by human beings, which result in 'messages' [meaning] being received by one or more persons" (p. 25). In Redding's view, a person "has communicated . . . as soon as at least one other person derives some *meaning* from his words, his actions, his silences, or his inactions. Similarly, communication takes place if at least one person derives meanings from inanimate objects, intangible events, or indefinable 'climates'" (p. 26; emphasis in the original).

A few things about this definition should be mentioned here. First, the idea is implied that the basic or requisite unit for communication is one person, not two (or more) people. With communication, it doesn't take "two to tango." One will do. And interestingly, that one is not a so-called "sender." The one is really not even a "receiver," in the sense of receiving meanings from anywhere outside the one's own head. In fact, "sending," "senders," "receiving," and "receivers," like many other ordinary expressions of the communication literature, are basically the workhorses—the *Trojan* workhorses—of the conduit view of communication. I'm not suggesting that we somehow try to banish them from our language about communication, just that we recognize their origins and their "cargo."

As implied by this view, the essential person for communication is a *perceiver* or, more awkwardly, a sense maker: someone who observes something—words, acts, silence, things, and the like—and creates some personal "sense" of it. Redding's definition of communication stands traditional—that is, "conduit"—thinking and talking of communication on its head, placing most of the explanation for what happens when we communicate largely in the hands and heads of what he calls receivers, and what I call perceivers. It only takes a little thought about this point for the conceptual and practical lines between so-called "senders" and "receivers" to become blurry. The roles, whatever we call them, are not sequential, or discrete. If *you* ultimately determine messages from things I say, don't say, do, and don't do, and *I* ultimately determine messages from things you say, don't say, do, and don't do, then that means there is an incalculably immense number of messages, ongoing and simultaneous, that *we* "communicate" to one another, the "meanings" of which almost certainly we know little or nothing about. What I "communicate" to you is more under your control than mine, and what you "communicate" to me is more under my control than yours.

Redding's definition of communication is much more expansive, more connected to the whole—rather than just a narrow part—of our lives, than conduit oriented definitions. It implies a link between potentially any human experience and communication, and therefore between potentially any human experience and the attendant communication responsibilities of the people involved. That's why a book like this can examine the communication dimensions of such topics as leadership, empowerment, building teams, and managing change, among others. From the conduit perspective, communication boils down to "sending" and "receiving." And the expectation is that "receiving" occurs only under the narrowly circumscribed conditions of a sender's choosing.

Who's "in charge" of meanings makes a big difference in how we approach the communicative world. A working definition of it that puts "senders" in charge makes the communicative world an ordered, predictable, and safe place. In such a world you and I can take greater comfort in the things we say and do, because we know what their impact will be. We can believe that communication is riskless, and so we can act accordingly. We can take it easy.

The world where so-called "receivers" call the shots, however, is a much "messier" and unpredictable place—where you'll never know for sure "what" you're communicating at any time, and the odds are that none of it is exactly what you think or intend. In such a place neither of us can ever afford to drop our guard or feel secure in what we say and do, because we don't know the impact of our actions.

Which "world" would you rather inhabit? The more pertinent question is, "Which world *do* you inhabit?" The available evidence, and even common sense, argues strongly for the latter. In his 1972 book, *Communication Within the Organization: An Interpretive Review of Theory and Research*, Redding organizes a sizable portion of his review of nearly 600 sources around a number of "firmly established principles of human communication" (p. 27), so thoroughly documented or self-evident that virtually no controversy about them exists. Likewise, Watzlawick, Beavin, and Jackson present several "axioms of communication" of special relevance here, based on a wealth of clinical research on communication "pathologies," from their pioneering *Pragmatics of Human Communication* (1967). A number of these principles, from Redding and from Watzlawick et al., would be worth looking at here, in the context of the previous discussion of the conduit metaphor and what communication "isn't." By contrast, they can help us know what communication "is."

Principle 1: Meanings are not transferred—they are created in the minds of perceivers (Redding, 1972). The first part of this principle refutes the first assumption of the conduit metaphor, that meanings are transferred. The second part centers meaning in the heads of perceivers (or what Redding calls "receivers"). Whether this seems common sensical or not, it can be a startling realization for many people (see Chapter 2). In training seminars, I often use two or three simple exercises to demonstrate graphically that perceivers create meanings, rather than receive them from someone or somewhere else. One variation of the first exercise is shown in Table 3.1. Before going on, take a minute and see how you respond.

The expressions in Table 3.1—and hundreds of others—never fail to show dramatically how *different* people make different sense of the *same* words. A quick sample of ranges is: "Young," to some, is 30 years or less, but 50 years or less to others. "Middle-age" begins at 35 and ends at 50 for some, but runs from 50 to 70 for others. "Senior citizens" are over 55 for some, but over 70 for others. A "child" is 10 or less, or 20 or less. "Seldom" is 5 of 100 for some, but 30 of 100 for others. "Usually" is 51 of 100 for some, but 90 of 100 for others. "Usually not" means that something happens 1 of 100 times for some, but 20 of 100 times for others. Something happening "much of the time" happens 20 of 100 times for some, and 80 of 100 times for others. "Substantially" means at least 10% to some, but at least 51% to others. "Mainly" means anywhere from 51% to 95% Your definitions, of course, might be altogether different from these. And that, substantially (to me, 60%), is the point. If meanings were transferred, then you and I would know, without ever having to ask one another, "how frequent" frequently is, or "how rare" rarely is, and so forth.   And of course, frequently we don't.   Sometimes it makes no difference.   But occasionally it does.

A second exercise which shows graphically that meanings cannot be transferred employs a line drawing like the one in Figure 3.1.   In a workshop setting, a participant is asked to describe the drawing for others so that they can reproduce it exactly.   The stipulations imposed are that only words can be used (no hand gestures, etc.), listeners can't ask questions, although the speaker can repeat instructions as many times as seen necessary, and speakers aren't allowed to inspect drawings as they are drawn.   When the instruction-giver feels that he or she has said enough for listeners to faithfully reproduce the drawing, we then show the group the original drawing and compare their drawings for accuracy. "Accurate" reproductions in this case mean that figures and lines are essentially at the same angles, spatial relations, and size proportions to one another as in the original drawing.   This is a pretty generous definition of "accuracy."   But a number of results are predictable, in my experience with the hundreds of managers and supervisors who have done it: (1) although listeners often feel frustration at not being able to question the instruction-givers, the majority of listeners feel confident, before they actually get to see the original drawing, that their reproduction is accurate; (2) the majority of instruction-givers feel confident, before they get to see the results of their instructions, that the reproductions will be accurate; (3) only a very small percentage of drawings (maybe two or three drawings, in a 30-person group), and often zero, will turn

Table 3.1
What's It To You?

Below are a number of commonly used expressions.   For each one, use the blank to specify what it means **to you**:

_____1.   "Young" (What's the age range of someone who's "young"?)
_____2.   "Middle-aged" (What's the age range of someone who's "middle-aged"?)
_____3.   "Senior citizen" (What's the age range of someone who's a "senior citizen"?)
_____4.   "Child" (What's the age range of someone who's a "child"?)
_____5.   "Seldom" (How many times out of 100 would something happen if it happened "seldom"?)
_____6.   "Usually" (How many times out of 100 would something happen if it happened "usually"?)
_____7.   "Usually not" (If something does "usually not" happen, how many times out of 100 *does* it happen?)
_____8.   "Much of the time" (How many times out of 100 would something happen if it happened "much of the time"?)
_____9.   "Substantially" (If something is "substantially" this or that, what percentage does that mean?)
_____10.   "Mainly" (If something is "mainly" this or that, what percentage does that mean?)

Figure 3.1
Line Drawing

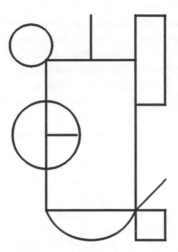

out to be accurate; and (4) the drawings that people produce are often wildly different, but each is a legitimate interpretation of the words that everyone was exposed to.

Try this on someone, with yourself as the instruction-giver. It's a virtually fail-safe way of teaching humility about making yourself understood. In workshops, the ideal instruction-giver is someone from the group who has shown the "gift of gab" and who seems confident and articulate in his or her verbal skills. That's what makes it such a compelling demonstration that language doesn't transfer meanings: We've got someone who's obviously a facile verbal communicator, and who tries to accomplish just about the simplest communication task imaginable—describing a simple line drawing so that others can reproduce it accurately. It's not like we're trying to build a rocket together, much less develop a shared understanding of something truly complicated like "justice" or "democracy" or "prejudice" or "love." Yet this simplest of communication tasks produces overwhelming failure rates, when accurate reproduction is the criterion for "success" (and great diversity of "meanings," which of course could itself be a criterion for "success" under some communication conditions)—because people take the symbols they perceive and create, idiosyncratically, their own meanings. And even in those rare instances where drawings do match up (by the relatively "loose" standards previously mentioned), that's not because a "transfer" of meanings took place. It's because one person was able to create meanings that were close enough to the creations of another to reproduce a more or less accurate line drawing. But keep in mind that such outcomes have been, in my experiences with hundreds of supervisors and managers, the exception. The rule in this—and every—communication exercise is inaccuracy and diversity of meanings, not accuracy and uniformity.

One final point needs reiterating before moving on to the next principle: If meanings were "transferred" in communication, then misunderstanding simply wouldn't occur, whether it's over line drawings, over instructions to "knock hell out of" some gussets "with a hammer," over what "participative management" or "in a little while" means, or over any words. But just like that young welder's helper that summer, people get "bonked" on the head all the time, figuratively and literally, by assuming that communication transfers meanings—or really, by the easy confidence and corresponding lack of communicative effort that such an assumption ultimately engenders. Make no mistake: "transferred meaning" is a seductive and comfortable notion—but unrealistic and often downright dangerous.

Principle 2: Anything is a potential message (Redding, 1972). This principle makes communication a wide-open proposition, fraught with uncertainty and the potential for surprise. But many people forget this, assuming that the things having message value—or lacking message value—for them will have the same value for others. This principle reminds us that anything "perceivable" can be made meaningful by someone. There are the obvious "intentional" message sources that come to mind immediately: what we say and write—the actual words we string together. Many people want what they say and write—their words—to be the exclusive sources of their messages. This is understandable, since our "word choices" help us believe, comfortingly but nonetheless mistakenly, that we're ultimately in control of what we communicate. This principle reminds us that such control is largely illusory. It reminds us that so much of what we "communicate" to others is "unintentional," because people can and will make meanings—messages—from anything . . . *Anything*:

Take the case of a professor who, when he lectured, liberally punctuated his sentences, through and through, with the phrase, "sort of." As in, something has "sort of" this quality, or "sort of" that quality. Things didn't *do*—they "sort of" did. Ideas weren't good, bad, strong, weak, brilliant, bone-headed, and the like, they were "sort of" those things. Virtually everything he said was, well, "sort of" qualified in this way, often several times in the same sentence. That phrase and the number of times he used it—yes, its recurrence practically demanded, "count me"—acquired message value for a number of his students. The "messages" ran from, "he's nervous" to "he's unsure about everything" to "he won't take a definite stance on anything" to "he's entertaining" to "how can he be unaware of this mannerism?" to "what a scatterbrain" to "fifty-seven times in three minutes—a new record!" He probably didn't know his actions had such message value, much less what the "messages" were that others made of his actions. I doubt, also, that he intended to communicate what he communicated to his students.

The same could be said for Smokin' Moe and the difficulties described earlier between him and the people he supervised. With Moe, his verbal "okay, it's your baby" meant, among other positive things, "I trust you." But much of his "hovering" and "about-faces" meant, for some, that he really didn't. And eventually, because of enough inconsistency between words and deeds, his verbal approval by itself came to be viewed suspiciously, even before he had the opportunity to affirm or disconfirm it behaviorally. This meant that his crews spent lots of time and energy watching their flanks and repeatedly checking with him about plans—instead of doing the job—because they didn't believe him when he said, "okay, it's your baby." Probably Moe did not *intend* his actions to undermine and negate his words. Nor did he intend the resulting frustration, mistrust, and inefficiency that came to define many of his working relationships.

Finally, I frequently have the opportunity to visit with employers who recruit students on college campuses. In these visits I've always tried to learn something from the recruiters, in the form of advice, that I can take back to my students to help them prepare for that crucial "first interview" they'll have. The advice collected isn't as important here as the fact that it underscores the very points that anything can have message value, and that even momentary and seemingly minor lapses in attention to this truth—not to mention complete ignorance of it—are indeed consequential: Recruiters routinely disqualify applicants whose garb or personal appearance is "unbusinesslike" or "unprofessional" (which, as you might imagine, has as many different definitions as definers); they "make something" of handshakes, of eye contact during the interview, of fluency, vocabulary, and vocal mannerisms, of whether applicants know anything about the organization (and what, specifically), of what kinds of questions applicants ask, and of many, *any* other behavioral, artifactual, and contextual cues that can be made meaningful; resumés can be "too long" or "too short," "insufficiently detailed" or "excessively detailed," or "unprofessional" in appearance, organization, print quality, paper texture and weight; a single grammatical or stylistic oddity in a resumé signals, to many recruiters, "not smart enough or conscientious enough to work for us," and lands the offender in the "circular file," regardless of content or qualifications. More than an interview prep guide, this catalog of what can and does have message value—it is a reminder that "anything is a potential message." Those who remember the lesson can better use it to their advantage—"how" comes later—rather than be victimized by it.

This principle of human communication—anything is a potential message—accounts for an enormous number of the "headaches" and unpleasant "surprises" people experience in their personal and professional lives. (On the other hand, of course, it helps explain much of why "art" speaks with so many personalized voices; and keep in mind that many communication "surprises" are in fact pleasant.) There are hundreds of examples, but the most convincing ones will be your own. So please, think of two or three recent instances where you as a perceiver, or someone you know, "made the message." And because we're saying that anything can have message value, the farther you look from the "traditional" sources—words—the more compelling the demonstration. Do these questions help?

1. What conclusions ("messages") have you "made" based on how someone's office or room "looks"—type and arrangement of furniture, neatness of objects, presence of artifacts (pictures, books, signs, "stuff"), and the like?
2. What conclusions ("messages") have you "made" based on someone's facial expression—a smile, frown, quizzical look, expressionless stare, glower, and so forth? Has anyone recently looked at you in that tone of "voice"?
3. What conclusions ("messages") have you "made" based on someone's appearance—clothing, jewelry, grooming, size, and the like?
4. What conclusions ("messages") have you "made" based on someone's food preferences, or "how" they eat?
5. What conclusions ("messages") have you "made" based on someone's "entertainment" preferences—TV, types of programs, reading, types of reading, films, types of films, music, types of music, "live" entertainment and types, and so forth?
6. What conclusions ("messages") have you "made" based on "how" someone said something or on their mannerisms?

This list could go on and on. That's because we do these things—*make messages* from everything imaginable—all the time. The idea of a so-called "sender" communicating only what he or she wants is a happy thought—but it just doesn't happen that way. And that's because anything is a potential message, and because perceivers ultimately determine what has message value.

Principle 3: The message perceived is the only one that "counts" (Redding, 1972). This principle simply means that when perceivers have determined the message value of something, *those* perceptions are the bases for further thought and action, not any intended meanings or lack of intended meanings on the part of other persons. And in view of the earlier point that "received" ("perceived") meanings are *never* exactly the same as "sent" ("intended") meanings, this principle takes on special importance. Think about the implications: I will always be off, sometimes more, sometimes less, in matching my meanings (as I create and understand them) perfectly with your meanings (as you create and understand them), and because of the uniqueness of perception and the nature of symbolic behavior (discussed in Chapter 2), I can act only on the basis of mine, not yours. Sometimes it matters, sometimes it doesn't. Sometimes it's funny. Sometimes it's deadly serious:

There's a form of "miscommunication" that Haney (1986) calls *bypassing*. Bypassing occurs when people ("sender" and "receiver") "miss each other with their meanings" (p. 250). (Note the "conduit" imagery and assumptions implicit to *missing someone with your meanings* and even the term, *bypassing*, as though meanings can somehow be aimed and projected toward others, and passed right by others. This operationalizes assumptions 1–3 of the conduit metaphor, Chapter 2, and is an especially compelling testament to Reddy's claim that it's nearly impossible for English speakers to avoid conduit-based terms. For if ever there were a thinker who is both sensitive to the influences of language on our behavior, and philosophically antagonistic to the conduit metaphor, it is assuredly Haney.) In other words (there's another conduit expression!), you make *this* sense from our communicative exchange, I make *that* sense, while we both assume we're making the *same* sense, but neither of us recognizes that we're not. Often we don't realize that it happened, because the consequences of our communication don't call attention to it. But there are assuredly other times when consequences—bonk!—cause us to wonder "what happened" or "what went wrong."

Sometimes the latter is just funny, as much as anything else. David Ricks's book, *Big Business Blunders* (1983), is loaded with examples that you'd almost have to cry about if they weren't just a little funny:

> The naming of a new automobile model to be marketed in Germany by Rolls Royce was a difficult undertaking. The company felt that the English name "Silver Mist" was very appealing but discovered that the name would undoubtedly not capture the German market as hoped. In German, the translated meaning of "mist" is actually "excrement," and the Germans could not possibly have found such a name appealing. Unfortunately, the Sunbeam Corporation did not learn of this particular translation problem in time and attempted to enter the German market advertising its new mist-producing hair curling iron, the "Mist-Stick." As should have been expected, the Germans had no interest in a "dung" or "manure" wand.
>
> A British and U.S. joint venture proposal ran into serious difficulties . . . when the U.S. firm requested that certain key points be "tabled." The British firm agreed and both parties prepared for the negotiations. When the British team brought up for discussion those topics which had been "tabled," both parties became highly irritated. It seems that in the United States "to table a motion" means to avoid discussion of it, but in England, the same phrase often means to bring the topic to the table for discussion. The Americans had requested the exact opposite of what they had really wanted. (pp. 39–40, 56)

As a final example of how bypassing sometimes produces comical results, it's hard to top a story recounted recently on a late-night talk show by the well-known network sports commentator and (then) himself a late-night talk show host, Bob Costas. Costas was describing one of the funniest "bloopers" he had ever witnessed first-hand in the broadcast booth. It seems that two of his colleagues were broadcasting a baseball game from St. Louis during National Dairy Week. As part of the promotion of the event, a very attractive "Miss Cheesecake" representing a dairy association visited the broadcast booth toting a cheesecake for the broadcasters. At some point after Miss Cheesecake's departure from the booth but before the cheesecake had been served to the broadcasters, one asked the other, on air, "what do you think of Miss Cheesecake?" To which the other man replied, apparently believing that he had been asked, "what do you think of *this cheesecake*?": "I'd like to have a piece of that right now" (used by permission).

The serious side of bypassing shows all too clearly that "the message perceived is the only one that counts." The near-disastrous "head-bonking" described earlier affirms the truth of this principle. It mattered not in the least what Sam, Ed's supervisor, meant by those fateful instructions. What ultimately mattered was what *Ed meant* by Sam's instructions, and their mutual ignorance that Sam meant one thing and Ed meant another. Ed acted on his meaning, not Sam's.

The same was true for the pilot of a United Airlines DC-10, after aborting at the last second his plane's takeoff from the Philadelphia International Airport on February 3, 1982. A picture of the aftermath, as shown in the *Chicago Tribune* (February 5, 1982), bears the caption, "Takeoff aborted after false alarm," followed by:

Some of the 144 passengers from a United Airlines DC-10 walk through the fog after sliding down emergency chutes at Philadelphia International Airport Wednesday. The unidentified pilot told officials he heard a radio report of an engine fire and, assuming it was for his plane, aborted the takeoff. The plane, bound for Los Angeles, went off the runway and sank in mud. No serious injuries were reported. Investigators say there was no apparent sign of an engine fire on the DC-10 and that the broadcast was probably intended for another aircraft. (p. 4)

It didn't matter if the broadcast was intended for another plane. What mattered was that *that* pilot thought it was intended for him. The message he perceived was the one that counted, for him, for his passengers, and for United Airlines.

And so, too, in the case of "Room 406," a tragic but true story described in Haney (1986, pp. 293–294). This case describes an actual hospital incident in which two nurses bypassed one another in a complicated exchange of comments that, so the case strongly implies, resulted in the death of a patient's wife, after the patient himself had expired in the hospital.

We act on the messages we perceive, which *we* create. Meanings are never the same from person to person, and the message ("meaning") perceived is the only one that counts. Lots of times it doesn't matter whether anyone remembers these truths. But lots of times it does.

Principle 4: Interpersonal messages have "content" and "relational" components (Watzlawick et al., 1967). This principle is based on the clinical work of Paul Watzlawick and his colleagues. When we speak to one another, there are simultaneously two levels of "messages" involved. One involves the "content" of our messages. (Note that "content of messages" is clearly a "conduit"-oriented expression—operationalizing assumptions 2 and 3 of the conduit frame-work—even though these authors' thinking is anything but conduit oriented. Again, in talking about communication, it's exceedingly hard to avoid reinforcing, at some level of consciousness, the tenets of the conduit metaphor, because its imagery is everywhere in our language.) "Content"—sometimes called the "report" element of a message—simply refers to the "what" of a message. This level of message is purely "informational"—our words taken more or less at face value, stripped of the myriad other things that can color our interpretations.

It's the aforementioned "other things" that make up the trickier "relational" elements of communication, sometimes called the "command" elements. The relational or command elements of a message give us two kinds of clues: "how" to interpret the "content" part of the message, and "how" we each define our mutual relationship, in terms of equality or differences between us. Watzlawick et al. (1967) put it this way:

> The report aspect of a message conveys information and is, therefore, synonymous in human communication with the *content* of the message. It may be about anything that is communicable regardless of whether the particular information is true or false, valid, invalid, or undecidable. The command aspect, on the other hand, refers to what sort of message it is to be taken as, and, therefore, ultimately to the *relationship* between the communicants. (Watzlawick et al., 1967, pp. 51–52; emphasis in the original)

The content or report aspect "conveys the 'data' of the communication," while the relational or command aspect, "how this communication is to be taken" (p. 53). Words do the work of the "content" aspect. Everything else does the work of the relational or command aspect. The latter, of course, encompasses a gigantic number of things potentially affecting the relational or command dimensions of communication. Some examples of content and relational elements in communication will help. Let's start closest to home.

The words you're reading in this book make up the content part of my (intended) message to you. But there are numerous features besides words alone that shape your interpretations of the "content" here—such as the way certain expressions are used and emphasized, the structure of the writing, the degree of formality (or informality) in my "voice," the kinds of stories and examples given, and so forth. Several features that might have relational message value for you are purposeful on my part—others aren't. And regardless of which is which, the fact remains: What they are and what they "mean" is ultimately up to *you*.

Vocal "emphasis" colors our interpretation of spoken communication all the time. For instance, consider the following question someone might ask: Why do you believe that's true? Pretty neutral content, as is. But how does interpretation of it change, even if only slightly, when different words are emphasized? In the list below, the informational message—content—of each question is identical. But in each case, there's a message about the informational message that differs from one to another. Look at each question and "ask" it aloud, emphasizing the highlighted word each time. What, to you, is the "message about the informational message" in each instance?

Why do you believe that's true?
Why *do* you believe that's true?
Why do *you* believe that's true?
Why do you *believe* that's true?
Why do you believe *that's* true?
Why do you believe that's *true*?

Granted, any number of additional cues perceived in an interpersonal situation would affect interpretation of this question, such as "who" asks it that way (a boss, a subordinate, a child, a loved one, a stranger), other dimensions of "how" it is asked (shouted, whispered, through clinched jaws, dead-panned, wide-eyed, glare-eyed, with a smile, a frown, etc.), and the referent or subject of the question (is someone's ego tied to it?), to mention just a few. But all of those other things aside, just emphasizing different words within a string of words can *mean*, to a perceiver, something "relational" that qualifies and elaborates the purely informational "content" of the words.

People get excited all the time over the relational elements of communication. Take the expression, "in that tone of voice." Looking and speaking "in that tone of voice" are both relational elements of communication. Like so much concerning communication, the relational dimension is so "ever-present" as to be unnoticeable, except when circumstances call attention to it. One such circumstance is when people are at serious odds over something. In such situations, we often will comment *explicitly* that the relational elements of the communication trouble us: "Don't speak to me that way!"; "Oh sure, your words say one thing, but your actions say something else"; "You sound like you're mad at me"; "You say you're sorry, but you don't look like it"; "You sound like it's my fault"; "The way you say that, it sounds like you're blaming me"; "Say it like you mean it"; "Why do you always have to talk down to me?"; "Why do you always have to have the last word?"; "Your apology sounds phony"; "The way you said it just set me off"; "You don't have to be sarcastic"; "You don't have to talk to me like I'm a child"; "Don't be so superior-sounding"; "If only you sounded the least bit sincere"; "If you talk to me that way again, you'll be sorry"; and the list could go on and on.   Keep in mind that the "content" part of these expressions explicitly concerns relational communication and perceptions (definitions) of the particular relationship in question.   On top of that, "how" the expressions themselves are uttered—intonations, volume, rate, word emphases, physical actions, posturings, and the like—will add layers of relational meanings for each perceiver. Finally, one additional point about these examples must be made: the relational dimension of communication is very often both "cause" and "effect" in interpersonal disputes.   Anyone who's had experience with verbal head-knocking will smile at the huge number of times they've heard both the other person and themselves saying, "I was just reacting or responding to *you*."

The content and relational dimensions of communication are crucially important in both how they characterize and shape relationships between people. For the moment, I hope that I have shown these elements at work in our communication. We return to them in more depth in the next chapter.

Principle 5:   Communication interaction can be either symmetrical or complementary (Watzlawick et al., 1967). This principle is related to the previous one in that it speaks directly to the "relationship" side of communication. Its focus is broader, however, in that it applies to strings or, more accurately, *patterns* of communicative "acts" between people, called *interacts*, rather than to isolated communicative acts. Specifically, the patterns of interaction between communicators reveal their ongoing definitions of the relationship, particularly their relative status, in terms of either *equality* or *difference*. "Equality" and "difference" in this case have special meaning. They do not in any way imply "goodness" or "badness" or "strength" or "weakness" of one pattern relative to the other. Rather, "equality" means that the communicators mirror one another's communicative behavior with regard to the relational "direction" of their respective communication acts. Interaction like this is "symmetrical," in that the communicators attempt to "match" relational definitions, act to act to act. "Difference," on the other hand, means that communicators differentiate themselves from one another with regard to the relational "direction" of their respective acts. Interaction based on differentiation is "complementary," in that each communicator defines the relationship in a way that differs from that of the other, but that also *interlocks* with the definition of the other, act to act to act. The following demonstrates these patterns.

Researchers who study the relational patternings of communicators use the symbols, ↑, ↓, and →, to show the status patternings of relational definitions in a given sequence of communication acts. ↑ is read as "one up" and means that the communicator is attempting to define his or her relative status in the relationship as "superior" or "primary." ↓ is read as "one down" and means that the communicator is attempting to define his or her relative status in the relationship as "inferior" or "secondary." → is read as "one across" and means that the communicator is attempting to define his or her relative status in the relationship in "neutral" or "equal" terms. These symbols, and the relational definitions they portray, are most interesting when strung together to depict a pattern of interaction between people. That's where patterns of "symmetry" and "complementarity" can be seen. Figure 3.2 shows five common patterns—three symmetrical and two complementary.

The first row of symmetrical arrows, where all arrows are ↑, shows a pattern of interaction sometimes called "competitive symmetry." The sequencing of arrows shows the alternating utterances of two people, with each utterance (↑), except the first and last, connected (by an arc) to both an immediately preceding and a following utterance. In this pattern each communicator is attempting to define his or her status in the relationship as "primary" or dominant. Here's a "mild" example of what it could look like (keeping in mind that many forms of competitive symmetry can become much more explosive and hostile in "tone"):

HUSBAND: "We're going to the Yen Ching for dinner tonight." (↑)

WIFE: "No, I'd rather get Mexican food." (↑)

HUSBAND: "That won't work for me. We'll get a steak instead." (↑)

WIFE: "We did it your way last time. I want Mexican." (↑)

HUSBAND: "You're wrong about that. We both decided." (↑)

WIFE: "Like hell we *both* decided!" (↑)

These two are struggling over who has the superior status in this relationship at this time, and over who's in control.

The second row of symmetrical arrows (all ↓) shows a pattern very different from the first, and is sometimes called "submissive symmetry." In this case, each communicator basically attempts to defer to the other, to define oneself as secondary or submissive in the relationship. It could look like this:

HUSBAND: "Do you think maybe you'd like to go out to dinner?" (↓)

WIFE: "Gosh, I hadn't thought about it much. Does that sound good to you?" (↓)

HUSBAND: "I guess so. What do you think?" (↓)

WIFE: "Sounds okay to me. Is that what you'd like?" (↓)

HUSBAND: "I don't know. Where would you like to go?" (↓)

WIFE: "I don't know. How 'bout you?" (↓)

The struggle among these two is also about status and control, but flip-flopped: who will be made to have superior status, and therefore made to control in this instance.

Figure 3.2
Relational Patterns of Interaction

Symmetry:

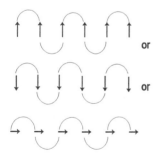

Complementarity:

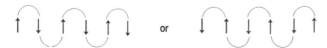

The third row of symmetrical arrows (all →) shows a pattern sometimes called "equal symmetry." Each communicator attempts to define his or her status in the relationship on equal terms. There's neither the relational "wrestling" that goes on with competitive symmetry, nor the "whatever-you-say" qualities of submissive symmetry. Sometimes single utterances within an "equal symmetry" sequence will show elements of both ↑ and ↓, such that they more or less cancel each other out to create an overall impression of neutrality, or →. It could look like this:

HUSBAND: "How 'bout going out to dinner tonight?" (→)

WIFE: "That sounds good. I'm really hungry for Chinese. What are you up for?" (→)

HUSBAND: "Chinese sounds good to me too. Although we haven't had Mexican for a while." (→)

WIFE: "You're right. Unless you have a strong preference, though, I'd rather go to the Yen Ching." (→)

HUSBAND: "That's great with me, too." (→)

WIFE: "Then let's do it." (→)

Both examples of "complementarity" (↑↓) show the same basic pattern, with just the first and last communicative acts reversed in terms of ↑ or ↓. The idea here is that one person wants to be primary, which appears to be just fine with the other, in the exchange. Each one's communication "fits" the other's wish. The first pattern could look like this:

HUSBAND: "We're going to the Yen Ching tonight for dinner." (↑)

WIFE: "Okay." (↓)

HUSBAND: "You can make the arrangements for the sitter." (↑)

WIFE: "Alright. Do you want me to make reservations?" (↓)

HUSBAND: "Yes. Seven o'clock." (↑)

WIFE: "What else do we need to do?" (↓)

And the second pattern could look like this:

HUSBAND: "Do you think maybe you'd like to go out to dinner?" (↓)

WIFE: "Yes. We can go to the Yen Ching." (↑)

HUSBAND: "Okay." ($\downarrow$)

WIFE: "Make the reservation for seven o'clock." ($\uparrow$)

HUSBAND: "Alright. What else?" ($\downarrow$)

WIFE: "I imagine you'll wear something other than those jeans you've got on?" ($\uparrow$)

   Strings of interaction often show more variation than any of these "pure" symmetrical or complementary strings. For example, an argument between you and me which first "simmers," then "boils," and finally "cools" could appear this way (M is me; Y is you; we alternate, with my statements being the "odds" and yours the "evens" throughout):

$$\uparrow(M) \rightarrow(Y) \ \uparrow(M) \ \downarrow(Y) \ \uparrow(M) \rightarrow(Y) \ \ldots \ \uparrow \uparrow \uparrow \uparrow \uparrow \uparrow \uparrow \uparrow \uparrow \rightarrow \uparrow \downarrow \rightarrow \rightarrow(M) \rightarrow(Y)$$

At the beginning of our exchange, it looked like I was "pushing" something—my first three statements were $\uparrow\uparrow\uparrow$. You, at first, were somewhat accommodating and apparently wanting us to interact as equals—your first three statements were $\rightarrow\downarrow\rightarrow$. But I must have pushed too far, because after my fourth consecutive "one-up" utterance, you essentially jumped into the fray and we competed for our next nine statements, at which point *I* moderated a bit, as did you eventually, but only after getting in one last $\uparrow$. We finished up talking to each other on more neutral or equal terms.
   And any other patterning of $\uparrow$, $\downarrow$, and $\rightarrow$ is possible. Because these aspects of communication—the symmetrical and the complementary—play a very important role in determining the quality of our professional and personal relationships, we'll return to the relational dimension of communication in the next chapter, where its impact on the development of solid working and personal relationships is a central topic. The brief examples given here, however, have hopefully foretold some of the ways that symmetrical and complementary communication can work to our benefit *and* to our detriment. We'll discuss this further in the next chapter ($\uparrow$).
   Principle 6: Effective communication is hard work. In reality, this principle of communication is a logical "summing up" of the previous five, as well as an antithesis of everything said up to this point about the conduit metaphor. One of the objectives in this chapter has been to describe different features of human communication that, taken together, help reveal at least something of what communication is. As said earlier in this chapter, no single picture or graphic model or "map" can adequately capture the complexity of this particular territory. By extension, nor could a single metaphor reveal the complexity and subtlety of human communication. So none are presented here. In effect, I'd rather us traverse a labyrinth, with uncertainty as our most accurate map, than I would with a crystal-clear but inaccurately simple map that fails to show the countless

blind alleys, brick walls, and drop-offs awaiting. The uncertainty is far less dangerous.

The preceding five principles show just what a slippery, complicated proposition human communication is, and how easily and consistently we underestimate both its complexity and its difficulty. The ideas and principles I've discussed in this chapter contrast dramatically with the "teachings" of the conduit metaphor, discussed mostly in the previous chapter. To help pull these contrasting views into focus, Table 3.2 shows the most important points of difference between the conduit perspective of communication, and the perspective described in this chapter.

DOING HARD TIME: VIGILANCE AND ACTION

The conduit view of communication—the right-hand column of Table 3.2—has powerful friends in "language" and in the easy "comfort" it bestows.   The perspective here, summarized in the left-hand column of Table 3.2, has no such allies or allure. If anything, the opposite is true. Subscribing to the views of the left-hand column of Table 3.2, taking them to heart, and living their implications philosophically and behaviorally, in effect sentences you to "hard labor" from that point on:

1. Hard labor in your roles as a "message source," because you appreciate the complexity and uncertainty of the simplest communicative act, and therefore are better equipped to translate your awareness into increased vigilance and requisite actions.
2. Hard labor in your roles as a "message perceiver," because you appreciate the biases and idiosyncracy inherent to perception, and therefore are better equipped to translate your awareness into increased vigilance and requisite actions.
3. Hard labor as a "language user," because you recognize our dependence on it, its power as a tool, and its subtle but compelling influences as a teacher, and therefore are better equipped to translate your awareness into increased vigilance and requisite actions.
4. Hard labor in "spreading the word" to others about what communication is and isn't.

But the fruits of your hard work will be mainly of two varieties: more accuracy in your communication activities (fewer "bonks" on the head) and stronger, more productive and constructive relationships (fewer Smokin' Moes in your life). These outcomes will serve any communicator and any organization well. The next chapter describes both the nature—the "how to"—of this "work," and its beneficial consequences.

Table 3.2
What Communication "Is" and "Isn't"

This	Not This
• Meanings are not transferred—they are created in the minds of perceivers.	• Communication involves the transfer of meanings from person to person.
• Anything is a potential message.	• Messages are what "senders" intend.
• The message perceived is the only one that "counts."	• The message "sent" is the only one that "counts."
• Miscommunication is the rule, and perfect communication is the exception.	• Perfect communication is the rule, and miscommunication is the exception.
• Interpersonal messages have "content" and "relational" components, determined by perceivers.	• Interpersonal messages have "content," determined by "senders."
• Communication interaction can be either symmetrical or complementary.	• Not applicable; symmetry and complementarity are "relational" terms.
• Effective communication is hard.	• Effective communication is easy.

Chapter 4

Communicating for Accuracy and Strong Relationships

> I'll be up there around 6:00.
>
> Wife to husband
>
> Okay, I'll be waiting.
>
> Husband to wife
>
> I hope you're happy with it.
>
> Merchant to customer

EVERYONE'S STORIES

Everyone has at least one story about recent events like the following, experienced either first- or second-hand:

I'LL BE UP THERE AROUND 6:00

He had timed it before—at a brisk walk it's about two minutes from the parking lot, into the building, up the stairs, to the office where he was working. So it must have been about 6:15 p.m. when she finally "blew" and started up to get him. First, he heard the door at the end of the corridor of offices "whoosh" open with great force, and then "bang" against the wall as it was flung open. The approaching "footsteps" told a similar story. On the tile floor of the corridor, the high pitch and quick tempo of hard-soled shoes told him the footsteps weren't those of a heavy or large person, yet there was nevertheless a large "attitude" or "assertiveness" about their sound even from a distance. As they grew nearer, the "attitude" became an aggressive "stomp, stomp, stomp!" More ominous yet, as they neared he heard low-pitched, angry muttering coming from the stomper. "Boy, someone's mad," he mused.

She was. At him: "I've been waiting down in the parking lot for twenty minutes!" his wife snapped as she whirled into the office doorway. "What in the hell have you been doing up here? It doesn't even look like you were thinking about coming down any time soon."

"What do you mean, what have I been doing," he defended himself. "Waiting for you. You said you'd come up here to get me at 6:00. I've been wondering where *you* were! And since you weren't here when you said you'd be here, I thought I might as well get something done while I waited."

"Excuse me, but we said *around* 6:00, and anyway, I didn't say I'd come *upstairs* to get you—just that I'd come up to get you at work. Meaning, 'You come down around 6:00 and I'll be waiting for you in the parking lot.' And by the way—6:20 is just a little later than *around 6:00*, don't you think?"

"But you didn't *say* any of that to me on the phone," he accused.

"And neither did *you!*" she practically spat back at him. (Used by permission of the author, whose name has been witheld by request.)

She had him. More accurately, they had each other. He had meant one thing by his words and by her words; she had meant something else by her words and by his words. They each believed they meant the same things, and didn't recognize their differences. No different in origin, really, from that unfortunate but nonetheless self-inflicted "bonk" on the head of Ed, the welder's helper in "The Four-Pound Pinball" (Chapter 3). The consequences of bypassing (see Chapter 3) in this instance were relatively harmless, though: some lost time, some frustration between loved ones, some argument over how it happened (whose "fault," especially).

It is worth noting here that episodes like this can't be prevented altogether, even by concerned, vigilant communicators. But with concerned, vigilant communicators, they *can* be made both less frequent and less momentous than they otherwise would be. We'll see how, a little later. But before that, have you ever met a businessperson this nice?

I HOPE YOU'RE HAPPY WITH IT

Mitch Browne was looking for a twin bed set for his young daughter. He'd seen the ad of a discount store in the area and went to check it out.

The man at the store appeared to be 20 years or more Mitch's senior, and was the owner. They pieced together a mattress, box springs, and frame, which all had prices visibly displayed. The headboard did not show a price, but the man told Mitch what it was. Mitch hadn't been keeping a precise subtotal of items in his head, but he nevertheless had a general "feel" for what kind of money was involved up to that point. He knew it was less than $260 but more than $230. The man told him the entire set would cost $250. Mitch took the deal.

In making out the invoice, the owner lumped the set together without itemizing prices and wrote a price of $250. So as to have a reference for the prices of the individual items, Mitch asked the man to itemize their prices somewhere on the receipt. Without looking at those prices, Mitch wrote a check for the $250 plus $15 and change sales tax—a total of $265 and change.

Practically as an afterthought, later that evening after setting up the bed for his daughter, Mitch was looking at the receipt the man at the furniture store had given him: "Hmmmm. The four pieces of the bed, sold as a set: $250. The total of those four pieces, summed individually: $237."

Back to the furniture store went Mitch the next morning. Through the front window of the store, the owner saw him get out of his car to come in. He met Mitch right at the front door. His very first words:

"You got a problem?" the owner said flatly.

"I was looking at the receipt you gave me yesterday and wondered why the bed as a set cost more than the individual items added together," offered Mitch.

The owner sounded irritated: "I just shot you a price for the set; if you're not happy with it you can bring it back."

Mitch hadn't expected "take it or leave it." Thinking that maybe the owner didn't understand his genuine puzzlement, Mitch tried to explain himself more: "I guess I assumed that the $250 *was* the sum of the individual parts. I've never really seen a package deal where an unassembled set costs more than just the individual parts added together."

Without a word, the owner continued frowning and motioned Mitch to follow him into his office a few feet away. For about three or four minutes, he calculated and re-calculated the numbers at his desk, saying nothing to Mitch, not even looking up. The owner then reached into his middle desk drawer, into an envelope containing cash and some checks, took out $13 and some coins, and put them on the desk, still without saying a word to Mitch or looking at him even once.

Mitch fumbled, reaching to pick the money up off the desk: "I'm sorry if this causes you any bookkeeping problems—and by the way, I *am* happy with the set. My daughter loves it."

The owner's face was expressionless, and he said flatly: "I hope you're happy with it."

Mitch thanked him and left. (All names are disguised. Printed by permission of the author, whose name has been withheld by request.)

Happy with it? What do you think? In this case, the relational aspect of the merchant's communication with Mitch turned out to be much more important than any refund. Most customers are looking for → or ↓ ("the-customer-is-right" sort of a response) from merchants in such situations, especially if their own approaches are conciliatory. Instead Mitch got "↑ed," start to finish. How many customers enjoy being "↑ed"? Yet businesses drive customers away just like this everyday. Many become one-time customers. And one-time customers always have the last ↑.

These two little cases are identical in kind to hundreds more heard from supervisors and managers, and they probably conjure similar stories from your personal and professional experiences. They describe the two major ways in which communication affects us: through the relative *accuracy* with which we make sense of others' actions—the "fit" between what we perceive and what others intend to communicate; and through the impact of our communication on our relationships with other people. Communicative actions without regard for how accurately a manager's (i.e., a communicator's) intentions are interpreted will guarantee later "surprises," some that are funny and some that are not. Communicative actions without regard for how they affect relationships will produce relationships that, when viewed as a form of *resource* for managers to draw upon, are less than they could be at best, and actually destructive at worst.

The questions become, then, what can we do to improve the accuracy of our communication (when we want it to be as such), and to promote strong, productive relationships? The rest of this chapter is devoted to these two topics, which we will take up in turn.

COMMUNICATING FOR ACCURACY

The central theme of this book that I hope sticks with you is that *communication is complicated*, not simple. In his playfully evocative little book about organizations and "organizing," *The Social Psychology of Organizing* (1979), Karl Weick tells us something important about complicated things, processes, and people—that it takes complication to understand and manage complication. In this case, Weick is talking about what he calls the "variety" or the "diversity" in any given things. Technically, variety and diversity refer to the *dimensionality* of something. Varied and diverse things, whatever they are, have more possible dimensions or states they can assume than things that are less varied and less diverse. The "match" between the variety of things to be sensed in this world and the variety of whatever we use to sense them is crucial. Weick uses the example of a camera that must photograph subjects at 20 different distances from the camera. Unless the variety of the camera's lens settings (i.e., number of distinct settings) can accommodate the variety of the subjects to be photographed (i.e., their differing distances), the camera won't be up to the photographic task. So, some images will be inaccurately registered because they are more complicated than the camera.

Weick applies this idea of variety and "match" to a host of interesting phenomena: things, processes, people. The idea is simple but profound. Complicated, multi-dimensional cameras will be better at photographing more of complicated environments than will be simple, few-dimensional cameras. Complicated, multi-dimensional languages will be better at describing more of complicated phenomena than will be simple, few-dimensional languages. Complicated, multi-dimensional thinkers will be better at understanding more of complicated ideas than will be simple, few-dimensional thinkers.

By extension, complicated, multi-dimensional communicators will be better at understanding and managing more of complicated communication than will be simple, few-dimension communicators. And what do "complicated" and "simple" mean in this context? Essentially, there is hardly a "simpler"—low in variety—conception of communication than the popular conduit views described in Chapter 2: "what communication isn't." Indeed "complicated," on the other hand, are the counterpart principles of communication described in Chapter 3: "what communication is." What makes each perspective simple or complicated is not just the relative uncertainty—the variety—implied about the nature of communication by each view, but also the variety and amount of actions implied for success in communication by each view. "Easy" does it for the conduit view, because communication is seen as simple. But "difficult" does it for the alternative—and more realistic—perspective on communication presented in

Chapter 3, because communication is seen as complicated.

Table 4.1 summarizes a number of specific tactics that can improve your accuracy as a message source (communicating more consistently with your intentions) and as a perceiver (interpreting more consistently with a message source's intentions), primarily by "complicating" you—reminding you of the ways that communication is complicated, and of the varied actions you must undertake in order to better manage its complexity. The advice begins with assumptions, ends with specific behaviors, and incorporates the ideas on what communication is and isn't that we have discussed up to this point in the book.

Question Your Answers

Questioning your answers involves, foremost, "doubt": consciously, diligently, and vigorously doubting those comfortable old assumptions about communication that many of us have spent a lifetime nurturing. Here's a good start.

Blow up the "communication pipeline." To "blow up the communication pipeline" means to deny the major premises of the conduit metaphor that we discussed in Chapter 2, especially the first assumption. Remembering that communication does *not* involve the transfer of meanings from person to person is probably the most important preventative mental step a person can take, because it implies so many other mental and behavioral preventative measures. Although in a sense symbols can be "sent" and "received," meanings cannot. They must "get" to perceivers some other way, which is itself a reminder that meanings come from within perceivers. This in turn reveals the complicity of terms like "sender" and "receiver" in helping ourselves maintain the illusion that meanings are sent and received—transferred. In the interest of improving communication accuracy, the biggest favor we can do ourselves is to mentally "blow up the communication pipeline." Until we do, there will be too many good reasons to take it easier than we should in communication situations.

Table 4.1
Communicating Accurately Is Complicated—
So Complicate Yourself

QUESTION YOUR ANSWERS
- Blow up the "communication pipeline"
- Assume "miscommunication"
- Think "perceiver" instead of "sender" control

WORK YOUR ASSUMPTIONS OFF
- Use redundancy
- Ask the question
- Sniff out miscommunication opportunities
- Be approachable
- Work at listening

Assume "miscommunication." This is another implicit by-product of blowing up the communication pipeline, but it is important enough on its own to be considered separately. It is not, as some might interpret, simply a version of "assume the worst and you'll never be disappointed." Rather, it's just an explicit acknowledgment of what actually happens when people try to share meanings—communicate—in that meanings from person to person cannot be identical, for reasons we discussed earlier. Assuming miscommunication reminds us that your meanings for something, anything, will never be *identical* with my meanings, and vice versa. If we truly believe that miscommunication is the rule rather than the exception, and act that way, it will change our orientation to communicative episodes, as well as the expectations we have for them. Because we expect miscommunication, we'll be more likely to pay attention to contexts and to the possible consequences of miscommunication. In those situations where our miscommunication will have serious results, we'll know we have to work harder at anticipating what they might be, and at minimizing the differences between our meanings. When we expect miscommunication, we'll expect "surprises." Expecting surprises is a prerequisite to anticipating what the possibilities might be in any given communicative situation, and to taking preventative measures as needed. When they're expected and accounted for, surprises aren't surprises, or as surprising. Assuming miscommunication is a necessary step to this kind of proactivity in communicating.

Think "perceiver" instead of "sender" control. In the balance between message sources and perceivers, the latter exercise ultimate control over what is "communicated." Obviously there is a degree of initial influence exercised by sources, in the sense that they choose words and actions that they believe or hope will convey their intentions. But what happens beyond that is determined by perceivers. And of course very often, message sources have no inkling that they have in fact "communicated" something to others, because they habitually equate their intentions to communicate with whether or not communication occurs. That is, they mistakenly assume that they're the ones in control of what's communicated and what's not communicated. So they go happily along, "communicating" all sorts of things out of line with their intentions, and oblivious to it, precisely because they think that if they don't intend something, then it doesn't get communicated. Thinking "perceiver" control instead of "sender" control helps break this risky habit, because it makes us explicitly acknowledge that *other people* ultimately determine *our* meanings. And if that last thought doesn't make you want to do everything within your skills and power to influence others' perceptions in ways that are consistent with your desires, I don't know what would.

Work Your Assumptions Off

Communicating so as to minimize the difference between your meanings and your perceivers' meanings requires more than just new assumptions. To be sure, it will help to "think" differently. But there are also specific actions that, when made an habitual part of a person's communication efforts, help message sources to further influence others' interpretations of their messages as much possible, within the limits ultimately imposed by perceivers. Each one means more "work" for communicators, but the payoffs can certainly be more than cost effective.

Use redundancy. In the name of "efficiency," we've been conditioned to equate redundancy with superfluous waste or needless duplication—something we generally want to avoid. But in language and communication, redundancy is useful, even necessary. Without *some* repetition, both of letters within words ("repetition" has 2 e's, 2 t's, and 2 i's; up to the end of this parenthetical comment, there are 20 t's so far in this sentence) and of words within our expression of ideas ("words" is used four times in this whole sentence, as is the root "with")—that is, if we *never* duplicated our letters and our words—our language would be so complex as to be virtually incomprehensible. Psycholinguists tell us that language must be redundant to a degree to allow comprehension.

Making your communication redundant doesn't just mean repeating letters or words. That's unavoidable. Here, "redundancy" means restating, paraphrasing, and using redundant channels to help expose and minimize differences between people's meanings. For instance, restating the most important parts of something you've said, using more or less the same words, is one way of giving your perceivers a second chance to hear, read, or see the essentials of your intentions. And the very act of highlighting—remember, anything is a potential message—can help perceivers realize that those parts of the message are evidently more important to you than other parts, and should receive special attention.

Simply restating something may not materially reduce wide differences between a message source's meanings and a perceiver's meanings. The perceiver will have created particular meanings based on certain words and, upon hearing or seeing the same words again, may simply become more comfortable that the chosen interpretation is "correct." That's where paraphrasing can play an important role in exposing differences in meanings. To paraphrase is to try to say essentially the same thing, but with different words. Paraphrasing gives the perceiver an opportunity to hear or see what the source intends as the same message, only expressed differently, so as to provoke the perceiver's comparison of the versions and, ideally, convergence of meanings. The goal is to let different versions of the "story" help expose important discrepancies in meaning between source and perceiver, which ideally will motivate clarifying questions and comments from both.

Just as we can say something in more than one way, so can we use more than one channel or medium to say it. Educational psychologists say that for most people, "seeing" instructional material in addition to "hearing" it presented promotes more accurate understanding, deeper comprehension, and greater retention than does either channel used by itself. Writing it out for me to see and also saying it to me presents me with duplicate signals, but which I perceive differently. Not only does one channel serve as backup for the other(s) in case I don't see, read, or hear well, but each one also reinforces the message of the other. And, keeping in mind that channels themselves often have message value, the act of repeating in writing all or parts of a spoken message will very often elevate the perceived importance of the duplicated parts, and consequently provoke greater care by perceivers to understand them accurately. None of this is intended to suggest that organizational communicators should put almost everything in writing that they communicate orally. Far from it. Rather, remember that in situations where shared understanding is most critical, using redundant channels—putting the word out orally as well as in writing, and so forth—will help ensure greater exposure of the message as well as accuracy in understanding the source's intent.

Ask the question. Questioning is, of course, the common sense and time tested method of clarifying uncertainties between people. But here, I mean two variations of the same question, one for the role of message source, and the other for that of perceiver. In any communication situation where differences between source and perceiver are potentially important, the key question, from the source's perspective is: "Does the perceiver make of it what I intended?" However unusual the wording of this question, it epitomizes—and forces the source to acknowledge—the ultimate control that perceivers have in the transaction. Put most straightforwardly, this question means that as a message source, when something important is on the line, you'll do well to ask your perceivers to tell you what something you said or wrote means to them.

For the perceiver's role, the counterpart question is: "Does the source intend what I make of it?" Again most directly, this means that when differences in meaning will be costly or otherwise important, as a perceiver you'll want to ask your sources how closely your meanings for their words and deeds square with their meanings. For both source and perceiver questions, the answers will help reveal differences between your and others' meanings.

Sniff out miscommunication opportunities. People are pretty good diagnosticians of miscommunication problems—after the fact. Among the hundreds of managers and supervisors I've interacted with on the subject, hindsight on personal miscommunication episodes is good. But with miscommunication, it's of course foresight that really saves money, time, feelings, "bonks" on the head or worse, and anything else of value. Spotting the opportunities for costly miscommunication before we turn them into *enacted* costly miscommunication is an important key to minimizing problems. Remember, all communication is technically miscommunication, in the sense that meanings are never the same between sources and perceivers. The main thing distinguishing one episode from the next, and the next, and the next, then, is just how costly the consequences of the miscommunication are each time. Many times miscommunication doesn't matter. But often enough, it does. Raising your vigilance in four areas will improve your odds of minimizing costly miscommunication: people, language, behavior, and contexts.

The particular people involved in a given communication episode can, of course, make *the* critical difference in whatever understandings result. Personal qualities and background factors influence the interpretations and meanings created by sources and perceivers. These factors are unquestionably too numerous for anyone to catalog even just the most important ones. Probably a very few of them would include such things as hearing and visual ability, intelligence, vocabulary, educational background, values, and needs. Obviously we don't have systematic ways of instantaneously assessing these and other important qualities in others as we attempt to communicate with them (although some of us are better than others at intuitively "reading" other people). But we can be aware of the constant need to "size up," to the best of our ability, other people with whom we attempt to communicate. *Knowing* yourself and others—your customers, your subordinates, your boss, your team members, and so forth—is a necessary step toward anticipating what others will make of your messages, and toward anticipating their intentions as message sources.

"Watch what you say." Everyone has heard this advice before, and it makes great sense—if only we were better at following it. Language greatly complicates communication. And though all language creates miscommunication, certain language creates more than others.

Qualifiers, jargon, and *idiosyncratic usages* are especially slippery. Qualifiers are the kinds of expressions seen in our "What's It To You" exercise of Chapter 3: young, middle-aged, seldom, usually, substantially, mainly, and similar words. And the list can go on, endlessly: heavy, light, dark, bright, fat, thin, often, frequently, not much, so much, much more, much less, a great deal, commonly, commonplace, knock the hell out of, just a little, smart, dumb, costly, pricey, inexpensive, cheap, a modest amount, pretty, ugly, fast, slow, detailed, sketchy, soon, after a while, a little later, a long time, a while ago, recently, poor, wealthy, some, to a great extent, hardly ever, hardly, just about done, not quite, almost, practically, virtually, pretty much so, pretty good, pretty bad, alright, not really, rarely. The sneakiness of qualifiers derives from their ubiquity: certain ones are so much a commonplace of expression that we hardly notice them, and even less frequently recognize their fundamental ambiguity. Which keeps us from recognizing the need for elaborating on them when we use them, and from taking steps to determine what they mean more specifically to others who use them. That, and the time and effort involved: if we took the time and effort to expand on every qualifier we used or heard used, understandings would be much clearer and more specific, no doubt. But communicating practically everything would take more time and effort than any busy person can expend.

We can, however, be especially vigilant in those situations where miscommunication will be important. Those are the times when we should be on the lookout for any qualifiers that heighten the opportunities for miscommunication. *Frequently*: how often is that? *Not much*: how much is that? *Soon*: how much time is that? *Commonly*: what percentage is that?

Knock the hell out of . . . : how hard is that, and how do I do that? *A modest amount*: how much is that? *Young*: how old is that? *I'll be up there around 6:00*: where do we meet? Find a way to spot the qualifiers that make messages more ambiguous, and, as both source and perceiver, make them more precise, even quantitative.

Jargon and idiosyncratic usages are essentially variations of the same thing: linguistic expressions that have very specialized applications. The former mean something special to particular people, such as medical professionals (the "thrill" of mitral stenosis), financial analysts ("leverage" ratios), electricians (making up a "joint"), pilots ("deadheading"), plumbers ("sacrificial anode"), management trainers ("TQM," "OD"), and so on. The latter include things such as expressions that are unique to certain regions of the country, to specific groups of people in the country, and even just unique to a certain person. The problem, of course, with jargon and idiosyncratic usages, occurs for people who aren't "in the club"—from the region, a member of the group, one of the professionals, and the like. Recognizing your own and others' jargon and idiosyncratic usages is important to making sure that these expressions help minimize differences in meanings rather than magnify them.

Our behaviors, and the contexts within which they occur, add yet another layer of demands to sniffing out miscommunication opportunities. Vigilance in this sense means constantly monitoring your "message value": your actions, the artifacts around and about you, and the contexts associated with you, all of which can have message value for someone else. It means reflection on the potential message value of what you *do* in relation to what you *say*. Do you "walk the talk?" Do you want to? Do your actions and artifacts support your intentions, as to how you want to be seen? How can the relational dimension of your communication ($\uparrow$, $\downarrow$, $\rightarrow$) color others' perceptions of you and your messages? Is your relational communication consistent with the content dimension?

To help sensitize you to these demands, try this little exercise right now, before reading on: Think, in detail, of a recent communication episode of consequence that you participated in. Identify five actions on your part—not words—or features and artifacts of the context (spatial orientations, clothing, time, objects, smells, etc.) that, in that episode, could have had message value for the other person(s) involved. Itemize them, along with one potential message *as possibly seen by the other person(s)*. This is the kind of circumspect vigilance, practiced at least when it matters most, that puts you just a little more in control of your communication destiny. Fundamentally, this means recognizing, in all its ramifications, that "anything can and does have message value." And though you can never anticipate every possibility, just being mindful of even a few will improve your foresight, your chances of being perceived in ways that square with your intentions, and probably the consequences of your communication activities.

Be approachable. This advice applies especially to communicators in positions of authority. One of the biggest "stiflers" of asking for clarification or interacting in a way so as to clarify misunderstanding is fear. Many times, subordinates who have gotten instructions but suspect that they don't truly understand are fearful of asking questions or making comments that will reveal their uncertainty. They fear someone's perception and resulting judgments about why they didn't "get it." Everyone has heard that "little voice" insistently pushing for more certainty and clarity about some instructions or message. But the voice of fear pushes back, more ominously.

One of the keys to silencing the voice of fear in your subordinates, in your kids, or in anyone else who views you as an authority figure, is to be approachable. And what does "being approachable" mean, or look like, behaviorally?

It means showing people: "You can be open with me; you can trust me; you can reveal yourself; you can ask me about what's important to you and get honest answers without being judged for asking." These things are *demonstrated*. Said and done. Approachable managers definitely "walk their talk" of approachability. When they're put to the test, their actions are as good as their words. Their demonstrated receptivity—which itself has strong positive message value about the relationship between the people involved—promotes greater volume of "upward communication" of all sorts, good news, bad news, and in-between news. An approachable manager will be approached more often, to hear what someone's "little voice" has to say. The benefits can be tangible and important.

Too often though, managers espouse their "approachability," but without really being approachable. It's self-flattery and self-delusion, basically. But these managers inevitably show their colors when someone, sometime, really puts their professed approachability to the test. Then the unfortunate person who tested it learns the awful truth, along with a personal price of trusting the words. And worse yet, that "mistake" won't be likely to happen again. And people who got burned "talk" to their peers. The result? Unapproachable managers—in "approachable clothing" only or even flying their true flag—eventually isolate and insulate themselves. People would rather risk screwing up due to miscommunication than invite certain disdain or wrath by seeking clarity. Unapproachable managers might like the false security and power of the walls they build between themselves and their people. But they must remember: their fortress can also be a very real and escape-proof prison.

Work at listening. Communication isn't just speaking and writing. The forgotten part of it for most people—largely due to "conduit" influences—is listening. So much potential for miscommunication could be thwarted with more effective listening. Studies have shown that a large percentage of people listen less effectively than they believe, and many in fact are poor listeners. To give yourself a quick "read" on your listening skills, take the little listening inventory shown in Table 4.2, developed by Glenn and Pood (1989). Please do this before continuing.

You can score yourself using two methods developed by the authors. The first is based purely on how satisfied you are with the "yes" or "no" answers you gave. To get it, simply add up the total number of minuses you had, multiply that number by 7, then subtract the result from 105. We'll call this score your "Satisfaction" score. For your Satisfaction score, the authors say that if you scored 91–105, "you approve of your own listening habits" (p. 14). And scores of 77–90 show that "you have some doubts about your effectiveness" (pp. 14–15), while scores below 76 reveal that "you do not like the way you listen" (p. 15).

Table 4.2
Listening Inventory

Go through the inventory twice. The first time, check (✓) the "yes" or "no" column next to each question, in light of your behavior in the last few meetings, gatherings, or communication episodes you were involved in. The second time, mark a plus (+) next to your answer if you are satisfied with that answer, or a minus (-) if you wish you could have answered that question differently.

	YES	NO	+/-
1. I frequently attempt to listen to several conversations at the same time.			
2. I like people to give me only the facts, and then let me make my own interpretations.			
3. I sometimes pretend to pay attention to people.			
4. I consider myself a good judge of nonverbal communication.			
5. I usually know what another person is going to say before he or she says it.			
6. I usually end conversations that don't interest me by diverting my attention from the speaker.			
7. I frequently nod, frown, or whatever to let the speaker know how I feel about what he or she is saying.			
8. I usually respond immediately when someone has finished talking.			
9. I evaluate what is being said while it is being said.			
10. I usually formulate a response while the other person is still talking.			
11. The speaker's "delivery" style frequently keeps me from listening to content.			
12. I usually ask people to clarify what they have said rather than guess at the meaning.			
13. I make a concerted effort to understand other people's point of view.			
14. I frequently hear what I expect rather than what is said.			
15. Most people feel that I have understood their point of view when we disagree.			

Source: Adapted from Glenn and Pood (1989). Used by permission of the publisher.

According to the authors, the second scoring method draws upon "listening theory" to determine "correct" answers, or how you "should have" answered if you are a good listener. Table 4.3 on page 80 shows these so-called "correct" answers, along with brief justifications. For scoring yourself using this method, count the number of "incorrect" answers, multiply by 7, and subtract the result from 105. The same scoring ranges as with the first method apply, but with these interpretations provided by the authors: 91–105, your listening habits "are on the right track" (p. 14); 77–90, "your knowledge of the listening process is somewhat skimpy" (p. 15); below 76, "your friends and colleagues probably do not think much of you as a listener" (p. 15).

Listening effectively is one important way of improving the accuracy of communication. As you can see from the different items of the Listening Inventory, being a good listener is, like everything else involved in effective communication, hard work. It requires focus, resistance to internal and external distractions, and genuine, demonstrated concern about what others have to say. It takes practice.

As Table 4.1 states earlier in this chapter, communicating accurately is complicated. First, it's a matter of constantly challenging those comfortable old assumptions about communication: blow up the communication pipeline, assume miscommunication, and think "perceiver" instead of "sender" control. And second, hard work and constant vigilance are necessary to promote greater correspondence between our and others' meanings. Use redundancy; ask the question; relentlessly sniff out miscommunication opportunities in people, language, behavior, and contexts; be approachable; and work hard at listening. Only hard work makes communication work to your advantage.

But the other area of outcomes for communication is nonetheless important—relationships. Effective communication practices affect the quality of our relationships just as surely as they do the accuracy of our messages from source to perceiver. And solid relationships are just as important in determining the success of managers. We now turn our attention to the ways in which communication practices shape our relationships in organizations.

COMMUNICATING FOR STRONG RELATIONSHIPS

Everyone has experience with "power" in human relations. Power, most simply, is the ability to influence. This ability, in turn, depends on the presence and manipulation of certain resources: outcomes that are attractive, outcomes that are unattractive, information, beliefs in the legitimacy of "hierarchy," expertise, affection, love, liking, approval, respect, trust, admiration, and so on. As such, almost every form of interpersonal behavior involves the resources connected, however blatantly or subtly, to power: We do this because someone we perceive as an "expert" advises it, and because it can benefit us in some way. We do that because we're fearful of the consequences if we don't. We do this because we respect someone. We do that because we don't respect someone. Because we love someone, we act this way. Because we dislike someone, we act

Table 4.3
"Correct" Answers to Listening Inventory

Answer	Justification
1. No	Limited listening capacity; spreading yourself too thin.
2. No	Others' interpretations can improve clarity.
3. No	You get caught.
4. Yes	Nonverbal cues are critical to interpretation.
5. No	You're probably using incomplete information.
6. No	Diverted attention guarantees lack of clarity.
7. No	Evaluative feedback can "shape" speaker's comments.
8. No	Time is needed to think and to form your response.
9. No	Evaluation should occur only after the full message.
10. No	Planning like this interrupts listening concentration.
11. No	Disrupts concentration on the message.
12. Yes	It's best to be sure.
13. Yes	This benefits clarity and relationships.
14. No	This kind of selective perception can be risky.
15. Yes	Again, this benefits clarity and relationships.

Source: Adapted from Glenn and Pood (1989).

that way. We do this because we accept someone's legitimate right to expect it of us. We do that because we don't accept the expectation as legitimate. Because we want someone's approval—even our own—we do this. Because we fear their—or our—disapproval, we do that.

Of course the cause-effect chains depicted here aren't nearly this simple, but the point is valid nonetheless: power pervades interpersonal behavior and interpersonal relationships. The key questions, then, are "What kinds of power, and therefore, resources, best serve the interests of our relationships?" and "How does our communication affect the development of those resources and, therefore, that power?"

Although perhaps not everyone would agree, most people would concede that it's better to be trusted than distrusted, liked than disliked, respected than disrespected, loved than hated, and so on. Relationships based on "positive" power resources such as trust, liking, respect, and love are both more efficient and effective for the people concerned than those based on "negative" power resources such as distrust, dislike, disrespect, and hate. Efficiency is an expression of a ratio of inputs to outputs. An efficient process is one in which the amount or quality of the output is commensurate with the amount or quality of the inputs. An inefficient process produces outputs that, for whatever reasons, either dwindle in comparison with the amount or quality of the inputs, or produce both unwanted by-products in addition to or instead of desirable ones. Relationships characterized by distrust, dislike, disrespect, and the like—negative resources—are inefficient in that lots of energy gets expended (i.e., wasted) second-guessing intentions and motives, protecting ourselves, maintaining appearances, and covertly or even overtly antagonizing others, instead of in more productive pursuits. On the other hand, relationships characterized by trust, liking, mutual respect, and the like—positive resources—are more efficient, in part due simply to the lack of these diversions. More energy is available for other things. Plus, such relationships can themselves be great motivators to accomplish agreed-upon goals.

Effectiveness, as it applies to relationships, refers to an ongoing ability to draw upon the resources of the relationship to accomplish goals while enhancing or maintaining the strength of the relationship. Here, the idea of an "emotional bank account," popularized by Stephen Covey in *The 7 Habits of Highly Effective People* (1989), provides a useful metaphor. Covey says that we maintain something akin to an "emotional bank account" with everyone we interact with. Like any kind of bank account, we make "deposits" to and "withdrawals" from our emotional bank accounts. Deposits and withdrawals stem from what we say and what we do—how we treat others. The actual "balance" in the account is *trust*, probably the ultimate interpersonal "currency" we amass to varying degrees for use in the "exchange" transactions of our relationships. Those actions resulting in deposits of trust are good; in withdrawals of trust, not so good. So minimally, relative to the important people in our lives, we want our bank accounts to be positive, and large.

While Covey discusses emotional bank accounts as they apply to people individually, there are several possible combinations of accounts *in relationships*, shown in Figure 4.1.

For some relationships, each person's "balance" with the other might be positive, or in the "black" (Cell 4). For other relationships, each one's balance of trust with the other could be zero, or even in the "red" (Cell 1). And a third possibility could find one person in the "black" with another, while the other has zero balance or even a deficit with the first person (Cells 2 and 3). Relationships characterized by caring, honesty, liking, respect, expertise, and the like, will produce hefty, high-trust emotional bank accounts (Cell 4) for everyone concerned because people tend to appreciate the use of power based on these qualities (resources), and tend to reciprocate their use. Relationships charac- terized by indifference, dishonesty, animosity, disrespect, authority, and the like, will produce impoverished or bankrupt, low- or no-trust emotional bank accounts (Cell 1) because people tend to resent the use of power based on these qualities (resources), and tend to reciprocate their use. The rich get richer and the poor get poorer. Effective relationships promote trust promotes effective relationships promote trust, and so forth. And ineffective relationships promote distrust promotes ineffective relationships promote distrust, and so on.

Trust is the bedrock of any strong interpersonal relationship. And importantly, trust is shaped largely by communication. Table 4.4 summarizes a number of communication features that either "build" or "erode" trust. Let's review them.

Figure 4.1
Emotional Bank Accounts

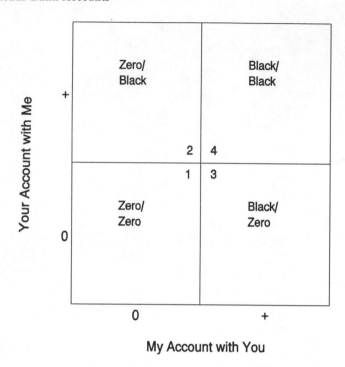

Adapted from Covey (1989).

Table 4.4
Communicating for Strong, Productive Relationships

Erodes Trust	Builds Trust
•Chronic communication "surprises"	•Few communication "surprises"
•Words/deeds don't match	•Words/deeds match
•Content/relational elements clash	•Content/relational elements mesh
•Poor "relational" listening	•Good "relational" listening
•Judgmental	•Nonjudgmental
•Disconfirming	•Confirming

Minimize Communication "Surprises"

One of the quickest ways to build trust is to understand and be understood. One of the quickest ways to subvert confidence is to chronically misunderstand and promulgate misunderstanding, however unintentional. Here, we're talking "accuracy" again. The trust involved here is not so much a matter of character as it is simple confidence that when we communicate, both of us "get it right." People who "get it right," with very few communication "surprises," especially when it counts, earn our confidence, our trust that communicating with them is predictably safe. People who chronically "get it wrong," especially when it counts, make us skittish about entrusting words—ours or even theirs—to them.

So the recommendations earlier, on "complicating yourself" to communicate accurately (Table 4.1), apply here as well: "Question your answers" and "Work your assumptions off." The hard work will not only benefit the accuracy of your communication with others. It will help fatten your emotional bank account with them, too, because they'll be able to count on you to "get it right."

Walk the Talk

Do you remember Smokin' Moe, from Chapter 3? His relationship with the people who worked for him was less than it should have been because he didn't "walk his talk." His words and deeds were inconsistent often enough to make his crews eventually doubt the "talk," and resent its dishonesty, however unwitting it was.

"Walking the talk" is both simple and hard to do. For the easy part, it's first a matter of telling ourselves not to "*say* it" unless we're going to "*do* it," because people pay attention to discrepancies. Honoring our words with consistent actions puts money in our "trust fund," so to speak. The real trick, however—the hard part—is appreciating other people's role in writing the check. In other words, because others ultimately control what we've really "said," what our words and deeds mean *to them*, we must be ever vigilant of whether we're in fact communicating our intentions in the first place. If we're reasonably sure that others do understand our intentions as represented by our words, then it's easier to act consistently with them—although actions are messages, too, and must be monitored as to their meaning for others. If we're uncertain as to others' understanding of our intentions, though, behavioral consistency becomes more of a moving target, and much, much more difficult to achieve.

So again, we find that building relational strength depends in part on doing those things that promote accuracy—remembering that anything can have message value, thinking "perceiver" control instead of "sender" control, asking the question, and so on. How can we truly act purposefully and consistently with our words until we know what our words mean—to the people who consume them? How can we "walk" the talk until we know what the "talk" *is* to the people who count?

Get Your "Content" and "Relational" Stories Straight

The merchant in the furniture store, beginning this chapter, lied to his customer twice. The first time was when he charged $250 for an unassembled bed set, the separate parts of which summed to $237. The second time was when he said, "I hope you're happy with it," just after pushing his customer's money across the desk. In the first instance, he tried to get the customer to pay more than the listed prices totalled. *Caveat emptor*, sadly enough—just the way some people do business. But the second instance was hardly "just business." It was a businessman and a customer trying to work through something that was an issue to the customer. It happens everyday, everywhere. But one of them used the situation as an opportunity to establish his relational status as superior to the other, to put himself "one up" (↑), while cloaking the attempt in words of accommodation (→ and ↓). In that second instance, the merchant tried to convince his customer *informationally* of something—"I hope you're happy with it"—that he contradicted *relationally* with the way he spoke and with his actions. The only statements he made in the entire several-minute exchange were "You got a problem?", "I just shot you a price for the set; if you don't like it you can bring it back," and "I hope you're happy with it." The informational or content dimension of these statements is pretty harmless, even deferent: → or ↓. But the *way* he uttered them—zero eye contact, deadpan, free of any nonverbal hint of sincerity, and with a scowl—was, on the *relational* dimension, pure ↑.

Sarcasm and "mixed messages" like these are variations on dishonesty. Sometimes the contradiction is unintentional, and sometimes, purposeful. But no matter what the intent, dishonesty, when recognized, usually exacts an interpersonal price in the form of trust. It makes us wonder which of the multiple messages we should believe, and *what else* to believe of another person. A seasoned and very successful manager I once worked with said it best: "I don't mind being told 'no,' but don't insult us both by trying to make it sound like 'yes.'" People appreciate the honesty of getting your "content" and "relational" stories straight. They reward it with their respect and trust.

Hear "Me" in Addition to My Words

Ask employees what behavioral skills distinguish great managers from okay managers, and near the top of every list will be the ability to listen empathically. It's also true of great communicators versus okay communicators in general.

Stephen Covey (1989) has this to say on the subject of empathic listening: "If I were to summarize in one sentence the single most important principle I have learned in the field of interpersonal relations, it would be this: *Seek first to understand, then to be understood.* This principle is the key to effective interpersonal communication" (p. 237; emphasis in the original).

Empathy is the ability to understand someone or something, as near as is possible, *from another person's perspective.* It's not the superficial "I know what you mean" or the reflexive "I know how you feel" that we all hear so often.

It's the sincere and sustained effort to get outside ourselves and into another person's head and heart—to appreciate how and why another person interprets things, and to fully understand something the way that person understands it.

Not easy at all to do. So much mitigates against trying it in the first place, and doing it well even when we try. First, there's undiluted self-interest to contend with. *Me.* *My* interests. *My* problems. Second, there's "habit." From day one, I see the world from *my* perspective, not anyone else's. But once my world includes other people, *their* views must somehow be reconciled with my own. Their views seem to be just as important to them as mine are to me.

That's why empathy is seen as basically an expression of compassion, of caring, of respect. For me to see things only as I see them, denies you your "voice," your views, or at best subordinates them to my own. It separates us and says, relationally, "we are different," "my views count more than yours," and "I count more than you." It says ↑! But for me to work very hard, and to show you that I'm trying, to see things as you see them, joins us and our views. Relationally, it says so many constructive things, including: "I care about you." "I care about your views." "Your concerns are my concerns." "I truly want to know how you feel." "I know that your views are as important to you as mine are to me." "I'm like you." "You count as much as me." It says →!

"Doing" empathic listening is an act of communication. The idea of empathic listening is not at all new, and in the last 30 or 40 years there has been a wealth of good and not-so-good advice proffered on how to do it. Some of the most concise, sensible, and usable advice comes, again, from Stephen Covey (1989), and dovetails nicely with ideas presented earlier here. Covey says that the most sophisticated form of empathic listening involves rephrasing the content and reflecting the feeling of messages (p. 249). Earlier, this chapter talked about the value of using redundancy through paraphrasing as a means of promoting common understandings—accuracy in communication. So, accurately paraphrasing someone's intent does double duty. It promotes accuracy, and it can have empathic message value, in that the *act* of paraphrasing can convey sincere effort to appreciate the "informational" element of another's views. Reflecting the feeling of a message means making explicit what you believe to be the message source's feelings about the "informational" side of the message. This too shows your effort to understand, but to understand beyond the purely informational dimension of messages, to the personal and emotional sides. Most of us find it very gratifying when we are shown that another person really seems to understand not just our words, but also the emotions—the person—behind them. As I said, we recognize it as an expression of compassion, of caring, of respect. We'll look for ways of justifying those sentiments, and of reciprocating.

Describe—Don't "Judge"

Here are two different ways of commenting on the same events. What's the main difference between them, and how are they likely to differ in the reactions they get?

MANAGER TO MANAGER: "Your domineering style in team meetings stifles participation."

MANAGER TO MANAGER: "In our 30-minute team meeting, you spoke for nearly 25 minutes, and when Sally and Mike offered their views, you interrupted them four times with questions and comments. I wonder how that affects participation?"

Have you ever interacted with someone who's appointed him or herself as your personal judge? How did you feel about someone adopting that role? What was it about that person's words or actions that made you feel "judged"?

The natural reaction to being judged, in a court or interpersonally, solicited or unsolicited, is to defend ourselves. Sometimes the defense is purely protective. But often, the most convenient defense is offense—the "judged" turn the tables.

Judgment and evaluation are unavoidable and necessary in organizations. We have to evaluate other people and their actions, and they, us and our actions. But some ways of evaluating are more effective, and less likely to provoke defensiveness, than others.

In the two examples above, what were the main differences? Among other possibilities, the second one was specific and almost purely "descriptive" in content, while the first contained two quite nonspecific, value-laden terms: "domineering" and "stifled." Although specificity can often be an issue in itself, our concern is with the "evaluative" dimension of the expressions. There are at least two reasons why the kind of "evaluation" of the first example has great potential to provoke some head-butting, or minimally, some private teeth-gnashing. Both have to do with "definitions," one relational ($\uparrow$, $\downarrow$, or $\rightarrow$) and the other, operational.

Judgment, by definition, implies something about the relative status of the judge and the judged. By passing judgment on you, I'm not only commenting more or less explicitly on something about you. I'm also implicitly, by virtue of judging you, defining my status in our relationship relative to yours. You've been "$\uparrow$ed." For lots of people, being "upped" is something only a legal judge can get away with. Pretenders, on the other hand, often provoke a "who-are-*you*-to-judge-*me*?" reaction, public or private. They, unlike courtroom judges, can more easily be dealt with in kind, on the spot.

The other feature of the first example above that makes it especially likely to arouse defensiveness is that its phrasing does nothing to operationalize the evaluative terms, "domineering" and "stifles." There's nothing to give them life or concrete meaning. They're simple abstract conclusions, and practically beg dispute, if only to find out what they mean. The second example, on the other hand, describes the evidence *instead of* the conclusion, leaving it to the person in question to help interpret the facts. Because it is descriptive and factual, the only thing subject to dispute is the evidence. There's no personal interpretation or conclusion to dispute or defend against. Just the facts. You and I are less likely to disagree on the fact that I've missed four out of five project deadlines this quarter than on your labeling me "unreliable."

As a rule, when you find yourself about to label others or their actions with evaluative terms—and this happens much more of the time than we think—back off from the evaluative "conclusion" or label and instead describe *just* the factual evidence that led you to that judgment. It makes the exchange and the relationship more egalitarian ("→"), more honest (less subject to personal biases of interpretation), and implicitly acknowledges people's ability to be responsible for and draw conclusions about their own actions. Fatter emotional bank accounts.

Confirm

A confirming communication style isn't based on "agreement" or getting others to say "yes" to our requests. It's one in which *equality* of others' status (→) characterizes the relational viewpoint of the communicator, as expressed through communication. It's one that conveys that the communicator is a *flexible* person. And it's one that shows the communicator to have *empathy* for others. By contrast, a disconfirming communication style essentially "invalidates" other people, by conveying a communicator's perceived *superiority*, *rigidity*, and/or *indifference* to them (Gibb, 1961; Whetten & Cameron, 1991).

How do confirmation or disconfirmation manifest themselves, communicatively? What do they "look" like? Although the clues are sometimes subtle—and sometimes almost unbelievably "not"—everyone has seen them before.

Most often it's the relational dimension of communication that conveys confirmation or disconfirmation. That is, relatively rarely does anyone actually say to others (the information or "report" dimension), "You are equal to me in our relationship" or "I am superior to you" or "I am flexible" or "I am rigid" or "I'm an empathic person" or "I am indifferent to you." Rather, most often others impute these qualities to us from the *way* we say things, from revealing quirks of our word choices, from features of the situation, from things we do or don't do, and so on (potentially anything's a message, remember).

There are so many different ways of expressing equality, flexibility, and empathy—or their disconfirmation counterparts—that any attempt to list them will by definition be incomplete. Nevertheless, hopefully you will consider the items in Table 4.5 as a useful starting point toward communication that shows equality, flexibility, and empathy. They are just a few of the ways we can improve the bounty of our emotional bank accounts. You will surely have other items you can add to the list.

THE HARD-WORKING COMMUNICATOR

These last three chapters have tried to show what communication isn't, what it is, why the differences matter, and what the implications are for us if we want to be effective communicators. "Effective communication" has been defined primarily in terms of what I see as its two major consequences: *accurate understanding* created between people and *relationships* that can be tremendous sources of satisfaction as well as personal and professional productivity. Effective communication is hard work. Hopefully this chapter has revealed some of the work involved, along with a few of the possible payoffs.

In *The Fifth Discipline* (1990), Peter Senge extols "effective design" (of organizations, of products, etc.) as something that, as much as "solving" problems, "dissolves" them—keeps problems from developing in the first place (p. 342). As such, he says, effective design often goes underappreciated, even though it may be the product of enormous effort, because it keeps the main things that would call attention to it—problems—from ever developing.

The same logic applies to effective communication. Granted, effective communication helps "solve" problems that occur between people. But equally important, it "dissolves" problems—either they don't develop or not as many develop into problems that cost money, time, emotions, and worse. For these reasons, effective communication is *the* most essential and versatile tool of effective management. Communication pervades almost everything important

Table 4.5
Elements of Confirming Communication

<u>**These promote perceptions of equality, flexibility, and/or empathy:**</u>

Language... Is understandable and simple instead of specialized and overblown.

Is descriptive instead of evaluative.

Emphasizes us, we, ours instead of I, me, mine.

Is qualified and provisional instead of unqualified and absolute.

Highlights commonalities instead of differences.

Context... Minimizes status differences instead of emphasizing them.

"Joins" instead of "separates."

Eliminates possible diversions instead of promoting them.

Actions... Center on listening and talking instead of just talking.

Are consultative and participative instead of directive.

Show appreciation of content and feeling instead of just content.

Demonstrate undivided instead of partial or half-hearted attention.

that managers do. The remainder of this book examines a number of essential managerial activities from the point of view of the communication elements and implications involved. We'll see that for numerous management practices known by other "names," success hinges on—and in many instances, simply *is*—effective communication as described in Chapters 3 and 4. Let's begin with that age-old but elusive requirement of managers, "leadership." Leaders do leadership by communicating.

Chapter 5

Leading through Communication

The essence of leadership is influence over followers.

Gary A. Yukl

The only vision that motivates you is *your* vision.

Bill O'Brien

A leader must be an outstanding communicator.

Kenneth J. Chenault

A leader is someone whose actions have the most profound consequences on other people's lives, for better or for worse, sometimes forever and ever.

Warren Bennis

FOUR LEADERS

To introduce this chapter, here are four short stories about leaders I have known. As you read about them, notice their methods. How would you evaluate them as leaders? What makes them leaders?

THE MENTOR

When I was in graduate school, I worked very closely with my advisor, a faculty member who oversaw my progress in the degree programs I pursued. Over five years of graduate work, I had five courses with him. Plus, he directed my thesis and dissertation work. It's impossible to work this closely for this long with someone and not be affected by the experience. Three things about him defined our working relationship, from my perspective: First was what I considered to be the great breadth of his knowledge. He seemed to have read everything ever written, remembered it in incredible detail, carefully examined its merits and limitations, and was ever ready to "talk" about it. A casual conversation with him could wind up as a lesson in Aristotelian logic, matrix algebra, philosophy of science, social psychology, political ideology, linguistics, and nearly anything else, it seemed.

The second thing about him was his remarkable command of language, and his use of it to help me learn. He was widely published, and I really enjoyed reading the books and articles he wrote. He amazed me with his powers of written and oral expression. But perhaps more immediately relevant to me was the excruciatingly detailed feedback and critiques he gave me on everything I ever wrote for him. I learned a great deal from having to paddle my way so often, in writing, out of a sea of red ink from his pen.

The third thing about him was a "composite" of everything else about our working relationship: he cared about me. He told me so a number of times. But he also *did* things that "said" it, such as "sponsoring" me professionally early on, when his status helped me to establish my own, such as running interference administratively, and such as taking a real interest in my life activities beyond the university.

The upshot of these qualities of our working relationship was this: The things he did and said influenced me dramatically, and I wished that I could emulate those qualities when I found myself on his end of a working relationship.

MAC

Mac was the general foreman and manager of all building trades in the same large construction company that employed "Smokin' Moe" (see Chapter 3). Unlike Moe, Mac was universally beloved. His way of managing set him apart from others.

Mac was a crusty old guy, a man of relatively few words. He was very easy to talk to, though, maybe partly because he listened much more than he talked, usually. Mac gave his men great latitude in managing their work. He was much more of a "question-asker" than an "answer-giver." In almost any work-related conversation between him and his people, he would explicitly reveal his operating philosophy: "I'm here to help you help yourselves."

Mac had come up through the ranks and was a master craftsman. There wasn't anything his foremen or any craftsmen could do that he couldn't do and wouldn't do, and hadn't done a hundred times before—and probably better. He always let people do their jobs, but sometimes really enjoyed—maybe for just an afternoon or a day at a time—pitching in, keeping the callouses on his hands "in shape," he'd say. When he "helped," he'd reverse roles with his men. They told him what was planned, and he became just another member of the team.

Mac made his men feel special. He showed his respect for their craftsmanship and his care for them as people. He was more tenacious and aggressive than a terrier when it came to doing right by his men. More than a few times he took on people of much greater hierarchical status in the name of something that was keeping his people from doing their work as well as he knew they could, and wanted to. Yet when anyone would attempt to somehow thank him with either words or deeds for just being the way he was, he'd growl back, with barely a hint of a smile in his eyes, "Hell, I'd do the same for a stray dog." Nobody bought it.

His men literally *loved* him. An old-timer who had worked with Mac for years and who had seen him accumulate responsibility to match the respect he commanded, put it best: "There isn't anything any one of us wouldn't do for that old SOB." When Mac retired, retirees and employees long gone from the company came back from all over to show him how they felt at a retirement dinner in his honor. (All names disguised.)

I CAN'T GO TO MY GRAVE KNOWING . . .

When I was growing up, I remember a number of momentous events in which my father was faced with personal circumstances involving choices that affected him and our family in important ways. The particular circumstances aren't as relevant here as their common context, as he explained to his kids what I now know were some very tough life decisions. These decisions all concerned matters of "doing the right thing" versus doing the expedient thing or knuckling under to the standards of others, although at the time I didn't recognize that. Somewhere in his explanation of why he had chosen a particular "road," and why it should matter to all of us, he'd say, "I can't go to my grave knowing . . . ," followed by grim speculation on consequences that would have befallen others had he chosen an "easy" way around the issue at hand.

"I can't go to my grave knowing . . ." eventually came to symbolize, once I was old enough to appreciate it, the simple honor and honesty of knowing what's important and of being true, in words and deeds, to one's values. Warren Bennis (1989), the eminent leadership authority, refers to a crucial difference between "doing things right" and "doing the right thing." It's one of the important differences, he says, between being just a *manager* and being a *leader*. In Bennis's words I imagine many of us hear distant echoes. Do you?

NOT SO CLOSE

Not long ago I was doing some diagnostic work with a team of managers in which we were generating feedback for members about their roles, as perceived by people reporting to them. Here is the essence of one manager's profile, as seen by his people:

He's a "by-the-book" guy. He does things and treats people absolutely "to the letter" of policy. He never lets the "personal" interfere with the "professional." He doesn't allow himself to get "close" to or to know his employees in any other than a professional sense. He doesn't know much about his employees' lives beyond work. He works very well within "structure," and can live with virtually any decision that is organizationally sanctioned. He expects the same from his people. He communicates with those in his role set—downward, laterally, upward—mostly by memo. His subordinates resent the hell out of it. And they don't much like him, either.

In an organizational belt-tightening move some months after my involvement, it seems this manager was considered expendable. No surprise.

LEADERSHIP AND LIFE

What do each of these stories have in common? First, we've all known people like those described here. More than that, these people show us everyday instances of *leadership*, broadly defined, each differing in outcomes and effectiveness. Also the stories are each an instance in which leadership was "done" essentially through communication of some sort. Leadership like that shown here happens all the time. It's as much a part of life as, well, communication.

As long as there have been groups of people trying to accomplish something, there has been interest in "leaders" and "leadership." To suggest the magnitude of this interest, there have been nearly 10,000 published books and articles on the subject of leadership. And that's just the published works that formally and directly address the subject. If we were to throw in published works that relate to the subject at all, however tangentially—for example, a vast amount of published history, political science, scientific-technological advancement, religious writings, and the like, concerns leaders and leadership, as do many novels, short stories, and poems—then we'd be talking about hundreds of thousands of published sources that deal with leadership. That's quite a bit of interest, from lots of places, over a very long period of time.

Leadership is one of those subjects that's too complicated for anyone to write the definitive work about but too important to shrug off with "leaders are born not made"—which happens to be untrue, anyway. So author after author steps up to the plate to take a few swings. I can't accomplish in one chapter what thousands of authors have written whole books about. But I can show you what leadership looks like from the "communication" perspective developed here, what a number of managers, authors, and I think effective leaders *do*, how effective leadership hinges on communication, and how to use communication to be a better leader and to promote better leadership in others.

LEADERSHIP—WHAT IS IT, ANYWAY?

Given the thousands of sources officially concerned with the subject of leadership, should it surprise anyone that there are more than a few definitions of it, with some big differences between them? Rather than get involved in a debate that might interest academics but few others, however, consider this: the definition that has the most utility for people wanting to "do" leadership centers around two key terms—*influence* and *goals*. Leadership, conceived most broadly, is the process of influencing people toward the accomplishment of certain goals. For a more specific but wordier definition, Gary Yukl's is serviceable: "Influence processes involving determination of the group's or organization's objectives, motivating task behavior in pursuit of these objectives, and influencing group maintenance and culture" (1989, p. 5). As noted, basically "influencing people toward the accomplishment of certain goals."

Now although the notion of "goals" is important in this definition—whose goals, what goals, and the like—the more fundamental term in leadership is "influence." Leadership is *first* influence, so to understand leadership, we must first understand how and why influence occurs. We'll return to "goals" later.

Influence is an unfortunate term. Most published treatments of it center around an "agent" of influence and a "target" of influence. Does this notion remind you of anything? These ideas of an "agent" and a "target" are really no different from conduit metaphor notions of message "sender" and "receiver," in that "actors" and "those acted on" are implied in both pairs. They conjure someone doing something *to* someone else. It's partly for that reason that so many managers view leadership and leaders almost exclusively in "action-hero" terms. In much the same way that their images of communication show someone "doing" communication to someone else—"sending" meanings to a "receiver"—their images of leadership show dynamic, hard-charging, swashbucklers "doing" leadership "to" followers. Leaders lead!

But in fact, it's not anywhere near that simple.   Just as communication ultimately depends on "receivers" (or perceivers), so does influence, and therefore leadership, ultimately depend on "targets" or those influenced. And that's mainly because the same processes operative in communication—perception, perceivers creating messages, and the like—are at work in what we commonly think of as leadership. Leadership isn't really something we do to someone else or something done to us by someone else, as much as it is something we ultimately and actively do to ourselves, with others' help. The whole mechanism of influence hinges on perception and communication processes. Accordingly, influence, just like communication, can be intentional and generally consistent with one's wishes, or unintentional and not necessarily consistent with one's wishes. Lots of times, what we would call "leaders," in the best sense of the term, take very passive, even unwitting roles. So the notions of "leader as active agent" and "leader as hero," are not just limiting. Often they're downright misleading and overlook real leadership. We're going to examine leadership with the wider-angle lens it takes to see its many manifestations.

The ability to influence requires power, which, as hinted at in the last chapter, centers around *resources*.   When I bring up the "need for power" among managers, they often view the subject in dark, sinister terms, rather than simply in terms of "the resources needed to do what needs doing." They often equate the exercise of power with strong-arming and coercion, or the carrot and stick, rather than just the application of different resources—some exceedingly pleasant and growth producing—toward the accomplishment of goals. Power gets a bad rap among many managers. And that's too bad, because the *key* to effective leadership, alongside communication, is an understanding of power, its different forms and expressions, consequences, and how to develop and use it. Each of the people featured in this chapter's opening short stories was a leader. Each one influenced people toward particular goals, through the intentional and unintentional use of resources—power. All were leaders, although the first three produced more favorable outcomes than the last. (But just because a leader leads an organization right over a cliff doesn't nullify his or her "leadership"—it just means the influence produced bad results.) All four undoubtedly accomplished some of their influences without even knowing that they had influenced, much less knowing the extent of "what" it was they had influenced.   To really understand leadership, we have to start with power and influence.

Power and Leadership

In his book, *Leadership in Organizations*, leadership scholar Gary Yukl (1989) says there are three possible outcomes of attempts to influence (keeping in mind that "attempts" is a limiting term, since some of the most important influence takes place without any conscious attempt at all on anyone's part): commitment, compliance, and resistance. The differences between these are pretty evident. With commitment, people "buy in" psychologically to the goals in question and will enthusiastically pursue them; with compliance, people are indifferent to the goals in question but are willing to expend minimal effort to accomplish them; with resistance, they actively oppose the influence. "Believers" are what leaders should be after. And the use of different forms of power—different resources—affects that likelihood in different ways. Table 5.1 shows different sources of power, along with the most likely outcome each will produce.

Power-holders in organizations generally rely on two main sources of power: personal and organizational. These are just what the labels suggest. Personal resources emanate from people. We create them by the way we are and the ways other people see us. Organizational resources derive from positions and organizations. Of course there is overlap between the two categories—for instance, people control rewards and punishments that come both from organizations (e.g., pay, suspension without pay) and from themselves (e.g., verbal praise, or the lack of it). But for our purposes of discussion, let's keep them separate.

Expertise. This type of power derives from the attribution that someone has superior knowledge or expertise on a particular subject of relevance. As such, "expert power" often can be a source of influence even without any conscious attempt to influence on the part of the "expert." My own belief that you know more about the subject than I do is what influences me, coupled with my belief that this knowledge or information serves my own best interests. Like the other "personal" sources of power, the real power of expertise lies in the fact that it originates from the attributions and beliefs of the person influenced. Because of this, commitment will be higher.

Friendship, affection, loyalty. This type of power lies in the relationship between us. Because you're my friend, or I like you, or have a certain sense of loyalty to you and our relationship, I usually will want to act in ways that are consistent with those sentiments. Again like expertise, there may or may not be any conscious attempt to influence, and the power itself originates from my desire to act consistent with my perceptions of our relationship. So unless I perceive that you're trying to manipulate me or to exploit the value I place on our relationship, I'll be committed to serving the interests of the relationship.

Effort, industriousness. This is the type of power ascribed to "early birds," "eager beavers," and such. We've all seen people at work who seem to really put an "extra something" into their jobs. Maybe they come in earlier, stay later than others, invest more of themselves in their work, or show more concern for quality or for satisfying customers, whatever. These perceptions of ours are sources of power for them. We're more likely to admire and respect such people, and to value their contributions. These sentiments are themselves a type of influence, and they undoubtedly make it easier for more conscious attempts to influence to succeed within relationships having these qualities.

Charisma. This is a "can't-quite-put-our-finger-on-it" term that we've often heard used to explain the appeal and influence of certain people. There may be a special persona, emotional magnetism, mysteriousness, personal flair, and the

Table 5.1
Sources and Outcomes of Power

| | Most Likely |
Sources	Outcome
Personal	
Expertise	Commitment
Friendship, affection, loyalty	Commitment
Effort, industriousness	Commitment
Charisma	Commitment
Organizational-Positional	
Positional authority	Compliance
Resources seen as rewards	Compliance
Informational resources	Compliance
Environmental design	Compliance
Resources seen as punishments	Resistance

Adapted from Whetten and Cameron (1991) and Yukl (1989).

like, which attracts us to an individual and makes him or her potentially very influential. This attraction is, as above, itself a form of influence, intentional or not, and often provides the emotional pull or basis for more overt and deliberate influence attempts, especially if the possessor knows he or she has it. For practical purposes the difficulty with charismatic power is, of course, its mercurial nature. Since it has that "I'm-not-sure-what-all-it-is-but-I-like-it" quality, no one can really "bottle" it in definitive form and dispense it as advice to would-be leaders. It is safe to say, however, that charismatic power isn't imposed on those who are influenced by it. It originates *within* them, from the meanings they make of someone's words and deeds. It's largely a product of behavioral and communication style.

Positional authority. Unlike the personal forms of power above, this one depends in part on a "position" for its influence. Sometimes called "legitimate power," this type derives from perceptions that someone occupying a particular position—manager, parent, teacher, government official, and the like—has a legitimate right to request or expect us to do something. It doesn't mean we necessarily want to do it, but that we will, because we respect the legitimacy of their expectation, due to their position relative to ours. That's why compliance is often a more likely outcome than commitment. "Just because I told you so" won't guarantee genuine commitment to a request.

Resources seen as rewards. Many positions in organizations provide the ability to control certain outcomes which are widely valued—money, assignments, access to equipment, information, and so on. Like positional authority, just because I do whatever it takes to get certain rewards doesn't mean I am personally committed to what I've done. Foremost is the simple contingency of receiving valued outcomes based on behaving in a certain way. This won't make me believe in what I'm doing, however. I'll do enough of what I have to, to get the rewards I want. And probably not much more.

Informational resources. As mentioned in the preceding paragraph, this can take the form of reward power, if information is valued and made contingent on certain behavior. But information power doesn't have to be contingent. It can simply be the control of information such that people are either made aware or unaware of certain things. People who occupy "gatekeeper" positions in informational networks are potentially quite powerful, because they can limit what others know and don't know about issues of relevance. If I am your only "window" on a particular situation, then I have the ability to frame that situation as I see fit, and exert tremendous yet subtle influence on you. I can manipulate your compliance with my wishes merely by what I choose to tell or not tell you about the situation. The risks in this should be obvious, not to mention the ethical issues. But of course it nevertheless happens often.

Environmental design. Like some forms of informational power, this type can be exceedingly subtle yet quite compelling in its effects. At the end of the previous chapter the subtlety of design was mentioned, and its role and effects were compared with those of communication. The same is true here, applied to features of our work environment. For instance, the physical layout of work areas will affect people's ability to converse during work. The technologies connected with particular jobs require that the jobs be done in certain ways, with little or no tolerance for variation or expressions of individualism. If I want to drive an American automobile, I'm usually going to have to sit in the left front seat of the car to do it. That's just the way they're usually made. But what appear to be "just the way things are"—therefore becoming almost invisible—are very often features of someone's deliberate environmental design. Like the rule structures governing all sorts of human pastimes—baseball, legal proceedings, business transactions, conditions of employment, and so on—environmental design is maybe the ultimate in subtle influence. In order to play the game, you must comply with the rules. Like the umpire says to the disbelieving batter on a called third strike, "you don't have to agree with me that it was a 'strike,' but you sure as hell can't take any more swings after I say it." But remember, even the umpire isn't the most influential character in this scene. The people who "designed" three strikes as an "out" and similar rules—who wrote the rules used by the ump—are ultimately influential in getting compliance.

Resources seen as punishments. This form of power hardly needs explanation. It's the flip side of reward power: the ability to use resources that have negative or punitive value. These can involve the threat or actual administering of certain negative outcomes, such as reprimands, suspension, and the like, or the threat or withdrawal of certain positive outcomes, such as pay, choice assignments, and such. Everyone knows—or should know—the main trade-off with coercion: you make many more enemies than friends with it. At best, any compliance will usually be only grudging. And at worst, the resistance will be much more creative, explicit, and costly.

Influence Tactics and Leadership

What operationalizes these power bases—bringing them to life—are the particular influence tactics chosen by a leader (when attempts at leadership are conscious). Figure 5.1, adapted from Yukl's (1989) work, shows the entire process, beginning with the influence tactics chosen by a leader and ending with either successful or unsuccessful group outcomes.

The general idea is that a leader's power bases—personal and organizational—moderate the ways in which his or her use of influence tactics affects the intervening outcomes of commitment, compliance, and resistance. In turn, commitment, compliance, and resistance then ultimately affect a group's successful or unsuccessful accomplishment of various tasks. The group's relative success in accomplishing its goals can then feed back to affect the leader's personal and organizational-positional power bases. Successful groups enhance the power of their leaders, and unsuccessful ones diminish it.

The five main types of (overt) influence tactics available to leaders are persuasion, reciprocity, promises, pressure, and legitimacy. Persuasion and reciprocity are linked most closely with reliance on personal power bases, and promises, pressure, and legitimacy with uses of organizational-positional forms of power (although as noted before, there may be overlap). Table 5.2 summarizes some of the key "how to" features of each tactic, along with trade-offs

Figure 5.1
Influence Tactics, Power Bases, and Outcomes

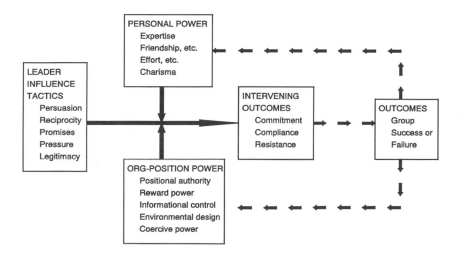

Adapted from Yukl (1989).

accompanying each.

Persuasion. Persuasion has an undeserved reputation as involving mostly variations on either sneaky verbal trickery or glad-handed hard-sell. Although it can take the form of both, persuasion is essentially just the use of argumentation to alter people's beliefs. So the elements making up persuasive appeals include the use of factual and nonfactual evidence, logic, rational arguments, and appeals to self-interest, among other things. With persuasion, I'm going to try to convince you of something, on the assumption that if you become a "believer," then you will act consistently with those beliefs. And this will serve our mutual interests.

Reciprocity. Reciprocity involves drawing upon our relationship to achieve influence. It means that because we mutually value one another in important ways—we're friends, we like each other, we're loyal to each other, and the like—we probably want to help preserve and strengthen the relationship. We can do this by reciprocating our help when we perceive that it's needed, which may

Table 5.2
Influence Tactics and Their Trade-Offs

Tactic	"How to"	"Trade-Offs"
Persuasion:	Use of evidence, logic; rational argument; appeal to person's self-interest.	Depends on credibility/trust; less certain than some other methods; time and effort consuming.
Reciprocity:	Appeal to friendship, affection, loyalty; show consistency of request with relationship.	Can be seen as manipulative or exploitive, if relationship seems "hostage" to request.
Promises:	Clarify the reward contingency—"if A, then B."	Must deliver on promises; must invoke meaningful rewards; must monitor compliance.
Pressure:	Clarify the punishment contingency—"if A, then B."	Must deliver on threat for noncompliance; must invoke meaningful punishments; must monitor; possible retaliation.
Legitimacy:	Invoke areas of perceived legitimacy—positions, rules, policies, etc.	Can backfire if request exceeds perceived legitimacy; can be perceived as impersonal.

or may not depend on a request. Requests don't even have to, and probably shouldn't, specifically mention the relationship as the reason someone should honor them. Drawing upon the relationship is most effective as an influence tactic when "the relationship" is contextual, unmentioned—but when its mutual importance can be safely assumed. The idea is that people will act in the interests of the relationship, because they want to, because "of us," or because "it's you," and so on. Reciprocity has the same "voluntary" quality as persuasion, but requires less "rationale," if any. Most of us have heard good friends say before, "no need to explain; just tell me what I can do."

Promises and pressure. Promises and pressure each take the form of an exchange: the promise of rewards in exchange for compliance with a request, or the pressure of punishment in exchange for noncompliance with a request. They mainly involve clarifying the particular contingencies for which someone will receive either valued rewards or important punishments—"if you do A, then I'll give you B"—and following through on the claim. Unlike both persuasion and reciprocity, which operate more or less on "internal controls" of those who are influenced, promises and pressure each require that people be watched, so as to administer the carrot or the stick. The dependencies and sentiments this arrangement creates can consume lots of energy and time.

Legitimacy. Influence tactics appealing to legitimacy trade on implicit or explicit references to external sources for their "oomph"—for example, to the fact that I'm your boss, to "the rules," or to "company policy," or to "the law." If the target of influence buys the legitimacy of the request in a given context or role arrangement, then compliance is quite likely. And depending on the nature of the request, maybe even commitment will be likely. But if the request is seen as exceeding the legitimacy of the context, then a backlash effect may be likely. Then not only will compliance suffer, but genuine resistance and even hostility can arise.

COMMUNICATION AND LEADERSHIP

Hopefully in our look at leadership as basically an influence process, the centrality of communication to the whole thing has shown through: The overwhelming majority of what we think of as "leading" and "leadership" either *depends* on or simply *is* some variety of communication activity or process. Leadership is almost entirely a communication activity, certainly more so communication than any other activity.

Virtually all of the power bases described above depend on someone perceiving them as power bases, with the exception of informational and environmental manipulation. Nevertheless, these two also depend on human perception for their power. And as noted in any number of places in this book, perceptual processes are inextricably linked with the "message making"—assignment of meaning—that comprises the central activity of communication.

Influence tactics and processes are also intimately linked with communication. Someone has to perceive and "make meanings" when the processes of Figure 5.1

and the tactics of Table 5.2 occur. We try to persuade with language and actions that are interpreted. We seek to create valued relationships that promote reciprocity. We promise, we threaten, we ask or direct because "I" or "the rules" say so. Communication is what enables influence. It is both the vehicle and an outcome of influence—of leadership.

What Effective Leaders "Do"

Not long ago, I published an article on leadership entitled "The Practical Qualities of Effective Leaders" (Axley, 1990) that is relevant here. It summarizes the views of almost 200 managers and supervisors—with cumulative managerial experience totalling more than 1000 years—on the basic question, "What do effective leaders *do* that makes them effective?" I provided no definitions of "effectiveness" or "leaders," but rather just asked that the managers let their years of experience guide them in listing and briefly explaining the most important things effective leaders do.

Their answers are listed in Table 5.3, in order of frequency of mention. The first five items were all mentioned by more than 70% of the managers, with each of the remaining items mentioned by at least 40%. These things that effective leaders "do" should be illuminating in the context of our discussion of power, influence, leadership, and communication. As you look at Table 5.3, how many of the items would you classify as either an explicit "communication activity" or as importantly "communication-dependent" in some way?

Communicate well. A cinch. The managers here meant specifically that effective leaders communicate clearly, in a timely fashion, and that they keep the people they lead informed.

Listen. Another explicit communication activity. Here, listening meant not just good "recording" skills, but also the ability to listen empathically. We covered

Table 5.3
What Effective Leaders Do

•Communicate well
•Listen
•Demonstrate approachability
•Delegate effectively
•Lead by example
•Read situations and people well
•Use a variety of power bases to lead
•Teach well
•Care about the people they lead—and show it
•Treat people fairly, honestly, and consistently
•Criticize effectively
•Accept criticism effectively

Source: Adapted from Axley (1990).

this in the last chapter.

Demonstrate approachability. Again, we "do" this through communication. This was considered important mainly as it related to leaders' need for information. We also discussed it in the last chapter as one of the methods of "working your assumptions off" in the service of accuracy and building strong relationships.

Delegate effectively. Delegation is one of the truly essential activities of any complex organization. It benefits both people and productivity in many, many ways. Delegation requires communication, start to finish. We're going to talk in much more detail about delegation and communication in the next chapter.

Lead by example. This, too, hinges on communication. Specifically it meant "walking the talk." To perceive that a leader has or has not "walked the talk" is basically communication.

Read situations and people well. "Reading" anything, whether things or people, involves a process of "making meaning." Here, the reference was specifically to a leader's sizing up the situational and/or personal factors that have important bearings on leadership needs and possibilities. Some situations will make certain approaches to leadership futile, as will some people. Effective leaders are good at detecting the relevant contingencies.

Use a variety of power bases to influence others. We've been through the connection of communication to power and influence. It's important to know here that these managers meant two things, especially: First, they acknowledged that leaders need power to lead. And second, connected to the "reading" item above, the best leaders possess and use a broad range of power bases, depending on situations and people.

Teach well. Good leaders are good teachers. It's part of developing people. Teachers teach by communicating.

Care about the people they lead—and show it. Simply caring about people doesn't necessarily require much overt communication. But showing it does. Effective leaders know that "anything can be a message," and they live their concerns.

Treat people fairly, honestly, and consistently. All of these are variations of "straight talking" applied to everyone. Not playing favorites among those they lead, no "sugar coating" in all matters, and consistency of words and deeds characterize the manner of effective leaders. Not surprisingly, these were often mentioned in connection with the respect—personal power—that accrues to such people.

Criticize and accept criticism effectively. The final two items on the list are both relatively pure communication skills. Criticizing effectively meant being able to criticize constructively, without provoking defensiveness. We considered related advice in the previous chapter, on the subject of building strong relationships. Accepting criticism effectively meant the ability to both "listen" to dissenters and to take direct criticism without "keeping score" or exacting retribution.

So What?

Remember, these were the views of experienced managers, on what they think effective leaders do to be effective leaders. And about the activities identified, three points must be made. First, as you look at the list of behaviors in Table 5.3 and their explanations, how many of them do you see exemplified by the four leaders who opened this chapter? Many of them are visible there, especially in the first three cases.

Second, it would be a very hard sell indeed to convince me that these aren't *all* communication or communication-dependent in various ways. Hopefully you feel the same.

Third, while only three or four of the category labels had a more or less explicit link to communication as is traditionally considered—as in basically just speaking and listening—every one of the ways the managers operationalized "effective leaders" incorporated communication, as the concept is treated in this book. I don't know whether managers appreciate just how much of what they seek to accomplish as leaders must be accomplished through communication. But when I've pointed out the findings of Table 5.3 and the attendant "communication connection" to managers and supervisors in workshops and consultations, it seems to be eye-opening for many. And that's primarily because most people's "working" definitions of communication—as extensions of the conduit metaphor, as argued here—would quite logically exclude all but those three or four items from Table 5.3 as something other than communication.

Ultimately, "work" in varying amounts is what any definition of communication is about. Doing all of those things listed in Table 5.3 is much harder communicative work than doing just the "sending" and "receiving" traditionally associated with communication. Traditional conduit-based definitions of communication treat communication as mainly just speaking, writing, listening, and reading—and leadership as mostly something else. Only a more realistic definition of communication—one that is as expansive and inclusive as the phenomenon itself—reveals leadership *as* communication, along with the behavioral implications of that understanding.

On the subject of communication as hard work, before moving on, the results of a very interesting study of 41 managers includes some who were apparently willing to work harder than others at the communication demands of leadership. Sponsored by the Center for Creative Leadership of Greensboro, North Carolina, McCall and Lombardo (1983) sought to determine why certain high-potential, fast-track managers fulfilled their potential and became "arrivers," while others with equal promise "derailed" somewhere well short of their potential. The top three reasons for "derailment" were all pure communication: (1) an insensitive, abrasive, intimidating, bullying style; (2) a cold, aloof, arrogant style; and (3) betrayal of trust. In fact, while each of these three kinds of behavior is intensely "communicative," each definitely goes "easy-does-it" on communication effort. Each hardly takes any effort at all. And what this easy-does-it approach to communication and leadership did for the "derailed" managers, quite expeditiously, was dynamite one of the tracks—the personal power bases—on which all effective leadership and managerial trains are run.

INFLUENCE TOWARD "WHAT"?
SHARED VISION AND LEADERSHIP

"Vision is the basis for the best kind of leadership." That's what Max DePree says in his beautifully written and insightful little book, *Leadership Jazz* (1992, p. 39). He should know, as the former "bandleader"—chairman and CEO—of perennial furniture powerhouse Herman Miller, Inc., an organization recognized by *Fortune* magazine for many years as one of "America's Most Admired Corporations." And Max DePree isn't alone in this sentiment. "Vision is key for any successful organization because it provides a 'magnetic north,' a true direction for people to follow," say executives and consultants Lynne McFarland, Larry Senn, and John Childress in their book, *21st Century Leadership* (1993, p. 94), based on interviews with 100 distinguished leaders of organizations in the United States. "Few, if any, forces in human affairs are as powerful as shared vision," says Peter Senge in *The Fifth Discipline* (1990, p. 206). The litany of quotable quotes could go on and on.

People are definitely "talking up" shared vision these days. Vision speaks to the "goal" component of leadership. It is a richer, broader term than goals, however. A manager with an annual sales target of 10% growth over last year's figure has a goal. A manager who wants to sell best-in-class products; to be the low-cost leader; to deliver unmatched after-sale service; to have educated, well-trained, fulfilled employees; and who wants to create a "customer-oriented" organizational culture has a vision. Vision is a "bigger" picture than goals. It subsumes them. The general idea behind the popularity of vision as a leadership tool looks something like the images in Figure 5.2.

As vision applies to leadership, it refers to a total image or picture of where someone sees an organization or a group going—where it will or should be, at a given time. Shared vision simply means that people have a more or less common picture of what they want. As Figure 5.2 suggests, an unclear, unshared vision leaves and even encourages people to pursue their own individual goals or to pursue goals that they mistakenly think are the group's goals. This can result in individual efforts that may well work against one another, or that at best are disintegrated with one another.

A clear, shared vision, on the other hand, exerts a common "pull," where those sharing it are similarly self-motivated and drawn toward its realization. This commonality is what allows individuals and groups with different preferences and methods for "getting there" to ultimately integrate—they all ultimately want the same thing, and are therefore more likely than otherwise to do what it takes to accomplish it. Shared visions get everyone directing their efforts, marching voluntarily—because they want to—in roughly the same direction, so to speak.

Peter Senge (1990) offers a helpful idea somewhat like the intervening outcomes of commitment, compliance, and resistance we looked at in our earlier

Figure 5.2
Benefits of Clear, Shared Vision

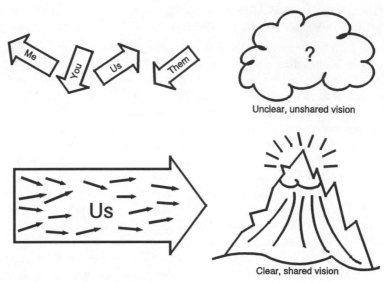

Unclear, unshared vision

Clear, shared vision

Adapted from McFarland et al. (1993) and Senge (1990).

discussion of influence. Senge says that visions can elicit enrollment, commitment, or compliance. Although we could add "resistance" to his list, let's
stick with the three conditions he describes. Both enrollment and commitment
mean that someone "wants" the vision. With enrollment, the person feels a part
of the vision, voluntarily. But with commitment, the person additionally feels
personally responsible for helping to bring the vision to reality. With compliance, the person just accepts the vision, doing what's expected, sometimes
grudgingly, and often no more, without identification with the vision. As before,
we'll do better with people at least enrolled in, and better yet committed to, a
vision. But remember, enrollment is voluntary. People have the choice. And
commitment will require more than mere choice. It will require, more often than
not, *ownership*.

That's why so many attempts to create vision eventually fail. They're often
based on a vision simply imposed from the top down, rather than developed
collaboratively from the bottom up. Only visions developed from the bottom up
will be owned by the only people capable of bringing them to realization.
Everything else amounts to renting someone else's dream. It's never the same
as chasing your own.

Integrating Visions

So what does seeking shared ownership of a vision imply? It means, foremost,
communication, communication, and more communication. For leaders at all

levels, it means doing what it takes, like old Mac at the beginning of this chapter, to make people say, "There isn't anything I wouldn't do. . . ." Mac's people felt that way because they owned the vision of their work. They owned their work. And this, in turn, was due to Mac's approach to leadership. For leaders, this means asking questions more than answering them. It means listening more than talking. It means finding out what people want, what they see, and then doing what's needed to "help you help yourselves," as Mac would say—to accomplish their own vision. This approach to leadership is fundamentally no different than that expressed by Warren Bennis: "I believe in helping people identify what they can do well and releasing them to do it" (1989, p. 161).

To be sure, this requires top-level support, and genuine respect for the visions people develop. One of the fastest ways imaginable of poisoning credibility and cultivating cynicism in its place is to invite people to own their work, but then do things that deny them ownership. I once heard a victim explain his bitter and deep resentment this way: "If you don't really give a ____ about my answer, then don't try to make me think you do by asking me in the first place." The dishonesty he experienced completely destroyed any personal power bases that might have been growing as a result of the initial "asking." The lesson couldn't be any clearer: if you ask the question, you'd better be ready for the answer. If you encourage people to dream their dreams, you'd better be ready to *act* in ways that preserve their ownership of them.

I have found that people differ more often on the "hows" than on the "whats" of visions. Who, after all, doesn't want to be good or competitive at something, profitable, to have satisfied customers, to be a market-aware organization, to have a fulfilled workforce, to have a productive workforce, or any other thing commonly seen in visions? Almost everyone, top to bottom, can fall in behind these visions. It's the "how we get there from here" that more often divides the ranks. And it's the "how" that ultimately determines both the desirability and the ownership of the "what"—of the vision.

Which is not to say that commitment to leaders' visions will follow simply by giving others a voice in how to accomplish them. True ownership is not just deciding "how" to climb the mountain in Figure 5.2. It's also deciding that *this* mountain is the one we want to climb, then how we'll do it. Whether to climb mountains at all—the fundamental purpose of a group or organization—is normally not an issue of ownership, as it is considered here. That has usually already been determined, and is a "given." When people select themselves into an organization, most of them tacitly understand that they're being hired foremost to help achieve the *organization's* purposes, which, if fulfilled, will also bring personal benefits (although many organizations do a poor job of conveying "purpose" to prospective employees during the selection process, so as to help prospects select themselves into or out of the organization). So encouraging individual visions doesn't imply the opportunity to meddle with an organization's fundamental purpose or mission. But for leaders it does imply working hard to nurture individual visions that are themselves integrated both with each other, and with the organization's purpose.

This is the biggest challenge facing leaders who hope to develop shared vision, at any level: reconciling the need for one coherent "statement" of vision, with the requirement that, in effect, it reflects the individual "voices" of many. Communication is the key to doing this. And it must start with the leader. The leader must initiate the integration of visions by expressing, as clearly as possible, his or her own vision for the group or organization, along with how it serves the purposes of the organization and the interests of everyone in it. The worthiness of this statement as a vision, and its accuracy in serving purposes and interests, must be assessed, from the perspective of the people whose efforts will achieve or not achieve it. This assessment may be formal or informal, but it must be done *publicly* if commitment is the objective. And it must be coupled with a sincere, demonstrated interest on the leader's part in collaboratively evolving a vision that everyone can appreciate. This sincerity means inviting and being responsive to suggested improvements and modifications to the basic vision. Above all it means that the vision cannot be imposed. It must be evolved—adapted and adopted.

Once the vision statement is clearly expressed to everyone's satisfaction—once the group sees the total picture of what it wants to or needs to become—then the leader must ensure that the group decides, owns, "how" the vision will be realized, and that implementation is left up to them. This is what will truly solidify the group's ownership of and commitment to the jointly created vision, when people "make it happen" from methods of their choosing.

Fundamentally, we're talking about *empowerment* in this process: how a clear, shared vision empowers and energizes people, along with the provision of all resources necessary for people to make their dreams happen. The next chapter takes up a more exhaustive treatment of empowerment. Hopefully, for the moment, this brief excursion into empowerment provides some suggestions for integrating visions.

Senge (1990) again offers some useful advice on the subject of enrolling people in a vision. And like my own ideas on the subject, communication plays the central role in all of it. Senge suggests three things (pp. 222–223): (1) "Be enrolled yourself." This is not unlike "leading by example" or "walking the talk" that those managers from my leadership study (Axley, 1990) saw as important things effective leaders "do." It means that leaders must show their own commitment to the vision. (2) "Be on the level." This compares nicely with the no-frills "honesty" mentioned by the same managers. It means basically, don't stretch or over-sell the benefits of the vision. In fact, the vision shouldn't have to be "hard-sold" at all. If its merits aren't reasonably accessible if not self-evident, then it's not going to "pull" people along in pursuit of it. (3) "Let the other person choose." This, according to Senge, is maybe the hardest of all to follow. Only with the freedom to choose will a person be able to own part or all of the vision, yet it is that same freedom that in a sense risks the vision. But really, which is riskier in the long run: mandating a vision and expecting people to care about it, or wrestling through the give and take, the clash of differing views, the discomfort and effort of accommodating others' needs and methods—that is, the communication—necessary to collaboratively develop a vision that is "owned" by everyone? No contest.

Another useful set of ideas on enrolling people in visions comes from David Armstrong's delightful and powerful book, *Managing by Storying Around: A New Method of Leadership* (1992). Armstrong takes "storytelling" as a time-honored instructional method and gives it even more credibility. His book is a collection of bite-sized, highly entertaining and illuminating stories about everyday life in organizations (his own company, Armstrong International, mainly). There are stories "to inspire self-management," "about core values," "about heroic people," "to honor quality and service," "to inspire innovation," and so on. A number of these topics are subjects commonly found in organizational visions. Armstrong claims that "storytelling" can do the following (pp. 7–9): pass along organizational traditions, train people, empower people, recognize people, spread the word, be fun, help in recruiting and hiring people, boost sales, and make key lessons memorable.

He's right. The stories and storytelling shown in Armstrong's book are powerful ways for leaders to express essential parts of organizational visions. Armstrong even instructs his readers in how to craft their own stories to meet their leadership needs. Storytelling offers leaders a very practical and versatile method of fulfilling their responsibilities as "teachers" (Axley, 1990) and "stewards" (Senge, 1990) of vision.

COMMUNICATION AND LEADERSHIP:
JUST THE BEGINNING

In a sense, all leaders are in part "born leaders," in that somehow "nature" plays a decisive role in their abilities and actions. But even more surely, no leaders could exist without being "made," in that the essence of leadership lies in what leaders *do* and in what they *say*, and in what others *make* of those actions. The essence of leadership lies within communicative processes. Things that can be learned. Bennis states it more unequivocally, but without the explicit connection to communication: "True leaders are not born, but made, and usually self-made" (1989, p. 42). To which I add: The most fundamental, essential raw material for "making" a leader is communication.

Leadership fundamentally involves influence. The ability to influence requires power. Influence processes and perceptions of power depend on communication. One important resource of leaders is vision, along with the ability to encourage and integrate individual visions into a compelling shared vision. The visions that leaders fashion and convey consist of symbols, of images, of language, of symbolic action. Visions, quite simply, are made up of communication.

This chapter marks just the beginning of our exploration of the connection between communication and leadership. The remaining chapters in this book look at "empowering others," at "creating culture," at "building teams," and at "managing change," respectively. These are all activities associated with modern leadership. And these responsibilities of leaders all depend in important ways on communication. Let's continue with a more detailed look at what most progressive organizational leaders see as *the* exigency of the modern organization: empowerment.

Chapter 6

Empowering Others through Communication

Of the best leader, when he is gone, they will say: We did it ourselves.

Chinese proverb

Ninety-five percent of American managers today say the right thing.
Five percent actually do it.

James O'Toole

You've got to recognize the genius in every man and every woman.

Patricia Aburdene

If you are planning for one year, grow rice. If you are planning for
20 years, grow trees. If you are planning for centuries, grow men.

Chinese proverb

THERE'S A STORM COMING

We examined the nature of power in the preceding chapter. For just a moment, let's reverse the terms and look at the *power of nature* to introduce this chapter. There's a useful metaphor in it for us.

Nothing teaches humility, respect, and appreciation for power quite like nature. Power is the ability to influence. And there's nothing more influential than nature. People who study the earth and the activities of its atmosphere are all the time calling our attention to the power of nature, often at nature's insistence and for our own protection. An earthquake here, a tornado there, a hurricane here, a volcanic eruption there, a blizzard here, a drought there, a flood here, global warming everywhere—they all show us that nature wrote the book on power.

Growing up where I did was an education in nature's power: If "Tornado

Alley" in this country were a bowling alley, then the little southwestern town where I was raised would be the headpin, Lane 1, at that bowling alley every Spring and Summer. And certain conditions during those seasons created "league night" at Tornado Alley. When a cool, dry air mass from the north collided with a warm, moist one from the south, look out! First would appear the little popcorn clouds way out on the horizon, changing into small snowy billows. Then they would grow up, becoming larger, more ominous looking bluish-gray thunderheads. And finally, they would burgeon into towering columns of swirling energy, and envelop the countryside in an awesome and incredible release of power—rain, wind, lightning, and thunder. Absolutely unstoppable, rolling over everything in their path.

Thunderstorms and the subject of this chapter, empowerment, share several qualities.

(1) They're both products of "collisions." A cold, dry air mass colliding with a warm, moist one can trigger the atmospheric instability that will produce a thunderstorm. Changing and accelerating environmental-competitive demands colliding with rigid, sluggish traditional organizational structures and methods can trigger the organizational instability and managerial exigency that will lead to empowerment.

(2) They both involve ordinary elements that, in synthesis, can produce extraordinary energy and power. Thunderstorms:

(a) Cool, dry air. Feels like the northern plains.
(b) Warm, moist air. Feels like the Gulf states.
(c) Cool, dry meets warm, moist. Feels like the headpin, Lane 1, league night, Tornado Alley.

Empowerment:

(a) Regular people. Found everywhere.
(b) Capabilities. Regular people possess these in abundance, and enjoy exercising and developing them.
(c) Resources to do what needs doing. Organizations and people have plenty of these.

Regular people, given the opportunity to exercise such capabilities as mature judgment, decision making, problem solving, initiative, innovation, and self-control, and provided with the necessary organizational resources, will accomplish amazing things.

(3) Both thunderstorms and empowerment have the potential for good and for harm. With the storm the best we can do is *readiness*, which won't change the nature of the storm, but which will help us anticipate and even benefit from the awesome and varied expressions of its power, not to mention save property and lives. The same is true for empowerment. Except that "preparedness" *will* make a difference both in the nature of the "storm," the energy it generates, and its effects on property and lives.

(4) They both frighten many people. The energy created and released by a thunderstorm worries lots of people. That's partly a function of their "readiness." The energy created and released by empowerment worries lots of people, many of them managers. That too is partly a function of "readiness."

(5) Thunderstorms and empowerment are *inevitable*. The "collisions" that produce thunderstorms are as certain as the next springtime. So are the "collisions" that will drive empowerment across the organizational landscape.

WHAT IS EMPOWERMENT?

What now goes under the name "empowerment" is one of those looming swirls of power—rolling onward toward us for many years—that is both inevitable and sure to change the look of wherever it goes. Empowerment is an extension and a manifestation of the leadership of an organization or group. In its simplest definition, empowerment is the broad distribution of resources— power—throughout an organization, so that people may first determine what needs doing and then do it effectively. The four key terms here are "power," "throughout," "determine," and "doing." They mean that all *enabling* organizational resources are shared widely in the organization or group, top to bottom. They imply decision making on important issues by individuals or groups at the points of greatest decision impact and most relevant information, top to bottom, as well as responsibility for implementing decisions by the people who made them.

Empowerment is not a new idea. There have been several forerunners in the study of it, two of the most noteworthy being Douglas McGregor and Rensis Likert. Who hasn't heard of McGregor's Theory X and Theory Y managers (1960), and the implications of those assumptive frameworks for managerial behavior? And although Likert's (1961) four "systems of management" are probably less widely appreciated among managers, his ideas, research, and prescriptions on "participative systems" were among the earliest and the most important on the subject.

The obstacles to widespread adoption of McGregor's and Likert's ideas were, ironically, a bountiful and friendly post–World War II business environment. American industrial organizations, having survived the great stresses of the wartime economy, found themselves stronger and more efficient for it, and virtual sole suppliers to the largest and fastest growing economy in the world. A huge labor force was returning from the military, hungry to consume the fruits of the newly won peace. And possibly most important, the new hires were already schooled in the legitimacy and the benefits of the military model of organization.

Against this backdrop, McGregor and Likert espoused their managerial prescriptions of empowerment during the 1950s and 1960s, an era known for its security-driven, authority-accepting "organization man." "If it ain't broke, don't fix it" was just as valid a rationale for inaction then as now, and it's small wonder that very little serious, widespread implementation of McGregor's or

Likert's ideas took place. Even if something would have been "broke" with American industrial organizations at the time, the business environment was placid, accommodating, and abundant enough to be quite forgiving. For sure, the highlights of McGregor's and Likert's ideas have stuck with us in that a good many business school professors, management trainers, and consultants still "talk their talk." But managers "walking that talk" on a widescale basis has only recently begun. The thunder of the approaching storm has made many seek the shelter of empowerment.

An Idea Whose Time Has Come

Empowerment's time has come, by necessity more than "niceness." Traditional organizational structures and processes have run head-on into new environmental demands, and the resulting inefficiencies and ineffectiveness of traditional forms of organization are coalescing the storm clouds, pushing managers to empower. Let's return briefly to some ideas from Chapter 1 to see what contributes to this.

Globalization of business and of economies has changed the name of the game for everyone. A manufacturer in Topeka has important rivals in Taiwan, Bangkok, Frankfurt, Osaka, Tijuana, and Buffalo, not to mention a hundred other far-flung places. Fierce worldwide competition has *pushed* American managers to view empowerment as a competitive tool.

Technological advances are changing the way work is done, and changing the demands placed on the people who do it. To stay technologically competitive, today's organizations increasingly need "knowledge" workers—highly trained, literate, knowledgeable employees capable of exploiting the potential of new technologies, particularly information technologies.

The pace of change is quickening. Environmental conditions change so fast anymore that only the fastest survive. The fastest organizations are those with many organization-environment contact points, flexible structures, and nimble decision and work processes that allow them to sense and exploit or at least adapt to important environmental dynamics.

Employee expectations are changing. Fewer employees today accept as a "given" the legitimacy of hierarchical authority. Additionally, many of today's knowledge employees insist that their work be more than "just a job" or "just a paycheck." Much more so than in the past, they want psychological and even literal ownership, self-control, and quality of life in the workplace.

Customers are growing pushier. As never before, they are demanding product quality, superior service, speedy delivery, and the like. And, due to the globalization of competition, they often have many, many choices among competitors. This just further stokes the fire under managers to do what it takes to get any kind of competitive edge.

What Else Is in It for Us?

More than environmental exigencies is behind the push for empowerment in

American organizations, however. There are some real "bottom line" benefits as well, accruing both to people and to organizations.

Benefits to people. The benefits of empowerment to people stem from two sources: self-control and use of abilities. Many people are highly motivated and committed to do a job well when they have the necessary information and training, lots of latitude in doing it, and when doing it engages their problem solving, decision making, communication, and other important human skills. Such situations provide more of an opportunity for people to "own" their work, to identify themselves with it, to develop their skills, and to be satisfied with themselves and their work experience. And besides, when an organization or a manager implicitly expresses trust in people's ability to solve important problems independently and values them *as people*, there is very often compelling incentive among those people to reciprocate—to deserve the trust and to prove their value. All of these add up to some significant motivational benefits of empowerment.

There are some who feel that a list of benefits of empowerment to people should also include—and probably even begin with—"long-term health." In a fascinating article provoking a lively and ongoing published debate among organizational scholars and managers, Marshall Sashkin (1984) states that empowerment, in the form of participative decision making, is, as much as anything else, an *ethical imperative* for managers. Strong words, but there is more than a little medical evidence to support him. The basic simplified linkage between empowerment and long-term health looks like this: the lack of self-control inherent to authoritarian arrangements is associated with more dissatisfaction, frustration of important psychological needs, and stress than is the self-control inherent to empowered arrangements; higher levels of dissatisfaction, frustration, and stress are further associated, over time, with higher levels of blood pressure, serum cholesterol, heart disease, and other health problems. Therefore, argues Sashkin, there are long-term and very serious health implications of working in empowered versus authoritarian environments. Hence, the ethical imperative of empowerment, according to Sashkin, is that even apart from all the other good reasons to empower, we should do it because, through our approach to leadership, we're literally affecting people's health and how long they will live. This puts a special kind of spin on the "human" benefits of empowerment.

Benefits to organizations. There are several important reasons, in addition to "people," that justify empowerment in today's organizations. A growing body of hard, "bottom line" evidence indicates that empowered systems outperform more traditional authoritarian or autocratic systems, on all sorts of important outcome measures. One of the most interesting of these studies compared "participative" management systems (organizations) with "authoritarian" systems on two "hard" financial outcomes, using Likert's taxonomy and operational definitions (Denison, 1984). On "return on investment" and "return on sales" percentages, the participative systems surpassed the authoritarian organizations to a significant degree over a five-year period, with the gap widening over time. And in one of the classic studies on empowerment, Bragg and Andrews (1973) found that empowered employees enjoyed significant long-term productivity and satisfaction increases over both their own long-term levels prior to participation, and over productivity and satisfaction levels of control group employees at comparable organizations. The results and research design of Bragg and Andrews' study offer strong support for concluding that empowerment produced objective, long-term improvements in productivity and employee satisfaction.

There are additional bottom-line outcomes of empowerment different from the productivity measures mentioned. Two of them concern employee absenteeism and turnover, both of which have very real labor costs connected with them, and both of which have predictable connections with empowerment or the lack of it. To cast it in the form of a crude syllogism: Empowerment satisfies people; satisfied people are absent and turn over less often than dissatisfied people; therefore, empowerment reduces absenteeism and turnover. The connection between empowerment, satisfaction, and absenteeism/turnover, while not completely uniform, is one of the more consistent findings in a very large empirical research literature on empowerment. For the most exhaustive reviews of research on the subject of empowerment and its outcomes, see the works by Lawler (1986) and Locke and Schweiger (1979).

Finally, there are two additional common sense and related benefits of empowerment to organizations. The first has to do with "speed." Remember, we live in an organizational world of essentially "the quick" and "the dead," with the former in no small way accounting for the state of the latter. In an empowered organization, the necessary things move along much faster than in an autocratic system. Decisions that could take weeks, months, or even years to inch up one autocratic cliff of approval after another, can take only a tiny fraction of that time when the people most affected by such decisions are empowered to make them and then jump right into action behind them. The quick and the dead.

The last benefit of empowerment to organizations concerns renewing and expanding the human resource base. Empowered organizations can't help but "grow" employees. Job experiences broaden and deepen, as do skills. People grow in interests, competencies, confidence, and other ways, psychologically. In short, empowered employees become more valuable and more versatile to their organizations as resources. As such, they are more likely to become "fixed" as "assets" to their organizations—dependable, productive, committed, self-renewing contributors, as depicted in cell 3 of Figure 6.1.

TYPES OF EMPOWERMENT

There are probably as many forms of empowerment in organizations as there are organizations. In this section I want to look at three of the most pervasive types. They have to do with (1) empowered work designs, (2) participative decision making (PDM), and (3) delegation. Many applications of empowerment

Figure 6.1
Human Resource Life Cycle

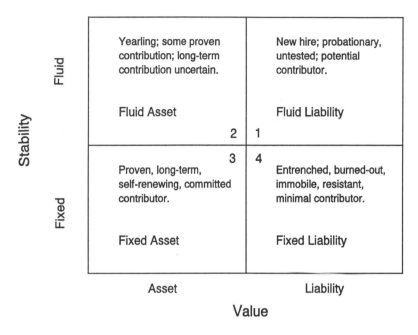

Adapted from Paul R. Craig, personal communication, April, 1994.

in organizations are variations on one or more of these.

Empowered Job Designs

Hackman and Oldham (1980) have proposed a model of work design that outlines the links between certain job characteristics; consequent intervening perceptions of meaningfulness, responsibility, and knowledge of results; and ultimate outcomes such as high internal motivation, high-quality work performance, and high satisfaction. For our purposes, the key items here are the job characteristics that trigger those intervening perceptions. They are empowering qualities, most people would agree, and they shape the way people experience their jobs. As such, they have "message value" of one subtle form or another.

Skill variety. Jobs that are high in skill variety require a number of different skills to perform them, as opposed to a very limited number of skills. High-variety jobs might require technical skills needed for operating different kinds of technologies, equipment, or tools; cognitive skills needed for planning the work and procuring the resources to accomplish it; and behavioral skills needed for communicating adequately with other people about the work. Low-variety jobs utilize a much narrower range of skills to perform them. The idea is that many people like the chance to use lots of different skills, versus doing only one or a few things all the time.

Task identity. One of the hallmarks of twentieth-century work design, pursued largely in the name of efficiency, has been task fragmentation: breaking jobs down into their smallest components, and then having different people specialize in performing only one narrow responsibility. It's more or less the "spark plug" approach to job design—spark plugs perform only one little function in a much bigger mechanism, over and over again, and are easily replaceable when they "foul." By contrast, the qualities of a job that give it task identity have to do with "wholeness," with designing work so that people complete whole jobs, getting a sense of closure on them. It's one order of meaningfulness when the part of the car you're responsible for amounts to three welds and three nuts. Or when the part of customer complaint processing you're responsible for is taking complaints and handing them off to someone who will further hand them off to someone else, and so on. It's quite another when you've built the entire engine, or the chassis, or the interior. Or you're able to examine the customer's problem, evaluate it, and personally solve it then and there, with a refund, a replacement, or a decision you make.

Task significance. A job has task significance when it is seen as "making a difference" to someone else. That someone else could be either an internal customer or (and) an external customer. The key thing is that if the job's performer sees the job as significant to others, that job will gain meaningfulness to the person doing it. It's the difference between knowing that if I don't do my job well, it won't matter in any important way to anyone, versus having my nonperformance cause real trouble for others. The simple truth is that most of us want our work to matter.

Autonomy. There's nothing mysterious about autonomy. It's the ability to call the shots on what we do and how we do it. More than any other job factor, autonomy is what allows people to "own" their work and its consequences. If I tell you to do something, how to do it, when to do it, and so forth, and you comply, then who's responsible for the outcome? Even if the work is successful by whatever measures we choose, who ultimately "owns" the success? I do. You're an instrument of *my* thinking and *my* authority. And psychologically, it's going to be difficult for me to acknowledge any but minimal talents and contributions when all you've done is what I've told you to do. But if you decide what to do, how you'll do it, when, and so on, whose work is it? I can own part of the success because I was smart enough to help enable the autonomy, but any good work and its outcomes are really *yours*—I know it and, best of all, *you* know it.

Feedback. Empowered jobs provide their performers with ongoing information about how effectively the job is being done. This can come from the work itself, if, for instance, the person completes operational or quality testing at the time the work is performed. Or it can come from other sources, such as internal or external customer service reports. The main requirement is that the people doing the work should be able to determine, in an ongoing fashion, how effectively they're performing it. This awareness allows them to feel further responsibility for the outcomes of their work, and to make adjustments as needed.

Participative Decision Making

A second and overlapping type of empowerment is PDM. PDM is not so much one style of decision making as it is one end of a continuum of possibilities. The clearest depiction of these possibilities I've seen is presented by Lorne Plunkett and Robert Fournier in their excellent book, *Participative Management: Implementing Empowerment* (1991). Figure 6.2, adapted from Plunkett and Fournier, summarizes the different decision making styles, along with some of the relevant issues attending each style.

Figure 6.2
Continuum of Participation

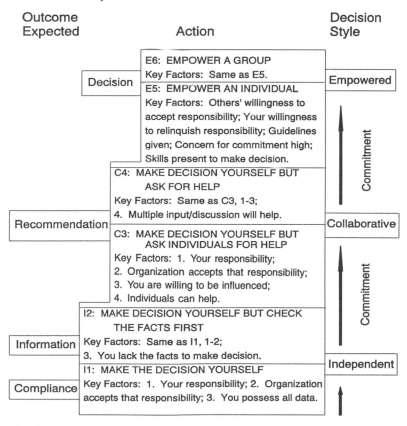

Adapted from Plunkett and Fournier (1991).

There are three broad categories of decision styles, with two types of each style, according to Plunkett and Fournier (1991): independent (I), collaborative (C), and empowered (E). Working from the bottom of Figure 6.2 up, independent (I) decisions are made by the manager, with either no input at all from others or possibly only factual information, which may or may not come from subordinates. With independent decision making, the outcomes expected by the manager from subordinates are simply factual information as needed and compliance with the manager's decision. Collaborative (C) decision making takes a step in the direction of participation by way of consultation, and involves asking either certain individuals or, more generally, a group for their input. The manager solicits a recommendation from individuals or the group, but still makes the final decision. Empowered (E) decision making completes the continuum. It is full participation, and entails empowering either an individual or a group to make final decisions. There are different key factors to consider with each decision-making style, and different levels of commitment to decisions that can be expected to result from each approach.

Interestingly, one of the obstacles to true empowerment among managers appears to be a puzzling kind of "confidence gap" that exists for many of us, with regard to our self-evaluations versus our evaluations of subordinates. In his book, *Theories of Management: Implications for Organizational Behavior and Development* (1975), Raymond Miles argues, on the basis of research and his own managerial background, that managers base their actions on personal "theories of management" they have developed through their experiences. As a manifestation of these theories, there's a curious "I'm-okay-but-you're-not" discrepancy that characterizes many managers' self-assessments versus their assessments of subordinates on the subject of empowerment, according to Miles. Managers tend to believe that they themselves are personally ready to take over decisions made by their own bosses, but that, sadly, their own subordinates just aren't up to it yet. When we extend the implications of this tendency up and down a hierarchy, is it any wonder that empowerment in the form of true PDM has been a long time coming to most organizations?

A Checklist of Requirements and Issues for PDM

Odd as it may seem, empowerment through PDM is no "easy sell," nor is it easy to pull off, particularly if a system must change from another established style of management to PDM. There may be very strong cultural forces as well as deep-seated and widespread suspicions about motives to contend with. Start-up groups or organizations, on the other hand, will have less historical inertia to overcome, and entering rationales, assumptions, and expectations can simply be expressed as a condition of membership. Every action right down to the people selected for membership can be planned and taken with the philosophy and needs of participation in mind. So we would expect an easier time of it all around for start-up systems than for ongoing systems. Systems that are changing from more autocratic management styles to empowerment might provoke resistance from different groups of people, for different reasons. Later in this chapter when we look specifically at "delegation," we'll discuss some relevant findings as to why managers feel they don't delegate as much as they should. These will have some application to PDM as well. But for the time being, we'll just look at the interests of the two major groups involved for sources of resistance.

From the viewpoint of managers, one of the big uncertainties of PDM is a feared loss of power that threatens their ability to control. From the viewpoint of those to be empowered, a legitimate concern about "What's in it for me?" often complicates the process. Managers hold the key to allaying both sets of worries. Unfortunately, many fearful managers forget that there are different kinds of power, and that feared losses in *organizational* power (via shared authority) often pale in comparison to potentially huge gains in *personal* power (respect, trust, caring, etc.). Additionally, managers often fail to fully communicate "what's in it for you," as it pertains to financial outcomes, personal growth, professional development, the opportunities and the risks inherent to participation, and so on. Both of these sources of resistance are communication-based, as are their solutions. We'll return to a more general consideration of resistance to change in a later chapter.

For the moment, however, there are several requirements and issues surrounding the use of PDM that we can examine in more detail. These are summarized more or less sequentially, as they become relevant, in Table 6.1. Let's briefly consider each one.

Reasons. The reasons behind PDM will affect everything connected with the initiative. Some managers and organizations get caught up in an idea more for its trendiness than anything else. It's a way of seeing themselves and being seen as "contemporary," and the real content and underlying philosophy of the managerial practice doesn't matter as much as doing the latest thing. So like some organizational equivalent of junior high school kids, their managerial "look" changes daily, according to whatever everyone else is wearing these days.

PDM requires a stable and genuine shift in mentality for managers, mainly regarding "who knows best?" and "why do it?" As for "who knows best?" without true belief in people's ability to act responsibly and independently, and to reconcile their own and the organization's interests, PDM runs the serious risk of becoming little more than a gimmicky, soft-peddled form of authoritarian management. Without this sincere belief, managers won't really "walk the talk" of PDM. Their *actions* will inevitably reveal their true lack of confidence, betraying any *words* of PDM as empty and manipulative. And as we saw in Chapter 4 and elsewhere, walking the talk builds personal power, whereas not walking the talk destroys it.

As for "why do it?" it's essential that PDM be approached and communicated as a "necessary" thing to do, rather than a "nice" thing to do. There are all sorts of "people" and "organizational" reasons to treat PDM as a competitive and ethical necessity. But as soon as PDM is viewed simply as something "nice" to do, then it's no different from traditional "carrot and stick" management, perhaps

Table 6.1
Ten Requirements and Issues Surrounding the Use of PDM

•What are the *REASONS* for PDM?
•What is the *COMPATIBILITY* of PDM with key contextual features and resources?
•What is the *PLAN* for implementing PDM?
•What *COMMUNICATION* is needed about the plan to implement PDM?
•What is the *PREPARATION* needed for implementing PDM?
•What are the *TIME* expectations for implementation of PDM?
•Have *DEFINITIONS* about scope, responsibility, and accountability in PDM been fully
 communicated?
•Is there an *INCREMENTAL* approach for implementing PDM?
•What kinds of *SUPPORT* for implementation of PDM are in place?
•What is the *ASSESSMENT* of the PDM initiative?

with a paternalistic veneer. When "niceness" is the known and true rationale for
PDM, there's always the implicit likelihood that management will have a "mood
swing" one day and withdraw it. But when necessity is the known and true
rationale, the initiative is not as subject to managerial whims. It's the logical
product of many larger issues. It's in everyone's best interests to pursue it
honestly and to make it work for everyone. The reasons behind PDM will
eventually make or break the effort.

Compatibility. There are a number of contextual and resource compatibilities
that can affect the success of implementing PDM: culture, structure, and
personal, to mention three of the most critical. The next chapter is devoted
exclusively to organizational culture. Suffice it to say at this point that for hope
of long-term success, the behavioral requirements of PDM and an organization's
culture must be compatible, for the same reasons that behaviors expected of a
person will be much more likely over the long-run if they "fit" that person's
values, customs, and personality. To ask an organization to adopt PDM in the
context of an unreceptive or antagonistic culture is like asking a person to do
something that challenges fundamental values and ingrained, lifelong behavioral
patterns. It might work okay for a while, but something's going to give sooner
or later. And because cultures, like values and personalities, are amazingly
stubborn in the face of change, it's not likely to be the culture of the
organization or the values and personality of the person. The *behavior* will yield
first. In the next chapter, we'll return to features of culture that have some
relevance to this "compatibility" question. The main thing here is, when cultural
incompatibility exists, then either PDM must be adapted to the limits imposed
by the culture—and run the risk of diluting its benefits to people and the
organization—or the culture must be altered to accommodate PDM. In either
case, we're talking about a long, arduous, communication-intensive transition.

    As both a cause and an effect of an organization's culture, structure must also
be taken into account. Almost by definition, broad-scale PDM means restruc-

turing: reorganized work processes, flatter organizations, cross-functional teams, self-managed teams, team-based incentive systems, and the like. Any serious PDM initiative must flesh out and evaluate the structural implications of the attempt, and the time and training it will take to accommodate them.

Restructuring also usually means some degree of "resistance." No matter how generally popular an initiative is, someone, somewhere in the organization, will fight the changes, either overtly or covertly. These are matters of personal compatibility with PDM, and several further questions will serve the interests of PDM: Who's on board and who's not? How do you know for sure? Among the unwilling, are there people who can single-handedly stymie the initiative? What are the options for dealing with them? There can be, of course, as many personal sources of incompatibility with PDM as there are resistant people. Some of the main ones are: perceived loss of power; history of similar but failed attempts; skepticism or cynicism about the sincerity or motives of the initiative; lack of understanding of the initiative; low interest in new expanded responsibilities; no perceived rewards or benefits of PDM; peer or reference group pressures; individual preferences for clearly structured work designs; individual preferences for directive management; individual preferences for working alone; weak growth needs; and many, many others.

The point in all of this is simply to remind PDM proponents that there are numerous cultural, structural, and personal "compatibilities" that must be assessed as part of the very earliest groundwork of the initiative.

Plan. PDM should be "pulled" along by a plan rather than "pushed" by edict. This means answering such standard questions as: What is it? Why are we interested in it? How does it fit into a larger vision for the organization or group? How can we do it, step by step? What changes does it mean for us? How will it affect you? What's the time frame for getting it going? These are only some of the more important questions that must be answered in detail. Others may arise from the particular situation. The point here is that many failed PDM attempts can be traced to insufficient planning. The old saying is still valid here: Plan your work, work your plan.

Communicate. Working your plan? It had better start and end with communication—specifically, communication of *all* the detailed answers to those "what," "why," "how," and "when" questions above, to those affected by the plan. People will have question upon question, and much of the uncertainty that fuels rumors and resistance can be headed off by thorough, open, honest communication, both of the one-way "information giving" kind, and of the two-way, face-to-face kind.

Preparation. One of the most common mistakes made in implementing PDM is trying to do it before the system and everything in it is ready. Readiness has several dimensions, among the most important being the level of trust and respect that exists, and the participation skills of affected managers and employees. A personal experience here will help demonstrate.

Several years ago I consulted, as part of a team, with a medium-sized company that was making the transition from traditional autocratic management to participative management. The initiative was "necessity driven," carefully planned and communicated, and long term in the making. My function was primarily in working with first-level supervisors and middle managers to help them dramatically redefine their roles—essentially from "cops" to "coaches"—and to help them acquire the skills needed to function effectively in these new roles. Before any meaningful change took place in any ongoing operations, each of these supervisors and managers completed almost eight months of intensive training on subjects like team building, interpersonal communication, power and influence, group dynamics, group facilitation, problem solving, decision making, conflict management, motivation, leadership, and many others. Their subordinates went through comparable training on many if not all of the same topics, in addition to some technical training mostly on using financial and production information that, before then, had not been shared with employees, but that would be essential to them in their new participative roles.

Maybe what's most amazing about that whole participation initiative is that it took root and evolved in a cultural context that could only be described as mutual union-management antagonism. But fortunately, the company was so pressured environmentally that just about everyone saw the writing on the wall, and wanted a better, more effective way of doing business. Largely due to their antagonistic history, from the very beginning there was an enormous amount of time and effort invested in *collaboratively* exploring and articulating the rationale for a change, developing the details of the plan, communicating them to everyone concerned, and only then beginning the lengthy and arduous training and informational programs that preceded the actual changes to participation.

Altogether, just the *preparation*—meaning, after the plan was in place and communicated, but before the beginnings of change to participation—took more than a year. The "rationale," "planning," and "communication" work prior to this took nearly two years. All three of those years were necessary to help lay even the shakiest of foundations of mutual trust and respect needed to sustain the initiative over the long haul. And even after all of that groundwork, there was still heightened sensitivity on everyone's part toward any visible hint that the program was either just a management ploy to weaken the union (among union members) or just a union ploy to selfishly exploit its members' new power (among managers). The participation initiative, by the way, has been a success by both "people" and "organizational" measures, and is still going strong and evolving now more than seven years after it was implemented.

If anything, hopefully this story shows the importance of preparing the system for participation. Organizations are like ships in that they cannot turn on a dime. There's just too much weight, momentum, and inertia to contend with. The system must be ready—readied—to participate. Readiness means thorough, painstaking preparation. *Readying* means communication.

Time. The story from the preceding section should suggest something about the time frame of participative efforts. For all but the smallest-scale initiatives, think *long term*.   Three to five years is not an unrealistic expectation for implementing large-scale participation; and longer, to fully institutionalize and acculturate the initiative, or if there are deeply entrenched and hostile cultural and historical forces to reckon with.

Definitions. Many managers confuse PDM with what has been called "laissez-faire" management, thinking that participation translates to "doing whatever you want" because managers leave employees alone to make whatever decisions they want.   This is not the case.   Participation takes place within some mutually agreed-upon domain of decisions, and empowered employees are made responsible for implementing decisions, and are held accountable for the results of their implementation.   That's most assuredly *not* "do-whatever-you-want." The point here is that the domain of decision activity, the responsibility for implementation, and real accountability for results must be *clearly* defined and understood—communicated—prior to participation.

Incremental. "Too much too soon" has done in many PDM efforts.   This obviously relates to the amount of effort and time spent preparing the system for participation.   But it also has to do with the kinds of tasks or decisions set in front of empowered employees at the very beginning of the initiative.   Too many organizations have, in effect (or sometimes even literally!), had their employees asking permission to visit the bathroom one day, and making purchasing decisions and setting production goals the next.   Just as an organization can't stop or change direction on a dime, so a radically new method of doing things can't be expected to go from zero to full speed in an organizational blink of the eye.

The tasks or decisions set before empowered employees should be incremental, in several senses.   First, skill demands shouldn't exceed the abilities and skills on hand in employees.   At the same time, tasks should be challenging enough for employees to get a true sense of accomplishment from managing them.   Over time, decision skills and other abilities will improve, as will confidence.

Another dimension of decisions has to do with their "scope."   It's often most "comfortable," and ultimately more productive and instructive, for everyone concerned to start with local issues and decisions—those that are often smaller scale and immediately relevant to employees—rather than large, big picture, distant decisions.   Unlike many big picture, distant decisions, local decisions are "sure bets" to play into the expertise and information of employees, and to hit employees right where they "live," organizationally.   Plus, their consequences, good and not so good, will often be concrete and visible—*soon*.   All of which should enhance employees' perceptions of self-direction and reinforce their commitment to make their decisions work.   Once mastery and successes have been achieved on more limited, local decisions, then movement toward bigger picture, more distant, decisions will be more likely to succeed.   The approach should be incremental.

Support. Empowered employees need several kinds of support, with some of the most important including: authority, material, informational, and incentive.

Authority support means that the empowerment is real. It is permanent, not taken back at the first sign of employees' methods or decisions which differ from management's preferences, so long as the decisions fall within the agreed-upon arena for PDM.

Material support means that empowered employees have the material resources they need—equipment, budget, and the like—to implement their decisions. For management to fail in supporting employees' decisions this way, is like putting a 250-pound jockey on a thoroughbred to run the Preakness. The horse might still finish, but don't bet on much else. True empowerment needs material support after decisions.

Informational support means making sure that employees who have the authority and responsibility to make decisions have all of the information needed to make *good* decisions. Serious empowerment requires serious information—often information that employees formerly weren't privy to, such as budgets, production and financial results, cost figures, customer satisfaction data, and even strategic planning intelligence. This, in turn, implies the personal, mechanical, and electronic means of delivering the information to empowered employees. Informational support means developing the channels of communication to deliver the relevant goods—information—to the people who will use it in their decision making.

Incentive support means hooking attractive incentives to the successful use of participation. PDM by itself may be motivating and satisfying enough for some. But meaningful extrinsic rewards will undoubtedly help pay the bills for everyone. Many successful programs lean toward "employee ownership" plans that translate successful participation into both money and literal ownership of the organization. Others tailor their incentive packages to group success versus individual accomplishments. Whatever the case, PDM needs important, attractive incentives behind it to help ensure its success. This usually will require asking people what they want as a result of their participation, and then making sure they get it for their successful efforts.

Assessment. Assessment refers to several related things. The first is the need to track the outcomes of participation. These should include measures of productivity, satisfaction, and any other outcome that makes sense. The initiative should be modified as results indicate. Assessment also implies publicizing and celebrating accomplishments connected with PDM, even small ones. Signs of success are important for everyone to know about, and for participants, this will help reinforce the felt efficacy of their efforts. Finally, assessment also means that the climate within which it occurs should be one where "mistakes are okay." Only such a climate, backed by actions—"walked talk"—will encourage the kind of innovative experimentation, risk taking, and learning from mistakes needed for participation to produce its ultimate benefits for people and organizations.

Delegation

Often, PDM is regarded as an organization-wide strategy of empowerment, where teams make decisions, and where the initiative pervades an entire organization. For this reason, many managers view PDM in self-limiting terms, as a kind of "all-or-nothing" approach to empowerment. There is some validity to this perception, in that the interconnectedness of organizational subsystems and the requirements of group empowerment make it challenging to have an oasis of team-based participation in a larger, thoroughly autocratic context.

But a special variety of empowerment can be applied in any organization, whether the organization as a whole is "empowered" or not. And in fact, this form of empowerment has long been considered an absolutely essential skill of management: delegation. Delegation coincides more or less with the "E5" decision style from Figure 6.2, which we considered earlier in this chapter: empowering an individual with authority to accomplish certain tasks or objectives, but with the person delegating the authority retaining ultimate responsibility.

Interestingly, while there remains quite a bit of ideological contention over the advisability of group-oriented PDM, management "prescribers" of all stripes and eras have been nearly unanimous in pushing delegation as a key to managerial survival and prosperity. Some of the evidence we've looked at in this book in connection with other topics, particularly leadership, shows the nature of this agreement about delegation.

Recall from our leadership chapter those high-potential managers who "derailed" before fulfilling their destiny (McCall & Lombardo, 1983). The top three reasons for their problems were mentioned as being communication-based. A little farther down the same list, still in the top ten "fatal flaws," was "the inability to delegate." And also from the leadership chapter, comes that list of things "effective leaders do" (Table 5.3), which emerged from my own questioning of almost 200 managers and supervisors (Axley, 1990). "Delegate effectively" was among the top five behavioral qualities mentioned. And finally, Whetten and Cameron (1991, pp. 7–8) describe an interesting study in which 402 "highly effective managers" were identified by peers and superiors. Interviews with these managers produced a lengthy list of characteristics which the managers themselves felt accounted for their success, with the sixth most frequently mentioned quality being "delegating." (And not surprisingly, the most frequently mentioned quality was "verbal communication, including listening.")

Along these lines, a few years back I undertook, in part as a follow-up to my 1990 "leadership" article, a closer examination of "delegation," again with the subject as seen by managers themselves, but with a different and slightly larger representation of participants. My interest was fueled only partly by delegation's top five presence on my 1990 "leadership qualities" list. More provocative to me was the sheer number of times in my training and consulting experiences that I'd heard managers talk about how necessary and what a big deal delegating is, while in the same breath they griped about their own or—much more likely—their boss's unwillingness or inability to do it.

More than 250 experienced managers and supervisors, from more than 20 organizations, were asked four questions: (1) Why should managers delegate? (2) Why don't they do it more often or more effectively? (3) What are the most important do's and don'ts to doing it well? (4) What are the essential steps in doing it effectively? The result was an article entitled "Delegate: Why We Should, Why We Don't and How We Can" (Axley, 1992), which, like some earlier articles of mine (e.g., Axley, 1990, 1987a) attempts to share advice about managers, mainly *from* managers. I believe that the delegation advice emerging from those 250+ managers is quite good and usable, and have received uniformly positive feedback on it from many other managers. So most of *my* advice on delegation highlights *their* advice.

Delegate: Why We Should But Don't

Table 6.2 lists the top five reasons the participants felt that managers should delegate, along with what they felt are the top five reasons that managers either don't delegate at all or do so ineffectively. Each item was mentioned by more than 50% of the participating managers, and we will review each one briefly. First the reasons why we should.

Productivity. Delegation boosts managers' productivity by getting others involved with what needs to be accomplished. It frees managers' time for other important responsibilities, by drawing upon a larger pool of ideas, methods, and other resources than those that just the manager can provide.

Satisfaction. Done effectively, delegation allows—requires—"ownership" of both the methods and outcomes of work. Many people find the ownership, autonomy, and responsibility to be very satisfying.

Trust and confidence. The overall personal power in a relationship expands as a result of effective delegation. It's the same "give-to-get" reciprocity that we've discussed elsewhere, concerning human relations. Delegating requires some initial degree of mutual trust. Delegation that produces successful results shows you the delegator that, yes, you can indeed count on me to deliver the goods, and shows me, the delegatee, that I can indeed count on you to use and develop my abilities and to support my efforts.

Table 6.2
Top Five Reasons Why We Should Delegate...But Don't

Top Five Reasons We Should	Top Five Reasons We Don't
•Boosts productivity; spreads the workload	•Lack of trust or confidence in others
•Promotes satisfaction of employees	•Fear of loss of control and authority
•Builds mutual trust and confidence	•Personal insecurity and threat to job security
•Promotes "team" concept	•Don't know how
•Develops employees	•Requires extra effort

Source: Adapted from Axley (1992).

Team. Because delegation involves enhanced responsibilities and autonomy, it enables a person to feel a greater sense of ownership in and contribution to the important work of the group or organization.

Development. Earlier in this chapter, we discussed that empowerment "grows" people, that it makes them more valuable, more versatile in organizations. Managers also increase their *own* power bases—both personal and organizational—by making themselves more productive, and their people more satisfied, valuable, and versatile through delegation.

These are all compelling reasons why we should delegate. But if it's so great, why then don't managers do it more, or do it better?

Trust or confidence. Here we are again. Without trust or confidence in others, delegation is extremely discomforting at best. The anticipated results are just too uncertain or threatening to many managers. Unfortunately, the same "you-get-what-you-give" reciprocity also works here: mistrust often eventually promotes the very behavior it assumes. So it's important for managers to know how much of their skepticism is fact- versus assumption-based.

Feared loss of control and authority. Delegation is an exercise in managing fear—our own fear that without our hands firmly on the "stick," the plane just won't stay in the air; and our fear, in effect, of losing our pilot's license, our authority to fly others around at all. So, many of us just decide to keep ourselves squarely at the controls. We try to do everything ourselves or, only slightly more generously, insist on co-piloting every "flight."

Insecurity. This is a special brand of fear. It has to do with "replaceability"—our own. It concerns the question, "By delegating, am I just making myself more replaceable?" The answer is: "No—but you are by *not* delegating, because you're squandering the human resources at your disposal and probably lots of your own and the organization's time to boot."

Don't know how. Lots of managers don't delegate because they don't know how. They've not seen much of it, haven't been shown how to do it, haven't done it, haven't done it successfully, and so on. So they stay away from it, given the choice.

Effort. "It's easier to just do it myself" is one of the truly classic excuses not to delegate; and most often, one of the truly short-sighted. Yes, there are costs in time and effort to delegate. But particularly if the tasks are recurring, and if the "labor costs" of the delegatee are less than those of the delegator, then it takes hardly any time at all for the pay-back "by the numbers" to exceed any real costs of delegating. In a way, this reason mentioned by managers fits quite nicely with the claim throughout this book that the "hard work" of effective communication reveals itself to us in most essential managerial activities. Many managers would rather "just do it myself" than work that hard at communicating.

Delegate: How We Can

There are a number of key "dos and don'ts" to delegating effectively, most of which have been implied already in the lists of Table 6.2. These were also mentioned by more than 50% of the participating managers. The most frequently mentioned one is to *know your people*. This makes sense, since selecting the right person to receive delegation depends on knowing who's who, with what attributes and skills, and so on. The second item on the list is to *have confidence and trust in your people—and show them*. With so much about delegation hinging on trust, this too makes sense as an essential "do." The third most frequent mention is another "do": *communicate thoroughly, throughout*. We'll learn more specifics about this a little later when we examine the steps recommended in delegating. The fourth most frequent item is both a "do" and a "don't": *allow "elbow room," without hovering*. In view of the issue of enabling people to "own" their work, this is also hardly surprising. And the final top five recommendation is also quite sensible: *delegate meaningful tasks*. This means not dumping trivial and insignificant work on people, but rather giving them challenging, personally significant work. The qualities of "empowered work," covered earlier in this chapter, are surely also relevant here.

The last question that the manager participants answered concerned each one's recommended step-by-step approach to delegation. As you might guess, this produced incredible variety among responses. Interestingly, though, the variety characterized the fine details and nuances more than the overall structures of recommendations. The latter were amazingly similar from manager to manager. Here is a "composite" created from their suggestions, taking into account the major elements that their approaches had in common. Table 6.3 summarizes the steps suggested by these managers. The process involves five general steps, with several requirements at each step.

Step 1: Define the task. The first step is to define the task so that it can be communicated later. This entails clarifying for yourself, so that it can be clarified to a delegatee, what the objectives are, and whether they can be negotiated with the delegatee. It entails knowing what the time frame for completion is, and itemizing the key resources that are available for doing the job—decision authority, support staff, budget figures, equipment, and the like. *You* need to know the relevant parameters of the job if you hope to convey them adequately to someone else.

Step 2: Review and select the recipient(s). Here, the answers to several questions will help you in your review and selection of prospective delegatees for a given delegation. First is, "What's your purpose in delegating?" Do you just want results more than anything else? Is "development" a concern? If the latter, then you might want to base your choice on whose skills would benefit most from doing the job versus who is most qualified at present to do it. An obvious concern is, "Who's able and willing to do the job?" And a third area of questioning is, "Are there special personal considerations that should be taken into account," such as relevant background experiences, credibility of prospects among key others likely to be involved, and special skills possessed by different candidates? The idea is to make your selection systematically rather than by default or convenience.

Table 6.3
How We Can Delegate

Step 1: Define the task
   •What objectives?
   •What time frame?
   •What resources are available?
Step 2: Review and select recipient(s)
   •What are your purposes in delegating (e.g., developmental, results, etc.)?
   •Who's able and willing?
   •Any special personal considerations (e.g., experience, credibility, special skills,
    etc.)?
Step 3: Inform and advise recipient(s)
   •Clarify boundaries of authority
   •Define resources available
   •Specify time frame
   •Agree on kind and frequency of progress reports
   •Advise on "what" is to be accomplished (objectives, goals), not on "how" it is to
    be accomplished (methods, decisions, etc.)
   •Highlights of delegation orally reviewed or written up by delegatee
Step 4: Follow-up support and communication
   •Honor your commitments for support
   •Don't interfere or snoop
   •Keep to your schedule for progress reports
Step 5: Final feedback and evaluation
   •Recognize and praise successes
   •Evaluate "what" (accomplishment of objectives) more than "how" (how objectives
    were accomplished)
   •Don't blame for mistakes; learn from them

Source: Adapted from Axley (1992).

Step 3: Inform and advise the recipient. Here's where the clarity achieved for yourself in steps 1 and 2 will pay dividends. In this step, you should meet with your delegatee to discuss the delegation. Sometimes this meeting will be very informal, even of the "hallway" sort, and sometimes it should be a more formal, "sit-down" in someone's office or work area. This discussion, wherever it occurs, should clarify these things: very specifically, what authority (decisional, budget, etc.) the delegatee has; what resources (staff, equipment, money, etc.) are available to the delegatee, how to get them, and how to get more if possible; the time frame for completion; the kind and frequency of any progress reports needed throughout the job; any known "potholes" or "traps" the delegator may know about—but not given as specific "do this" or "don't do that" advice. The one thing the delegator should be very careful *not* to do here is instruct the delegatee on "how" things should be accomplished, making even what seem to be the most harmless and best-intentioned suggestions. Too frequently, this is seen as, or actually is, a "do-it-my-way" intrusion into a process that must be owned by the delegatee. A final outcome that should result from this meeting, if the nature of the task warrants it, is either an oral or written cross-check of the agreement. The oral variety of this just has the delegatee orally review, to everyone's satisfaction, the specifics of the delegation. The written version has the delegatee create a concise document highlighting the agreed-upon specifics for review with the delegator. Either of these takes place before the delegatee is "turned loose."

Step 4: Follow-up support and communication. Primarily this means honoring your end of the agreement, as the delegator: make sure that whatever support you promised is there. And make sure that you don't interfere with the delegatee's actions or snoop around either pestering him or her, or doing "spy" work on the delegation. And finally, you must be sure to stick to the progress report schedule agreed upon. This will keep everyone accountable and head off any "surprises."

Step 5: Final feedback and evaluation. Everyone wants credit when they've got it coming. Make sure it's there. But also, be very careful about any critique of the "methods" of the job, particularly if they differed from how you would have done it. "What" was accomplished should take precedence over "how" it was accomplished, unless, of course, ethical issues are evident. One of the most nonthreatening ways of broaching the "how" part of the delegation, after the fact, is to say something like this to the delegatee: "Knowing what you know *now* about the job that you might not have known when you began, is there anything you'd do differently or improve on?" Everyone concerned will learn something important from the answer to that question. By all means, one of the very most important things *not* to do in a delegation is to blame your delegatee for honest mistakes. Look first to the delegation process itself or to yourself for ultimate causes. Learn from any difficulties, and structure your feedback nonthreateningly so that the delegatee can learn, too. Blaming just poisons the experience for the delegatee.

COMMUNICATION'S ROLE IN EMPOWERMENT

Empowerment appears to be *the* leadership strategy for the foreseeable future of most of our organizations. It is taking shape mainly through empowered work designs, different forms of participative decision making, and renewed attention to that old standby, delegation.

Doing empowerment is, more than anything else, a matter of communication. It is communication-intensive. The skill variety, "wholeness," autonomy, and feedback characterizing empowered work designs demand high information processing—and therefore hard communication "work"—of the people doing those jobs. The same goes for any type of participation in decision making. The whole process, from justification to ongoing assessment and refinement, revolves on communication activities. And in looking at the steps of delegation recommended by those managers questioned (Table 6.3), it's obvious that every single step in delegating hinges, most fundamentally, on communication of one form or another.

As this chapter concludes, the results of a study by Larry Greiner, published in the *Harvard Business Review* (1973), give us additional and strong testament to the link between communication and empowerment. Greiner asked 318 managers to identify what they considered "the concrete characteristics of participative leadership" (p. 113). The ten most prominent defining features are listed in Table 6.4, in rank order. Aren't they *all* communication-centered, communication-intensive?

COMMUNICATION AND CULTURE: A LEADER'S RESPONSIBILITIES

As we briefly touched on earlier in this chapter, one of the key elements in achieving empowerment, particularly at the organizational level, is culture. An organization's or a group's culture is both an antecedent *and* a consequence of empowerment. Culture's impact can be extremely subtle, and it can be "nose-on-your-face" obvious. In any case, its effects are pervasive and compelling. And it is management's responsibility to create and sustain an organizational culture that promotes the interests of people and the interests of the organization. Just like so many other important responsibilities of managers, it's not easily done. But like most of them, it is done through communication. Let's look at it, next.

Table 6.4
The Ten Highest Participation Characteristics

•Gives subordinates a share in decision making.
•Keeps subordinates informed of the true situation, good or bad, under all circumstances.
•Stays aware of the state of the organization's morale and does everything possible to make it high.
•Is easily approachable.
•Counsels, trains, and develops subordinates.
•Communicates effectively with subordinates.
•Shows thoughtfulness and consideration of others.
•Is willing to make changes in ways of doing things.
•Is willing to support subordinates even when they make mistakes.
•Expresses appreciation when a subordinate does a good job.

Source: Quoted from Greiner (1973, p. 114).

Chapter 7

Creating Organizational Culture through Communication

> What we are looking for, first and foremost, is a sense of humor. We hire attitudes.
>
> Herb Kelleher

> Good managers make meanings for people as well as money.
>
> Tom Peters and Bob Waterman

> Leaders do not have a choice about whether or not to communicate. They only have a choice about how much to manage what they communicate.
>
> Edgar Schein

THE BAZAAR

"This place has always been a kind of Turkish bazaar. Ever since I can remember, we've been in charge of our own shops. Now this. It's not going to work."

The three themes of this comment had been repeated to me over and over again in my interviews with the managers and other employees of SES (name disguised): (1) "SES as a bazaar"; (2) a recent upheaval in "the way we've always done things"; and (3) the trouble people saw in the works as a result.

I had been asked by the organization's CEO to help document and clarify what he intuitively felt was a "communication problem" that was, so he explained, becoming ever more complicated and nettlesome. Over the course of several months I "watched" things, interviewed a large diagonal cross section of employees, and created/administered a survey questionnaire for the whole organization in an effort to discover what was "bugging" people. Here's more context.

SES was a public agency of a southwestern state. In its entire 23 year history, it had had two CEOs or top administrators. The first was essentially the "founder" administrator, who was in on the agency's inception and charter, and who had shepherded its growth from just a handful of money and people to a hundred-million dollar budget and several hundred employees. By outsiders and insiders alike, the agency under his direction was considered very effective in fulfilling its mission. Approximately two years prior to my involvement, he died unexpectedly of a heart attack, in his early 60s. In my interactions with agency employees, he was described in uniformly glowing, even loving, terms both by those who had worked with him over the years and by those who had never met him. Time and again, employees summed up his managerial style with variations on *his* expression, "we're all entrepreneurs with a common goal." According to many of my interviewees, the agency was still mourning his death, after two years later.

Upon his death, a caretaker Administrative Council was set in place for about six months while a search was conducted for a new CEO. The committee overseeing the search consisted both of outsider officials from state government, in the majority, and SES members representing top and middle administration. There had been a few senior SES administrators vying for the position, but for whatever reason the job went to an "outside" candidate. This new CEO, in his middle 40s, had had his job for about a year and a half when he contacted me.

From what employees told me, the new CEO took about six months getting a feel for the terrain before he began "all-out dynamiting." Then over the course of the next year he instituted several sweeping changes in controls and reporting procedures that he felt would bring him in closer touch with what was going on in the agency's seven divisions. Simultaneously, he shifted a number of what had been divisional decision processes "upstairs" so as to personally address what he felt were coordination and competition problems between divisions. During this one-year period, two of the seven division directors resigned. And as near as I could tell at the earliest point in my involvement, practically one whole division, made up mainly of Ph.D.s and research scientists, was on the verge of either open revolt and/or mass exodus.

A "communication problem," indeed! But as it turned out, not nearly as narrowly bounded as the CEO initially surmised. He was concerned with *symptoms* of the problem, which were "mainstream" communication, alright: rampant rumors, nonexistent or severely distorted "upward" communication, pockets of ignorance and wild speculation throughout SES as to what really was going on, blatant expressions of resistance, and even some outright tangible hostility. And, he basically wanted help in treating those symptoms—ways of improving upward and downward communication, ways of reducing the resistance and improving morale, ways of doing a better job of informing employees about what changes were going to take place and why.

But the real problems of SES weren't going to disappear with the application of a few communication "Band-Aids." The real problems would simply pop up again in some other, perhaps more acute, form. That's because the remedies sought didn't address the causes of the problems. Now one interpretation of "causality" might be the CEO's actions flying right in the face of SES's customary ways of seeing and doing things. And that's true—they did. But there was a "cause" farther removed, a cause of this cause—a disposition, if you will, that made it much more likely that the CEO would fail to accommodate and would even antagonize, with his actions, the customary ways of seeing and doing things at SES. In turn, the consequences of his actions eventually came back to hammer him in the form of his communication headaches. SES's painful communication symptoms *originated* in the CEO's working definition of "what communication is and does." It limited his appreciation for the power of organizational culture, and therefore the conscious control of his own communicative activities in both adapting to SES's culture as needed and shaping it as possible.

This chapter examines organizational culture through the lens of communication, the message-related events and phenomena that create culture, constitute it, and express it.

WHAT IS ORGANIZATIONAL CULTURE?

In Chapter 2, we established the connection between metaphor, thought, and action. We spent most of our time on metaphors that frame our perspectives on communication, particularly the so-called conduit metaphor. But as mentioned, metaphor affects *all* of our thinking, not just that related to communication. Some of the most influential thinking around has concerned "organizations." Like everything else, that thinking too has been shaped by and expressed in metaphorical images. Historically, probably three metaphors have dominated thinking about organizations. The two timeless "standards" are "organization as machine" and "organization as biological organism." Each of these models has made some very useful contributions to our knowledge, design, and practices of organizations.

Most recently, a third very popular metaphor for organization has appeared: "organization as culture." This metaphor is "new" in its application to modern organizations, but not so new in its applications to the human race. Specifically, "organization as culture" was borrowed from cultural anthropology for the perspective it might render on understanding organizations, particularly business organizations. And like all metaphorical expressions, it suggests some immediate questions or connections about its subject.

For instance, in what ways are organizations "cultures?" The people of a culture are often connected by language(s). What kind of "language" does an organization develop to unite its members? Cultures develop and exhibit customs and traditions for doing things in certain ways. Do organizations develop and exhibit their own customs and traditions for doing things? The people of a culture have beliefs and values that serve, in various ways, the interests of the culture. Can the beliefs and values of organizational members promote the interests of the organization? Cultures have "norms" and "taboos," the things people must and must not do to stay in good cultural stead. What are the norms and taboos of organizations, how do they develop, how can they be changed, and what kind of influence do they have on organizational members? Cultures often develop subcultures and countercultures. Do organizations develop them too? Cultures socialize newcomers to their ways. How do organizations socialize newcomers to their ways? Cultures produce their own distinctive "artifacts," the "stuff" associated in all sorts of ways—functional, symbolic, physical, spiritual, and the like—with what the culture is about. What kinds of artifacts do organizations produce that reveal what they are about? This line of questioning could go on for quite some time, with the point being, again, that metaphors generate perspective.

There is much truth in the old saying, "necessity is the mother of invention." We saw in the preceding chapter that empowerment as a management innovation has been a product more of necessity than of anything else. The same goes for the popularity of "culture" as a metaphor for organization. Its "arrival" both for organizational scholars, and really, for everyone who works in organizations, was hastened immensely by a period of time centered in the early 1980s, and known, ominously, as "The Productivity Crisis."

The Productivity Crisis was the worst of times for American managers, who were losing their shirts to foreign competitors, especially the Japanese and (then) West Germans; and consequently, the best of times for authors and consultants who proffered relief from the humiliation American organizations were suffering. The one book, especially, that seized the attention of all those American managers in search of answers to the Productivity Crisis, sending them in search of "culture" for their own organizations, was *In Search of Excellence*, by Tom Peters and Bob Waterman (1982).

This book, riding an enormous wave of public anxiety and frustration over essentially being "↑ed" by the Japanese and Germans, mixed with more than a little nationalistic "let's do *something*, dammit!" became a best-seller overnight and went on to become the best-selling business book ever, with millions of copies sold. Shortly after its publication, I remember two students in a graduate class of mine, both middle managers in different Fortune 500 organizations, sharing identical stories with me. They each had been *required* to read *In Search of Excellence* by their managers, who had also been required to read it, and they themselves were going to require *their* managers to read it.

Peters and Waterman found exceptionally fertile soil for the seeds they planted. But the seeds themselves were, and remain, worthy. Their book linked the so-called "softer" side of management, the nonquantitative, "human" and symbolic side, with organizational "excellence," as judged by "hard" criteria. And more than anything else, their book seemed to connect organizational excellence with a somewhat mysterious yet powerful organizational quality called "culture."

Meanwhile, elsewhere in the early to mid-1980s, and partly because of Peters and Waterman, business magazines, trade publications, and scholarly journals began filling up with articles about "organizational culture" or its ancillary concepts, "norms," "values," "beliefs," "customs," "assumptions," "organizational myths," "organizational symbolism," "organizational ideology," and so on. As noted, it was the "best" of times for those with answers.

Interest in organizational culture as a fruitful metaphor hasn't really wilted much, all these years later. "Culture" has become a standard of organizational lingo, and is appreciated increasingly as something that must be reckoned with by managers. But "how" to reckon with it still troubles many managers. That's because many managers mistake the surface manifestations of culture for the culture itself, and neglect the deeper, less accessible causes giving rise to the more visible elements. Also, many managers simply don't understand the role of communication and assumptions about communication in accessing, shaping, and managing culture.

The definition of culture offered by Edgar Schein in his practical and insightful book, *Organizational Culture and Leadership* (1992), offers us the best point of departure: "A pattern of shared basic assumptions that the group learned as it solved its problems of external adaptation and internal integration, that has worked well enough to be considered valid and, therefore, to be taught to new members as the correct way to perceive, think, and feel in relation to those problems" (p. 12).

This is a "rich" definition of organizational culture. Rich for prospecting nuggets of communication gold that will have precious value in understanding and managing culture: What are basic assumptions? Where do they originate? How are they conveyed initially? By whom? How are they learned? How do they come to be shared? How are they taught? How do they affect individual and collective action? How accessible are they for conscious examination? How could this be done? Communication plays an essential part in answering each of these questions. And managers who appreciate the implications of them for communicative actions are much better positioned to harness and even direct the great power of organizational culture rather than to be subservient to it or victimized by it.

Getting to the Bottom of Culture: Basic Assumptions

Ascertaining an organization's "culture" isn't as easy as just standing around watching what goes on, although that can help; or asking organizational members how they would describe their "culture," although that too can help; or reviewing the founder's history, actions, decisions, managerial style, and the like, although that can help, as well. To return to Schein's definition, the essence of an organization's culture is a "pattern of shared basic assumptions." Those assumptions of the conduit metaphor reviewed in Chapter 2—communication transfers meanings, words contain meanings, and so forth—make up patterned, basic assumptions that are "taught," so the argument goes, first by the structure of the English language itself, and second, by our own repeated uses of it.

Basic assumptions operate below our conscious awareness. Like breathing, they once might have been "felt" or "understood" in some wordless experiential sense, but probably have not been clearly articulated and contemplated with words. We *experience* the "principle of gravity" first, then learn it intuitively, then assume it as a "given" of the world, and so don't fret or think about it, but live our lives very much counting on it to be true. Even though it's just something we pick up along the way, it nevertheless determines our actions. Basic assumptions are "gravitational principles"—subconscious, taken-for-granted explanations of the way the world, or something in it, *is* and/or *works*.

Figure 7.1 depicts three different "layers" of culture, along with their key features and relationship to one another. Basic assumptions are the least accessible but the clearest expression of an organization's culture. They are its ultimate source.

Figure 7.1
"Layers" of Organizational Culture

Artifacts   (discernible objects, events, symbols, etc.;
                                   easiest to see, but vague and incoherent
                                   indicators of essence of culture)

Values   (what the organization values; what it desires
Rules   and requires of members; accessible through
Behavioral Norms   careful listening/observation; can only infer
                                   basic assumptions supporting them)

Basic Assumptions   (subconscious "solutions" and "explanations"
                                   for organizational problems; most difficult to
                                   access, but clearest in revealing culture)

Adapted from Schein (1992).

According to Schein, the nearest we're likely to get to the shared basic assumptions of an organization are, first, its "artifacts," and second, its "values." These are the only visible expressions of basic assumptions, and they require a great deal of investigative and interpretive effort to decipher just how they reveal basic assumptions.

Artifacts are the easiest to see but also the most difficult to interpret as expressions of culture. Artifacts can be literally anything observable: physical features of a workplace, architecture, spatial arrangements, lighting, furnishings, ethnic and gender diversity, appearances and style of dress of people working there, technologies used, language and organizational symbols, policy manuals, presence or absence of time clocks, security systems, executive dining rooms, washrooms, parking facilities, employee benefits packages, corporate philanthropy programs, employee work-out facilities, softball teams, and so on. Anything—but also, of course, anybody's guess as to what in the world the basic assumptions from which they stem could possibly be.

That's where the values, rules, and behavioral norms espoused by the organization and its leader(s), or otherwise discernible, shed additional light. These may not be as readily visible—as "everywhere you look"—as artifacts. But through careful "listening" to organizational language, "sayings" and "stories"; through observing key actions, critical incidents, and detecting enigmatic artifacts; and through asking about the "whys" of those actions, incidents, and artifacts, "what" the organization values can emerge, which can in turn throw considerable interpretive light in the direction of the basic assumptions from whence the values derive.

Why Is Organizational Culture Important?

Peters and Waterman helped document the main reason why managers have begun paying attention to organizational culture: culture makes a big contribution in promoting organizational excellence. Or to turn it around, culture can make a big contribution in preventing organizational excellence. Because culture touches so many different parts of an organization's existence, it's going to influence, sometimes blatantly, sometimes subtly, practically everything an organization attempts to do.

In a sense, and ironically enough, "efficiency" is what's behind the link between organizational culture and performance. The organization where people share the same basic assumptions has definite efficiency advantages that, providing its assumptions are adaptive to the organization's environment, will be unknown to the organization with undeveloped or diffuse assumptions. Shared assumptions create *interpretive efficiency*, facilitating common understandings of *communication about* the organization's "world," why that world is as it is, what the organization's place in it is, and why the organization acts as it does in relation to its environment. When basic assumptions are shared, there will be less time and energy spent by members haggling over the nature of the organization's world, members' roles in it, and leaders' communication about both of these subjects.

Shared assumptions are also likely to promote *values efficiency*, in that values consensus will be more easily attainable when people operate from the same platform of assumptions about the organizational world. If you and I both believe that the world is a place of limitless physical resources and predictable environmental forces, it will be easier for us to agree on what we should value than if I believe the former but you believe that the world has only limited resources and unpredictable, constantly changing environmental forces. When people have trouble settling on "what's important," tremendous amounts of energy and time usually get chewed up in the process. Shared assumptions make it easier for people to agree on "what's important."

A third outcome of shared assumptions is *control efficiency*. This kind of efficiency derives from the common "meaning," sense of purpose, and direction implicit to sharing assumptions about the organizational world. As a "believer," I've got a powerful internal guidance system pulling me on, self-regulating my actions. The contributions I make are willful and willing products of my assumptions and values, as are the contributions of other people the products of their assumptions and values. If we all believe in and value the same things, there's little need for the kind of surveillance and control mechanisms found where people don't share assumptions and values.

ORIGINS OF ORGANIZATIONAL CULTURE

Organizational culture evolves from the interaction of five sources. The first two of them are external to the organization, and have broad but indeterminate influences on it: (1) the societal culture in which an organization originates and (2) the industry environment of the organization (Ott, 1989). The remaining three are internal, with some overlap with the two external sources: (3) the assumptions, values, and beliefs of leaders, and particularly founder leaders; (4) the things that organizational members learn through their work experiences; and (5) the assumptions, values, and beliefs entering the organization by way of new members, especially new leaders (Schein, 1992). The source having the most direct, visible, and far-reaching influence of these five is undoubtedly leaders or founder leaders. Although leaders are certainly affected by their societies and are more or less sensitive to industry dynamics, in a causal sense leaders' actions, decisions, words, and so forth, are much more closely linked to specific organizational consequences than either of the external sources. And as regards the other two "inside" sources of culture—what members learn, and what new members bring to the mix—leaders ultimately can control, with their actions, decisions, and words, both of them. But let's begin outside the organization, before coming back to leaders.

At the most inclusive level, an organization draws certain elements and standards from its societal culture in evolving its own culture. Some of the most ambitious and fascinating inquiry into this idea comes from the work of the Dutch social researcher Geert Hofstede (1984). Basing his conclusions on the results of an absolutely gigantic survey study—with more than 100,000 participants from 53 countries—Hofstede claims that societal cultures inculcate their populace, and therefore societal organizations, with the predominant assumptions and values of the given culture. Not much new there. But Hofstede's research takes this idea an intriguing step further. His data suggest that societal cultures can be distinguished on four main cultural assumptions or values: (1) the culture's stance on uncertainty—whether and how it tolerates uncertainty ("uncertainty avoidance"); (2) the culture's stance on the distribution of power—whether it tolerates power inequalities ("power distance"); (3) the culture's stance on sex role expectations—whether it divides behavioral expectations along gender lines ("masculinity-femininity"); and (4) the culture's stance on the individual—how it prioritizes individualistic concerns relative to group concerns ("individualism-collectivism").

Hofstede raises all kinds of implications of these assumptions and values. He groups different societal cultures having similar assumption profiles, and differentiates those with dissimilar profiles. The resulting cultural "map" of the world shows some interesting and sometimes surprising kinships and differences. He speculates on how certain societal cultural assumptions and values translate into unique customs, practices, and institutions, and even manifest themselves in management theories and techniques. He wonders whether certain theories and techniques of management, originating from particular societal cultures with unique assumption profiles (especially the United States), will be applicable in cultures possessing radically different assumption profiles.

The cultures of organizations can't help but show some of the shadings of the surrounding societal culture, since organizational members come largely or exclusively from that culture. Apart from Hofstede's cultural assumptions, some of the "lessons" imparted to us by our societal culture probably include assumptions about economic systems, the relationship between organizations and government, political systems, technology, the nature of people, ethics, competition, time, and the physical environment, to name a few.

A second broad cultural influence on an organization comes from the industry or organizational environment in which it operates. The dynamics of different industries are such that organizations operating in them must adapt certain qualities to survive. For instance, ferocious competition and very dramatic technological changes are two hallmarks of the personal computer software industry. The dynamics of the industry all but force member organizations to enter the arena with, or quickly cultivate, culture-centered appetites for the good fight, for constant technological innovativeness, and for organizational secrecy, because these cultural values buttress the organizational stance needed for survival. The same holds true for any industry. Certain industry dynamics require that member organizations adapt to them strategically, while other adaptations are more optional. The industry dynamics that *demand* strategic adaptation are the ones which will carry the strongest cultural messages for member organizations.

"Cultural *messages*?" Virtually the *entire* process of creating and shaping organizational culture centers around people doing things, or on things happening, which have message value for themselves and other people at some level of meaningfulness. Cultural lessons are crafted and enacted, wittingly and unwittingly. Perceivers themselves create, learn, and modify cultural lessons—"messages"—all of the time, from the events, actions, and words that make up their organizational streams of experience. The whole culture creation process is testimony to the validity of something said in Chapter 3: "Anything is a potential message."

And nobody's actions and words attract more attention or have more potential for cultural message value in the eyes of perceivers, than an organization's leaders. Leaders are by definition influential. They possess power of various sorts. People like them, people respect them, people identify with them, they're experts, they're charismatic, they own the place, they sign the checks. And part of exercising their powers includes influencing organizational members toward the most important elements of the organization's culture. This is not necessarily or even very often intentional. More often, akin to how we teach and learn "gravity," it just happens as a result of leaders' actions, decisions, and words. Like nearly everyone, most leaders are unaware of the basic assumptions they hold. Without some method for focusing their attention, they couldn't very well articulate and then "teach" people their assumptions any more than they could describe the surface details of Neptune for sure, never having seen either "place" except from a distance. It's much more likely that leaders can access their artifacts, values, and beliefs than their basic assumptions. Artifacts can more or less be seen "with the naked eye." It just takes a perceptive naked eye. And values and beliefs can be inferred from artifacts, decisions, life choices, actions, resource allocations (including time), even self-assessment instruments.

However, with some guidance, and intense, honest self-reflection, leaders *can* more or less "reverse engineer" their basic assumptions by identifying the prominent artifacts characterizing their activities and organizations, and then by questioning "why" those artifacts exist or occur as they do. The latter part of this process can reveal the basic elements of culture, and we'll return to it later in the chapter. It is an essential activity enabling leaders to get as close a view as possible of their basic values and assumptions. For now, the point is that leaders, particularly founder leaders who have the advantage of working with the organizational equivalent of a lump of clay, play the critical role in creating culture—largely, as we shall see, because "anything is a potential message."

For much the same reason, the learnings of organizational members also help create culture. That is, the things members experience, the actions of leaders, the words that determine and justify how organizational life will be lived, the artifacts around them—these are each the raw materials for cultural messages, some more explicitly meaningful than others, about what's important, what's desired, what's required of members; enacted values and norms that themselves whisper softer messages about *what's assumed*. Over time, indirect experiences with the organization's or leaders' basic assumptions, in the form of perceived actions, artifacts, words, values, and norms, will eventually, gradually, and subtly confirm or disconfirm for people the validity of the assumptions themselves.

The final source of organizational culture is new members, particularly those who establish themselves as leaders. Like founder leaders or other established leaders, new members and leaders will be in a position to influence the organization toward their own basic assumptions, through their values, norms, beliefs, and artifacts. The main obstacle to their success concerns whether their assumptions, values, actions, and words are compatible with those required by the organization's culture. If significant incompatibility exists, there will be tremendous resistance by the organization toward the person, and often tremendous pressure applied to change the new member's assumptions, values, actions, whatever. In the opening case, the CEO of SES experienced exactly this resistance, pressure, and hostility. In a recent interview, Jack Welch, Chairman and CEO of General Electric, also articulates this pressure (McFarland et al., 1993). Welch, one of most successful and innovative managers going, states emphatically that at GE, "living" the company's values is just as important as meeting the performance "numbers" in affecting a leader's future with the company. Figure 7.2 presents some of his views on the subject of evaluating different types of leaders. For this very successful CEO, it appears that his leaders either "buy in" to the culture's values—or are out.

In a way, of course, established leaders, and especially founders, hold the ultimate key to preserving their culture. If they've been effective in creating the kind of culture they want, they will have developed and refined methods to screen newcomers on "culture compatibility," administered at several points in the "joining up" phase. And those who don't fit are found out, and either simply not hired up front, or not retained after a probationary period.

Communication Elements in the Creation of Organizational Culture

The established leader(s) of an organization will be the most influential, wittingly or not, in shaping its culture, so it makes sense to focus on what leaders do and can do in that regard. Schein (1992) claims that leaders "embed" their own assumptions through six primary activities, listed in Table 7.1. If we consider each one in view of our communication principle (Chapter 3) that "anything is a potential message," a whole host of implications for communication emerges. Remember, one of the main themes of this book is that communicators need to be more vigilant, to work harder, so as to exercise more influence over the messages that others create from their words and deeds. Let's look at the potential for communication in each "embedding activity," in the interest of improving our vigilance.

Communicating about priorities. An age-old example of how priorities are conveyed comes from parent-child relations. It is invoked here, however, with the precaution that it is not meant to imply that leader-other relations are or should be paternalistic. The example simply is relevant and instructive here.

Figure 7.2
Values Buy-In, or Out: One CEO's View

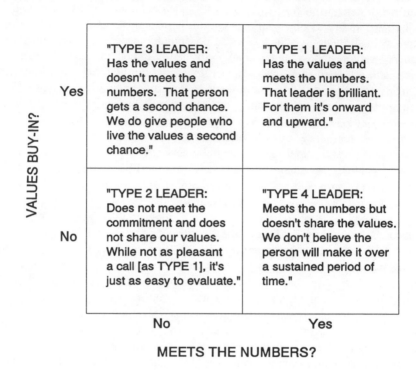

"TYPE 3 LEADER:
Has the values and
doesn't meet the
numbers. That person
gets a second chance.
We do give people who
live the values a second
chance."

"TYPE 1 LEADER:
Has the values and
meets the numbers.
That leader is brilliant.
For them it's onward
and upward."

"TYPE 2 LEADER:
Does not meet the
commitment and does
not share our values.
While not as pleasant
a call [as TYPE 1], it's
just as easy to evaluate."

"TYPE 4 LEADER:
Meets the numbers but
doesn't share the values.
We don't believe the
person will make it over
a sustained period of
time."

VALUES BUY-IN?   Yes   No

No   Yes

MEETS THE NUMBERS?

Quotes from Jack Welch, Chairman and CEO of General Electric (McFarland et al.,
1993, p. 153).

Table 7.1
How Leaders Embed Their Assumptions and Values

•What leaders pay attention to, measure, and control on a regular basis.
•How leaders react to critical incidents and organizational crises.
•Observed criteria by which leaders allocate scarce resources.
•Deliberate role modeling, teaching, and coaching.
•Observed criteria by which leaders allocate rewards and status.
•Observed criteria by which leaders recruit, select, promote, retire, and excommunicate
 organizational members.

Source: Table entries quoted from Schein (1992, p. 231).

Developmental psychologists and educators have long told us that kids learn
volumes about "what's important"—in effect, children "create" value-oriented

messages—by watching what their parents do: how parents spend time; doing what; what gets parental attention; what doesn't; what behaviors of children are required; how requirements are enforced; and how parental words about "what's important," if any, stack up against observed actions.

Exactly the same thing applies to leaders. What they do with their time, what they pay attention to, what they ignore, what they require, how they enforce it, and how their words about "what's important," if any, square with their actions, all have potential cultural message value for others.

The problem for leaders is twofold. The first, owing mainly to the slipperiness of nonverbal communication, is that actions by themselves offer a universe of possible interpretations as to "what's important," only a tiny number of which probably align with the *actor's* version. Sure, actions often do speak louder than words. But that just means they're often more compelling to a perceiver, not that the meanings created from them by perceivers are necessarily more faithful to a communicator's intentions. People who take comfort (or refuge) in "letting my actions do the talking" may be surprised at what gets "heard."

The second problem concerns whether anything at all gets "heard" by a leader's actions alone. People apprehend and process information in different ways, and with differing degrees of sensitivity. Simply put, what's meaningful or even noticeable to you as an actor or perceiver might be meaningless and invisible to me. Have you ever made a very big deal of someone's actions only to be asked by a fellow observer of those actions how you could possibly get what you got from what you saw? Or have you ever done the asking? These things happen all the time, and they simply verify what makes "action" such a communication ink blot test—we all have different "eyes" for what passes before us. Where you "see the writing on the wall" and I "see the light" in someone's actions, someone else might see just "huh?"

For these reasons, actions without words will leave more room for the communication of unintended values and assumptions than actions with words. Throughout this entire section are suggestions for opportunities for leaders to support their actions with words—opportunities for "redundancy"—so as to increase the explicitness of "cultural messages," with the hope of increasing the correspondence between cultural messages *as intended* by leaders and *as created* by others. The opportunities for a leader to *communicate about priorities* would include answering these questions, which should help clarify values and assumptions for everyone concerned:

1. Why do you spend your time as you do? Can you explicitly tell others why? Have you? If not, why not? Are your "stated" priorities about your time allocations consistent with your "enacted" priorities? Ask others if they think so.
2. Why do you measure what you measure in the organization? What are your priorities on what you measure, and why? Can you explicitly tell others your thoughts on these questions? Have you? If not, why not? Are your "stated" priorities on what you measure consistent with your "enacted" priorities? Ask others if they think so.

3. Why do you have whatever controls you have? Can you explicitly tell others
    why? Have you? If not, why not? Are the "stated" priorities for required
    behavior consistent with the "enacted" priorities as implied by your controls? Ask
    others if they think so.

Communicating values through incidents and crises. Chapter 5, on leadership
and communication, opened with stories about four different leaders. In "I Can't
Go To My Grave Knowing . . ." the story involved "crossroad incidents" that a
parent viewed as issues of doing the "right" thing versus doing the "easy" thing.
A father's decisions and actions conveyed messages that, taken by themselves,
were sometimes misunderstood by his family.   And the way his family
discovered their "misreads" was that he often at some point *explained why* he
acted as he did.   In doing so he shared his values and assumptions with his
family.   His words either clarified or drove the message home about what's
important and worth sacrificing for.
    There's a perfect parallel for leaders to communicate values in organizations,
through an explanation of why incidents and crises were handled as they were.
Again too often, we're content to let our actions do the talking. Answering the
following questions will help leaders clarify their values and assumptions, *using
incidents and crises as the opportunity for communication*:

What kinds of incidents or crises have you faced recently, that others have observed, and
which you feel showed your values through the way you handled them? Why did you
act as you did? Can you explicitly tell others why? Have you? If not, why not? Pick
a specific incident: what would you like others to have learned from the way you handled
it? Talk with them to see what, if anything, they "made" of your actions.

Communicating about who gets what resources. "Who gets what?" has always
divided people in organizations. So many of the important resources on which
organizations depend are limited and unevenly distributed, that the anxiety
underlying the question is not without legitimacy. And one of the sources of a
good deal of confusion, resentment, and conflict in organizations is that its
answer very often comes in the form of decisions made and announced,
unaccompanied by explanations of why resources were allocated as they were.
As noted above, actions taken and decisions made on resource allocation can sure
enough send a message. But what, exactly, is the message you as a leader want
created in your name? Let's look at an example.
    There are all kinds of allocable resources. In the last chapter, we discussed
delegation as a type of empowerment strategy. As such, delegation involves
allocating certain resources—authority, money, staff, equipment, time, and so
on—that are *not* made available to everyone. For sure, there are reasons
supporting a given delegation. They might be that you want to develop a
particular person. They might be that a particular person has a needed skill
advantage over other candidates. They might be that a particular person basically
"has it coming," having worked very hard and conscientiously on less appealing

jobs. There can be any number of reasons supporting this particular uneven, selective allocation of resources known as delegation.

The point here is that explaining to everyone concerned—those delegated to, and those who missed out—*why* the allocation was made, will accomplish two very important things: (1) it will let people know what kinds of behaviors, skills, attitudes, and the like, get linked to the receipt of resources and (2) it will leave the interpretation of decision actions less to chance—more to words—and clarify the values underlying them.

The example cited is delegation. Of course many people think of "hard," tangible resources when they think of allocation. Why can't the same apply there? Whatever the case, people want to know why. They might not agree with the reasoning, but knowing what it was, is, and will be gives them a much clearer picture of "what's important." Use the following questions to *communicate about who gets what resources*:

What are the resources that you have to make allocation decisions on (time, money, equipment, staff, authority, etc.)? Why did you allocate resources, or a given resource, as you did? Can you explicitly tell those affected by your allocations why? Have you? If not, why not? Are your "stated" reasons or priorities consistent with your "enacted" priorities? Ask those affected by your allocations if they think so.

Talking culture. Of all the activities and events connected with leadership that "embed" culture, role modeling, teaching, and coaching are possibly the most explicitly "verbal," and thus consistent with mainstream ideas on communication. The leader's intent is to deliberately instruct. The leader speaks, writes, and/or acts, and others listen, read, watch, and learn. As in any instructional situation, two of the main issues here are "what" to teach and "how" to best teach it.

Ideally, leaders know what cultural lessons need learning. This requires them to have a clear idea of the values they wish to be expressed in their group's culture. Even if leaders have a clear picture of what they value and want others to value, it's not just a matter of stating the values and expecting others to adopt them as guiding principles. As suggested elsewhere in this book, ownership is an essential condition for commitment. Yes, leaders can tell us what the "official" values will be, or what they want them to be, and print up a list of them for distribution among employees. But unless people can "own" them, those values will remain the "official" list, while the "unofficial" ones steer the organization.

The surest way for people to own an idea is to be a part of creating it. The implication of this for leaders is that when they deliberately try to provide cultural instruction, greater success will come from a "question-asking" approach than an "answer-giving" one. This has come up before, and we'll see it again. Leaders simply cannot tell people what to think, what to value. The best they can do is to create opportunities for thoughtful people to engage in dialogues with leaders about (1) what's important to them (the people) and (2) what should be important to an organization, with the purpose of identifying areas where value consensus exists and can exist. This isn't easy to do, and I'm certainly not suggesting that leaders simply take a passive "what should we value?" stance and see what happens. As leaders, their own ideas will probably count heavily in such dialogues, especially if their power bases are "personal." But it's important to remember that true commitment to any set of values can only come from within people. It won't result from values ordered from "on high," no matter what the external incentives.

Direct cultural instruction often comes in the form of officially sanctioned training. I have created and delivered many training programs having the intent of what I would call "cultural instruction." And along those lines, coupled with what was said above about "asking questions" versus "giving answers," let's draw a parallel here that can be instructive.

In virtually any training group of experienced supervisors and managers, there are good ideas about leadership, management, communication, motivation, time management, what have you, that are understood, valued, and successfully "lived" by individuals in the group, but not *collectively* shared. So an important part of facilitating learning in situations like these should be to provide a process by which group members can talk to one another to "share the wealth" that they possess. This objective is to help them draw "lessons" from their own experiences, worded as advice—in effect, to help them give themselves the best advice available in the group.

Now in any training context, I as a facilitator-trainer have ideas and advice of my own that I want to offer—ideas and advice that have both experience and research to recommend them. But over many trials, and many different kinds of behavioral skill training, I've noticed two curious things about my "good ideas" and my participants' "good ideas." First, their good ideas usually either replicate mine in important ways (with different words, maybe), complement mine in helpful ways, or even cause me to rethink mine. Second, they often get more excited about *their* advice and ideas than about *mine*. From my assessments of participants' reactions to our training sessions, there have been innumerable times when manager participants have stated some variation on the following to me: "I didn't know we had so much wisdom right here among us. I learned things that will help me every day." I agree with that general assessment. But the thing that really gives it energy for them is the fact that so much of what was learned was there all along, locked within individuals, awaiting collective expression. Awaiting *group ownership* of the good ideas.

From my experiences, a most effective method of "teaching" certain behavioral artifacts and values associated with culture relies on asking questions rather than giving answers. Leaders can use modified versions of the same techniques, in group settings, and emphasize dialogue—*not* one-way "telling" or "selling"—between themselves and others on subjects of importance. In most instances a skilled facilitator will help. In any event, questions and suggestions for leaders interested in *talking culture* include:

1. What values or cultural subjects should be talked about? What are the five most important to you? Why is a given value or subject important to you? What are your thoughts on these values or subjects—what "lessons" of yours do you think others would benefit from knowing? What are the best three pieces of advice you can think of on a given subject? Why are they "good advice?"
2. In a series of ongoing training session dialogues, get people talking about these questions. Listen to what they say more than talking yourself, and look for ways in which composites of "advice"—yours and theirs—dovetail. Someone other than the leader should compile what the group believes to be the "best" ideas and advice coming from a session or sessions, have them typed up, printed, and distributed to all participants as the "group's product." Do *not* "hard sell" your own advice.

Communicating about what gets rewarded, who gets status. Most accepted models of motivation these days have somewhere built into them, these two principles, among others: (1) rewarded behavior gets repeated and (2) highly valued rewards are more effective incentives than rewards that aren't as highly valued. These, frankly, are "Motivation 101" ideas, something we all learn growing up. Nevertheless, the communication implications of them are applied only infrequently in organizations. Often, managers more or less "make" employees discover the connection between doing something and getting rewarded for doing it—rather than go to the communicative work of explaining and showing exactly what the link is. As well, managers often make two mistakes concerning the value of rewards: First, they mistakenly assume that everyone wants the same kinds of rewards, often modeled on what the managers themselves prefer. And second, they very often take "incentives" to mean only organizationally controlled incentives such as money, which are frequently governed by policy more than by a manager's discretion. This ignores a huge number of incentives that are very frequently personally controllable by many managers, such as plum job assignments to those earning them, public and private recognition for jobs well done, symbolic rewards, recommendations for promotion, provision of special learning opportunities, and the like. Lots of managers overlook the communication needs implied by those two motivational principles above. Part of what "embeds" a culture is behavior that reinforces its values. And culturally motivated behavior is very much a matter of those principles above and their communication implications. The following questions will help with *communicating about what gets rewarded, who gets status*:

What gets rewarded in the group or organization? Why—what important values underlie what gets rewarded? Can you explicitly tell others your thoughts on these questions? Have you? If not, why not? Do people value the rewards you offer? How do you know? What else would they like? Are the "stated" criteria for rewards consistent with the way rewards are actually given? Ask others if they think so.

Communicating about who gets in, gets up, and gets out. This area of leadership basically concerns activities that convey "what it takes" for successful membership in a given organization or group: what it takes to get "in," to join; what it takes to succeed and advance within an organization; what it takes to get out successfully, to retire; and what it takes to get out unsuccessfully, to be fired or ostracized. Quite often organizations develop formal statements that speak, with greater or lesser detail, to each of these issues. Much less often do individual organizational leaders speak directly to or conduct face-to-face dialogues with members on them. To *communicate about who gets in, gets up, and gets out,* leaders should answer for themselves and talk with other people about the following:

1. What do we look for in new members? Why? Are our "stated" criteria for joining consistent with our "enacted" recruiting and selection? Ask others if they think so. In the recruitment process, do we give job candidates accurate and realistic job previews? Ask new hires if they think so.
2. What does it take to succeed and prosper here? Does our reward system show it? On what bases do people advance here? Are our "stated" criteria consistent with our promotion decisions? Ask others if they think so?
3. What does it take to retire from this place? What are the specific provisions for retirement? What do others think of them?
4. What is considered failure here? Why? What behaviors, outcomes, are not tolerated? What are the possible consequences of different offenses? Ask others for their views on the "fairness" of the organization on these questions.

Assessing Organizational Culture

In order for organizational leaders to more self-consciously and explicitly embed or convey their organization's culture, they must first know what it is. Knowing what an organization's culture is requires somehow getting a closer look at it. And getting this closer look is a communication-centered activity. The questions and suggestions offered in the preceding section will prove helpful to individual leaders in first *revealing* and then *conveying* cultural values and assumptions. Most of the questions ask "what" happens and "why" it happens, revealing artifacts, supporting values, and underlying assumptions. The suggestion is made repeatedly for leaders to share their views on the questions with others, and to ask others for their views. If we can liken culture to a "lens" through which we see our organizational experiences, then getting people to think and talk about these questions is akin to grasping the lens itself, pulling it off, and examining its properties to see how they affect us. Once the major values and assumptions underlying a culture become more accessible through cultural analysis, it is possible to evaluate them to determine whether they are in line with environmental demands as well as human interests and needs. Exposing the culture in this way is a necessary step in maintaining an organization's external and internal adaptability.

There are other ways of going about this process. Table 7.2, adapted from Schein (1992), highlights the major elements of an outsider-facilitated, group-

Table 7.2
An Intervention for Analyzing Organizational Culture

•Issue-based top management/leadership support.
•Group of "culture carriers" convenes.
•Leader re-states issue(s) precipitating culture analysis; outside facilitator introduced; discusses culture as artifacts, values, assumptions.
•Describing artifacts: What's going on here?
•Identifying values supporting artifacts: Why are we doing what we do?
•Articulation of assumptions: What statement(s) explains puzzles or contradictions between artifacts and values?
•Subgroups refine assumptions: Which assumptions "help" and "hinder" solving the issue that precipitated the culture analysis (2-3 of each)?
•Consensus on assumptions and analysis: What "helping" and "hindering" assumptions can we achieve consensus on, what are their implications, and what can be done about them?

Source: Adapted from Schein (1992).

based intervention he recommends for analyzing organizational culture. Schein's (1992) Chapter 8, "Deciphering Culture for Insiders," takes readers through a detailed explanation and justification of the formal process he suggests, including several cases. For leaders exploring the need and the possibilities for formal interventions that analyze culture, Schein's Chapter 8 is important reading.

COMMUNICATION AND CULTURE: INSEPARABLE PARTNERS

Leaders act, leaders decide, leaders use words, all in the service of building organizations that reflect their values and their images of the "good" organization. The actual construction gets done basically through communication processes. Actions, decisions, and words convey leaders' values and images, and from organizational members' subscription to those values and images emerges an organization's culture. As more people tacitly accept its values and underlying assumptions, organizational culture relies on different forms of the very thing that created it in the first place—communication—to perpetuate its unique, defining qualities.

Full circle. Communication gives rise to organizational culture, which gives rise to communication, which perpetuates culture. This self-reinforcing, reciprocal relationship between communication and culture can make a mature culture exceptionally resistant to change, unless change itself is one of its cultural values. In this book's last chapter, we'll return briefly to the role of both culture and communication in managing change. Communication holds the key to managing change, because the ultimate test for change—organizational culture—is communication-made.

We've got one other stop before arriving there, however. The next one involves another of the leader-manager's essential responsibilities: building effective teams. Hardly anybody does anything alone in organizations anymore. With the push toward empowered organizations and strong, adaptive cultures, organizations designed around teams and teamwork methods are becoming the rule rather than the exception. Increasingly, organizational effectiveness depends on team effectiveness. In the next chapter, we'll see why this is so, and how leaders must rely on communication to build effective teams.

Chapter 8

Building Teams through Communication

We need to honor our teams more, our aggressive leaders and maverick geniuses less.

Robert Reich

The amount of knowledge around that table . . . the potential! If only we could work together. The potential is thwarted by our unwillingness or inability to mesh.

Member of a "stuck" management team

The difference between great teams and mediocre teams lies in how they face conflict.

Peter Senge

GO TEAM!

In the early years, if the game was tight, the procession of events was as predictable as the sunrise: Get the ball to Michael and let him take over the game. The final outcome wasn't as reliable, however. Sometimes it worked. Sometimes it didn't. For lovers of applied physics and rugged individualism, it was simply poetry in motion to watch him go one-on-however-many with the game on the line. For one athletic shoe manufacturer, it was money in the bank. But for us fans of the Chicago Bulls, for lovers of "the game," and for the head coach or two fired from the Bulls during that time, the early years were frustrating. Despite having what more and more observers were claiming was the "best basketball player on the planet," the Bulls kept coming up short come playoff time. Too often, it just wasn't enough when Michael's 50 or 60 points outscored everyone else on the Bulls *combined*. Great entertainment. Early elimination. Maybe it would be the Cubs' year.

But then something happened. New head coach Phil Jackson put the "s" back in "Bulls." He found a way to use the talents of *all* of the Bulls; a philosophy and system designed to exploit not just the awesome skills of one all-world player, but also the considerable and diverse skills of the other guys, exploiting the power of *teamwork*. Michael, in his own unstoppable, inimitable fashion, continued getting his points—led the NBA in scoring average year after year after year. But the versatility and potency of the Bulls' arsenal and strategies had changed. Michael having an off night, with only 20–25 points? Not to worry. The team will step up. Michael in foul trouble and has to sit down? Not to worry. Other guys can get the job done. Double or triple-teams smothering Michael's usual end-of-game heroics? No sweat. There are four other guys there who can knock it down—from down low or downtown. And the most likely scenario of all: Michael having his "usual" spectacular night? Then it's all the worse for the opposition, because the team is pouring it on too. For three NBA seasons in a row, the Bulls became the best of the best.

Not that Michael wasn't *the* difference. The Bulls' failure to win a fourth consecutive NBA championship, their first season following his (temporary) retirement in 1993, proved that for some. But the 1993–1994 season proved something else about the Bulls. Despite the upheaval in team "chemistry," on-court leadership, and sheer firepower brought on by Michael's retirement, the Bulls made the 1994 NBA playoffs and lasted until the second round, losing to eventual finalists New York Knicks. Michael Jordan's singular talent was unquestionably a necessary ingredient to the Bulls' championship run—but just as unquestionably, insufficient. The frustrating, one-on-five, early years showed that. The three consecutive NBA championships showed something more: the awesome, unbeatable combination of talent and teamwork. Talent, of course, can take many forms, only some of which might be relevant to our concerns here. Talent is necessary. But teamwork is necessary *and* sufficient.

Let's take one more brief basketball excursion. I once heard an exceptionally flattering and credible compliment made about legendary and sometimes controversial Indiana University basketball coach Bob Knight. The comment was made by a network basketball broadcaster who himself was a former championship basketball coach. His comment had two themes: (1) Bob Knight can take a team of "average" players and consistently beat teams having much more talented players—due to differences in teamwork; and (2) Bob Knight's coaching skills are such that he could beat you with his guys one day; then he could swap players with you and beat you with your own guys the next.

Teamwork doesn't just happen. It begins with someone's leadership, someone's design, and ongoing fine-tuning. Make no mistake. Teamwork wins championships, on all fields of competition. And teamwork *always* means "communication." That's what this chapter is about.

WHY TEAM? BECAUSE "TEAM" WORKS!

This chapter is an extension of the previous three. Effective leaders (Chapter

5) earn that distinction largely by building teams that both get the job done better than others and that also provide for their members' social-psychological needs. The movement toward empowerment (Chapter 6) relies extensively, in its purest form, on teams, particularly self-directed teams. And leaders' efforts these days to build strong, adaptive cultures (Chapter 7) in their organizations very often emphasize symbols, themes, and work structures deriving from the "team" metaphor.

There are any number of reasons behind the popularity of "teamwork," certainly not the least of which is financial. Increasingly, evidence shows that teams very often make great "cents" for organizations. In their book, *Empowered Teams*, Wellins, Byham, and Wilson (1991)—human resource consultants— review some recent team initiatives, and attribute the following results to teams in different organizations: "reduced staffing needs, yielding a savings of $200,000 per year"; "increased productivity by 74 percent in three years"; "reduced unit turnaround time . . . from two weeks to two days"; "reduced defects by 90 percent"; "increased productivity by 250 percent"; "decreased defect rates from 1,800 parts per million to 9 parts per million" (p. 14). Even more recently, the work of McKinsey consultants Jon Katzenbach and Douglas Smith, described in *The Wisdom of Teams* (1993), offers further support that teams "work." From studying nearly forty different organizations which have adopted team methods, including numerous Fortune 500 companies, Katzenbach and Smith report these team-based results, among others: "substantially improved customer satisfaction and service in eleven key areas"; "1-year product rollout was fastest in Eli Lilly history for a medical product;" "$10 million savings in six months"; "became highest-revenue, most profitable division within 6 months"; "50% reduction in rejects and 70% reduction in late deliveries"; "designed and introduced new product in record time"; "absenteeism down to 1.6%" (pp. 268–272).

Time savings, reduced costs, improved product quality, more customer satisfaction, higher productivity, increased job satisfaction—these are a few of the reasons organizations are getting serious about teams. And they all have the added appeal of a common spelling: *m-o-n-e-y*.

Unrealized potential and, more to the point, even job security, figures into the picture, too. Earlier in this book, I mentioned a study by McCall and Lombardo (1983) documenting reasons why the careers of certain high-potential managers jumped the track. "Inability to build a team" was right there alongside "inability to delegate" in the top ten. More managers are getting the message from their organizations: "teams are our—*your*—future here."

Plus, several of the current "big ideas" on the business speaker circuits and management reading lists are team-oriented. "Organizational Reengineering" (Hammer and Champy, 1993) and "Horizontal Organizations" (Byrne, 1993), the hottest of the hot topics—and likely to remain that way for some time—are variations on the same theme: redesign organizations around core processes performed by teams. "Self-Directed Work Teams" (Wellins et al., 1991) speaks for itself as a team-centered practice, as does "Team Learning" (Senge, Roberts, Ross, Smith, & Kleiner, 1994; Senge, 1990). And don't forget "Total Quality Management" (Walton, 1986), the little snowball that became an avalanche, emphasizing both internal and external "teaming."

Just like the old saw that we've been "speaking prose" all our lives, teams too have been around forever. It's just that organizations are only now catching on to how teams can help them. But even if your particular work organization doesn't adopt formal team-centered practices, you rub up against teams or work with them informally literally all the time. Comments in Chapter 1 about the "organizational world" we inhabit apply equally well here. It's just not possible, as we approach the twenty-first century, to escape involvement with teams. A family is itself a team, a health care provider is a team or a collection of teams, as is an educational institution. And the same could be said for any organization—food suppliers, retailers, manufacturers, financial institutions, communities, and so on. Each of these entities incorporates elements of "teams," or "a team of teams," regardless of whether they think of themselves as such. So teams are everywhere. But what *is* a team?

"A team is a small number of people of complementary skills committed to a common purpose, performance goals, and approach for which they hold themselves mutually accountable." So say Katzenbach and Smith (1993, p. 45), and although I wouldn't disagree with them, I would stretch their definition in the following ways. First, we must remember that there are different levels of team analysis: teams of individuals, teams of teams of individuals, and so forth. A team of teams, or organization, can be just as much a "team" as a team of individual people, in the sense of fulfilling the other terms of the definition above—complementary skills, common purposes, goals, approaches, and mutual accountability. A second "stretch" stems from the first. Elsewhere in their book, Katzenbach and Smith stipulate that "small number" means typically less than 20 people (p. 21). Insofar as the size of a group affects certain processes and dynamics, it is perfectly valid to remind us that "size" has consequences. For example, as a group gets larger and larger, it tends to naturally break down into subgroupings due to these dynamics, whether anyone wants it or not. But the concept of a "team of teams" plays havoc with the stipulation of fewer than 20 people. There's no magic threshold number for what makes a team, and there's no guaranteed loss of "teamwork" stemming from size alone.

Those are my quibbles with the definition. There's really only one additional element that should be part of the definition of "team," to make what's implicit, explicit for leader-managers. I would propose to amend Katzenbach and Smith's definition of "team" as follows, with my modifications in italics: "A team is a *group* of *communicating* people with complementary skills who are committed to a common purpose, performance goals, and approach for which they hold themselves mutually accountable." "Group" instead of "small number" opens the concept a bit, downplaying size limits. A relatively minor adjustment, frankly. The more essential addition is the other one. "Communicating" reflects the activities necessary to bind people, allowing them to coordinate their efforts into a whole instead of functioning as a group of disconnected parts. It simply makes more explicit the one thing that enables shared purposes, goals, approaches, and accountability at all. Coordinated activity, the defining characteristic of teamwork, requires communication.

All of that being said, the most important terms in this definition of "team"—the terms that make *the* difference between teams and TEAMS!—are "communicating" and "approach," in that order of importance. Katzenbach and Smith explain "approach" to mean "how [people] will work together to accomplish their purpose," and "the specifics of work and how it fits together to integrate individual skills and advance team performance" (p. 56). Clearly, the success of a team hinges on the so-called approach it develops. But just as clearly, the approach itself, including what goes into creating it, hinges on communication practices. Try to establish a team "approach" without communication. Try to implement it without communication. Try to assess it and change it without communication. Teams that fully understand the role of communication in what they do, and that work hard at developing their team communication skills, will develop more effective approaches; teams that don't, won't.

QUALITIES OF EFFECTIVE TEAMS

There's no universal agreement on what *effectiveness* means with regard to teams, or even organizations. And although struggles with the latter have for years puzzled and polarized managers and scholars alike, there is a perspective that affords both scope and utility in helping us understand effectiveness. In Cummings and Worley's revision of Edgar Huse's classic *Organization Development and Change* (Cummings & Worley, 1993), the authors claim that organizational effectiveness rests on two assumptions (p. 3): "First, an effective organization is able to solve its own problems." The second assumption is perhaps a little more mainstream: "An effective organization has both a high quality of work life and high productivity." Substitute "team" for "organization" in these assumptions, and we've got an excellent working definition of "team effectiveness." Effective teams can develop and fix themselves. They do the job, well. They take care of their members. That about covers it.

The topic of teams is one, much like leadership, motivation, and job satisfaction, that has provoked a sizable and diverse research literature over the years, especially concerning group dynamics. Although it is not reviewed for you here, there are a number of practical conclusions drawn from that body of work, plus my own research and consulting experiences with more than 60 organizations and hundreds of teams, centering on qualities that distinguish effective teams from less effective teams. These qualities are summarized in Table 8.1. In a way, these qualities operationalize many of the important details of "approach" discussed above. That being the case, recall that a team's "approach" is made, implemented, assessed, and modified as needs be, through communication. Let's look more closely.

Clear, Shared, Communicated Purpose

"I still don't know what this group is *for*! How can we work together if nobody agrees on what we're trying to do?" This is what a member of a management team said recently about the struggles within his team, along with stories of the teeth-gnashing he and others experienced as a result of working in such a context. I heard the same tune, different musicians, virtually everywhere I listened in his group. His team had a formally designated organizational name, but not much else to go on. They lacked purpose.

The purpose of a team answers the question, "why do we exist?" Purpose functions like a fixed navigational point for the team. Chapter 5 discussed the importance of "vision" in connection with leadership and communication, and Figure 5.2 symbolized vision's role with images of a cloud versus a mountain. Those same images apply here, since purpose is certainly a central element of vision. Without purpose, or without clarity of purpose, a team's "navigational" point of reference offers nothing more fixed and substantial than that cloud for its members to orient toward.   So along with the misdirected efforts and individual pursuits this inevitably encourages, a floating, ever-changing point of reference prevents a team from evaluating itself. If we don't know "why" we exist as a team, then anything we do is okay. If we have no clear destination, then any direction we go and anywhere we are is okay.

Purposes that are clear, shared, and communicated, inside the group and out, promote team effectiveness. Teams without clear, shared, and communicated purposes will struggle. "Clear" means that the purpose has been formulated in terms—ideas, concepts, words—that are unambiguous to team members. "Shared" means that there is a common commitment among team members to the team's purpose. "Communicated" means that the team's purpose is explicitly conveyed, orally and in writing, to team members and to those outside the team whose roles and responsibilities have an important bearing on the functioning of the team. Additionally, the motivational "pull" in all of this, as well as the concentration of team efforts, will be strengthened by the team "owning" its purpose—having a voice in developing it—and by knowing how its own purpose "fits" larger organizational purposes and other teams' purposes. Developing and expressing purpose is a communication responsibility of team leaders.

Clear, Shared, Communicated Goals

If purpose is the "why" of a team's existence, goals are its "what." Goals should derive from purposes, specifying "what" a team seeks to accomplish, and should be stated as specifically as words and measurements will allow. Goals should reflect these things: *what* specific outcomes a team seeks; *how much* of the outcomes it seeks, in accepted units of measurement, as appropriate; and by *when* the goals are to be accomplished.

Table 8.1
Qualities of Effective Teams

•Purpose (clear, shared, communicated)
•Goals (clear, shared, communicated)
•Trust (absolute)
•Communication (open)
•Skills (diverse, relevant)
•Roles (clear, communicated, integrated)
•Norms (self-awareness and management)
•Conflict (appreciation and management)
•Decision Making/Problem Solving (methods which use the team's resources)
•Leadership (shared)
•Performance (challenges)
•Self-Analysis (ongoing, norm-based self-awareness and learning)

Goals should be formulated such that their accomplishment clearly contributes, in the eyes of team members, to fulfillment of the team's purpose. Their link with fulfilling the team's purpose should be explicitly articulated. Just as with purpose, goals should be clear, shared, and communicated, inside the team and, when appropriate, out. Also, "ownership" is just as instrumental with goals as with purpose in facilitating clarity, shared commitment, and communication. Getting goals that are clear, that enlist commitment, and that are communicated to the relevant people is hardly a problem when the people themselves have developed their own goals.

Goals make the team accountable. They give the team specific direction and specific targets for its efforts. The time spent developing and communicating about team goals will translate into team accomplishments and personal satisfaction. The time spent ducking these essential activities will translate into self-canceling efforts and the personal frustration that inevitably accompanies "going everywhere yet nowhere."

Absolute Trust

Trust is one of those qualities that affects almost everything of importance about human relationships. We behave differently toward trusted people than toward distrusted people. We speak differently to trusted people than to distrusted people. The actions of trusted people mean something different than the actions of distrusted people. With distrusted people, we "doubt" more, we "devalue" more, we "watch" more, we "distance" more, we "critique" more, and we "protect" more. With trusted people, we "accept" more, we "respect" more, we "participate" more, we "join" more, we "empathize" more, and we "share" more.

Distrust taints everything it touches in a team: communication, leadership, decision making, problem solving, even a team's very culture if it persists long enough. Amazingly, many teams become quite deft at "kidding" themselves when distrust is strong and pervasive. Although members might privately believe that the team is a "snake-pit" or that certain teammates can't be trusted, public behaviors, including actual team gatherings, sometimes reveal studious and determined efforts on everyone's part *not* to address the private issue head-on by explicitly talking about it. Some teams develop what Argyris (1990) calls "defensive routines" to protect themselves from having to confront sticky issues. These are unspoken yet seemingly unanimous "agreements" between team members to participate in a team delusion. In this case, teams often make their distrust an "undiscussable" subject, and even its undiscussability, "undiscussable." There is more to be said about this and what to do about it in the section on "norms."

In Chapter 4, a number of pages were devoted to features of communication that build trust in relationships versus those that erode it. Figure 4.1, depicting "emotional bank accounts" of trust in relationships, centered that discussion. The advice there, summarized by Table 4.4, is valid here: no communication "surprises," consistency of words and deeds, content and relational components of communication that mesh, good relational listening, and nonjudgmental, confirming communication practices will build trust among team members. The opposites will erode it.

Beyond these things, successful experiences in trusting are required. As circular as it sounds, trust grows or shrinks in part as a result of the outcomes connected with trusting. I have literally told team members who were paralyzed by their own mutual suspicions of each other, "to trust one another you must trust one another." After the nervous laughter and wise-cracking have stopped, I've gone on to say: "That's just another way of saying, to trust each other requires successful experiences with trusting each other. Only consistent successes over time will build lasting trust. There are no short-cuts. If you won't trust enough to try, you won't try enough to trust."

Additionally, it's a good idea for a team to develop "habits" of examining its existing own levels of trust. This is not easy to do, especially if the team has developed and entrenched only superficial methods for self-examination, or none at all. It likely will require some coaching from a skilled facilitator, in conjunction with other focused team development activities to begin with. But these habits can be learned and made a "norm" of a team's usual functioning. Self-consciously examining and building trust through regular team dialogue can be made just as "habitual" as evading it. We'll return to this later, when we look at "norms."

Open Communication

Communication is so much a part of the other qualities of effective teams that it might seem redundant to include it as a separate quality here. The type of communication found in effective teams is unique, however, in that its special features complement and magnify the powers of the other qualities which promote effectiveness. As surely as distrust poisons whatever it contacts in a team, particular team communication practices and features have the power to work just the opposite way—almost like some kind of all-purpose "tonic" that improves circulation, promotes healthy skin and muscle tone, stimulates good digestion, strengthens teeth and bones, lowers blood pressure, and boosts clear-headedness. Certain qualities of communication can improve the functioning of lots of other individual team processes, and the team as a whole.

These qualities center around the "openness" of a team's communication practices. "Open communication" has several operational dimensions, many benefits, and mainly one cause. Before we talk about any of those, though, we should clarify what open communication is.

Most basically, open communication is "unrestricted message making." We spent Chapters 3 and 4 considering the particulars of "message making"—communication. In a nutshell, message making is "perceiver" centered. We all "make" messages constantly, in that we create meanings from what others say and do and from potentially anything that happens or that we can be aware of.

"Unrestricted," on the other hand, needs some elaboration. Let's begin by narrowing the term a bit. Here is what "unrestricted" does *not* mean in the context of teams: It does not mean ungoverned or "mob" communication, some kind of chaotic "free-for-all" where everyone works hard to out-speak everyone else. Nor does it mean an uncensored mentality of "think-it-so-say-it," although that notion, coupled with empathy and sensitivity, is getting warmer to what "unrestricted message making" should be in a team.

"Unrestricted" message making means that when people consciously attempt to communicate, they feel no particular psychological restrictions on attempting to accurately convey their real intentions, other than those relating to politeness, courtesy, empathy, and the like. Unrestricted message making is "fearless" and "faithful" message making. It is free of the fear that "what we say can and will be used against us." It is grounded on the faith that what we say and do will be honestly perceived—as free of controllable biases as possible—and, above all, valued and respected.

From these views, it should be evident that trust is the gatekeeper of open communication, the ultimate source of honesty in a team. The products of trust briefly mentioned above—acceptance, valuation, participation, joining, empathy, sharing—are in fact expressions of open communication, and in their effects on teams, rewards in themselves: we accept each others' words and deeds as genuine, and show it; we respect each others' differences, and show it; we give more of our "selves"—our true views and our knowledge—to each other; we seek ways to collaborate; we listen empathically; we share what needs sharing.

The major beneficiaries of open communication are information and team learning. Teams that communicate openly become information dynamos, mainly because what members know will be made known. There was an "art-imitates-life" cartoon that sardonically depicted life in a "closed" management team. It showed a group of managers sitting around a rectangular conference table, and a man whose portrait was prominently displayed on the conference room wall, standing at the head of the table, glowering at the group, and saying something like this: "Alright, then. Let's decide. Those who oppose my recommendation signify in the customary way by saying, 'I resign.'" Teams that communicate openly are more information-intensive than those that don't. They can learn more, adapt more, *do* more, because more of what people know is made available through communication for collective learning.

Diverse, Relevant Skills

One reason why "two heads are better than one" is that a complicated environment supposedly will have a harder time throwing an unsolvable problem past two heads than past one head. The more variety of challenges that the environment can pose, the more variety of problem solving abilities needed to meet those challenges. This is the same principle brought up in Chapter 4, regarding "complication" and complicating ourselves so as to be better equipped to manage complexity. Its truth is all around us. Two favorite kinds of examples are from sports teams and from management teams.

In sports competition between two players (or teams), each player is basically the environmental "system" of utmost relevance for the other. As such, each "player system" often tries to challenge its competitor system with "variety" that its competitor can't accommodate. A baseball pitcher tries to "throw" variety—fastballs, curve balls, sliders, splitters (spitters!), screwballs, change-ups, knucklers, and the like—in the hope that batters can't accommodate it: "Steeeee-rike three!" Batters try to meet a pitcher's variety with variety of their own—switch-hitting if possible so as to bat opposite the pitcher's throwing arm, taking signed instructions from an on-field coach who should have the best idea of what's coming, reducing variety by "sitting" on (waiting for) a certain pitch, stealing signs from the catcher calling the pitches, repeatedly stepping out of the batter's box at crucial times to break the pitcher's concentration, and so on—in the hope of knocking the pitcher's variety "wherever they ain't": "Cccrraaaack!"

The same applies in all sports. A golfer's clubs are designed to meet the challenges of "variety" posed by a particular terrain. Play a round of golf with a set of clubs low in variety—just a driver and a sand wedge—and the variety of the course will make you pay in strokes. It's much easier to match the variety of a basketball player who can only leap and dunk, versus the "variety from hell" that must have described defending Michael Jordan. If a boxer's only punch is "a right hand," then the first step to victory is figuring out how to stay away from it. But if there's left-handed thunder should the right one miss . . . well, that's what makes boxing legends—variety that meets and overcomes variety; and really, all sports legends.

This same logic applies to teams. Sports teams, management teams, any organizational teams. Teams face any number of environmental challenges. The most important variety facing a team is reflected in whatever it is supposed to do or be. Teams that need to do or be only one thing or a few different things will need to meet that demand with their own "variety." Teams that need to do or be many different things will need to meet that demand with comparable variety. The key question is, "how numerous and diverse are the environmental demands placed on the team?" or "how many different problems does the environment throw at the team?"

The way a team deals with environmental variety is through its *content* resources and its *process* resources—"what" it does and "how" it does what it does, respectively. The technical content skills assembled in the team affect what it does most directly. The process skills present in the team affect how it does what it does most directly. Generally, diversity in both of these skill areas makes a team maximally adaptive—able to accommodate whatever variety is posed by a problem at hand. Figure 8.1 shows a simple match-mismatch combination of skill variety demands of the environment and skill variety in a group. From a human resource utilization, development, and motivational point of view, Cell 4 is the most favorable combination: having a broadly skilled team

Figure 8.1
Skill Variety Demands versus Skill Variety

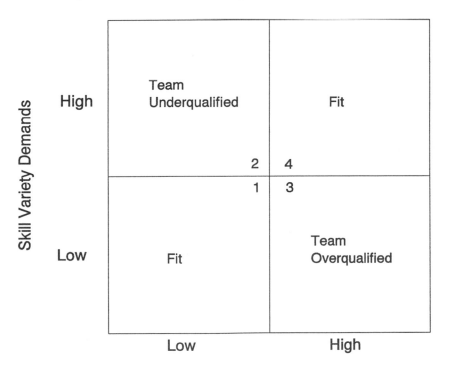

tackle a complex set of demands. This is similar to the empowered work design discussed in Chapter 6. Two of the other combinations will often produce frustration, stemming from: high skill variety teams taking on low variety problems (Cell 3), and low skill variety teams taking on high variety problems (Cell 2). The last combination, Cell 1, is a match that could produce short-term success, but doesn't really develop or motivate a team over time: putting a team of narrow specialists on a narrowly specialized problem.

For individuals, the price of skill variety can be shallowness: being pretty good at lots of things, but not very good at any. For teams, the price of skill variety is the process effort required to manage it. Diversity in skills almost always means diversity in values, assumptions, perspectives, language, cognitive styles, learning styles, and the like. While the breadth and depth of skills may be present in a diverse team, the processes of managing—to exploit—the diversity will often spell the difference between excellence and mediocrity or even failure. The process qualities from Table 8.1—roles, leadership, conflict management, decision making, problem solving, and *especially* communication—speak to the needed process skills for harnessing diversity.

Clear, Communicated, Integrated Roles

Different people bring different skills to a team. Increasingly, team designs emphasize the development of "generalist" skills among members rather than "specialist" skills, so as to make the team more flexible and adaptive. As we saw in the previous section, generalist skills enhance the "variety" within a team.

Team objectives usually require that members perform a variety of roles. Roles basically refer to the behaviors needed and expected from different positions within a network of positions. Obviously, different positions have different role expectations connected with them, regarding whatever it takes to complete the team's work. These expectations by definition revolve around the task at hand and getting it done. But there are other less officially sanctioned and articulated roles needed by any team, which have more to do with maintaining and building the team itself than with getting the job done. The latter roles won't usually show up in any formal statement of job descriptions. People most often just perform them, to greater or lesser extents, spontaneously.

For people to perform needed roles, roles must be clearly formulated. The expectations connected with different roles must be thoroughly communicated. And the different roles themselves must be integrated to insure that nothing essential to the team's success is left undone. All of these responsibilities require explicit team communication about the roles which members are and should be playing. Below, are two approaches for stimulating team communication about roles. The approaches are somewhat complementary, and each one can be used most productively under differing circumstances, with the second one being the more versatile in application.

Approach 1: Problem solving roles. Specifically regarding the special situation of problem solving discussions undertaken by teams, one of the most time-honored systems for classifying and analyzing the roles performed by members comes from an article by Kenneth Benne and Paul Sheats, published originally in 1948 and reprinted in many places ever since. Their system has provoked innumerable "spin-offs," which seemingly have produced very little real improvement on the original. The system is a comprehensive taxonomy of different team member roles, split up into three broad categories: task roles, maintenance roles, and individual roles. Task roles are oriented toward accomplishing the problem solving task of the team. Maintenance roles serve to maintain group-centered attitudes and behaviors among members. Individual roles are either irrelevant to the group's task and maintenance or antagonistic to them (Benne and Sheats, 1948).

Table 8.2 lists these roles, with the role names in most instances describing what the role "does." This system can be used with problem solving teams to help them learn about their own functioning, in the following two ways.

Prior to a team starting its deliberations, it reviews and discusses the three role categories, and the specific roles within them. It considers the merits of these ideas: (1) task and maintenance roles are functional, and individual roles usually less so, for the team; (2) good representation from both the task and maintenance categories is important across team members—balance between task and maintenance roles helps, and imbalance can hinder, the team. (The issue, again, is one of team "variety," although this needn't be explicitly examined.) This first application mainly heightens awareness of different roles, which also will stimulate attention to them as the team proceeds about its task.

The second use of Benne and Sheats' role taxonomy (within Approach 1) actually produces "on-the-spot" data for the team to evaluate its role functioning, and can be used with the application above or by itself.

First, create a "Team Role Matrix" like the top one in Figure 8.2, with three role columns labeled "Task," "Maintenance," and "Individual," and a fourth column labeled "Row Totals." Along the left vertical margin, list team members' names. Each member receives a blank matrix, along with a one-page list of the roles within each category and key descriptors. If need be, questions can be sought and clarification offered about categories and roles before proceeding. Members all use the same team activity as the frame of reference. For that period of the team's work, each member completes the matrix on everyone in the team *except* himself or herself. First taking the "task" category at the top of the page, group members privately run down through the names (excepting themselves), and simply check (✓) the appropriate space of members whom they feel performed *any task roles* during the group's working session. Then raters do the "maintenance" category for all members but themselves, and then the "individual."

A facilitator then gathers these simple checkmark "polls" and tabulates them across all team members, using the original matrix format to show composites on each team member as well as the group as a whole. The facilitator can prepare in advance a large blank matrix on newsprint, on which is then written

Table 8.2
Roles in Team Problem Solving Deliberations

Task Roles	**Maintenance Roles**	**Individual Roles**
Initiator-contributor	Encourager	Aggressor
Information seeker	Harmonizer	Blocker
Opinion seeker	Compromiser	Recognition-
Information giver	Gatekeeper-expediter	seeker
Opinion giver	Standard setter	Self-confessor
Elaborator	Observer-commentator	Playboy/girl
Coordinator	Follower	Dominator
Orienter		Help-seeker
Evaluator-critic		Interest pleader
Energizer		
Procedural technician		
Recorder		

Source: From Benne and Sheats (1948).

Figure 8.2
Team Role Matrices

	Roles			
Names	Task	Maintenance	Individual	Row Totals
Ron				
Jan				
Stu				
⋮				
Column Totals				

	Roles			
Names	Task	Maintenance	Individual	Row Totals
Ron	1	1	5	7
Jan	6	6	0	12
Stu	1	1	1	3
⋮				
Column Totals	32	26	8	66

Adapted from Benne and Sheats (1948).

the composites for all to see. A second blank copy of the matrix is handed out for team members to enter numbers themselves from the large copy when it's done. Even with fairly sizable groups, this tabulation doesn't take more than a few minutes. The bottom matrix of Figure 8.2 shows an example.

Cell totals within a person's row, with a maximum for each cell equal to the number of raters, will show how that person allocates "role time" among the three categories, as seen by team members. For instance, the bottom matrix of Figure 8.2 shows profiles on three members of a seven-person team. How do you interpret Ron's role activities? Five of the six raters see him performing roles that serve himself, with only one rater seeing task contributions and one seeing maintenance activities. You decide. Or what about Jan's? All six raters see her as contributing task roles and maintenance roles, with no one seeing her as self-oriented. Or how about Stu? For each role category, only one person sees him as doing anything there. These people show very different patterns of role activity in the team's work.

Summed across all three columns, row totals will give the team a rough idea of the overall role activity invested by each person. The maximum total possible for a row will be the number of columns (three categories) times the number of raters for each person (group size minus one, since members don't rate themselves). So with this seven member group, row totals can range from a high of 18 (3 x 6) to a low of 0. Zero role activity is highly unlikely, though, since the system is inclusive enough to incorporate roles that essentially mean passively "doing nothing." With role totals, it's important to look at the breakdown of contributing scores. For example, Ron's row total in Figure 8.2 is higher than Stu's. But the breakdowns reveal that the difference stems from more people seeing Ron as performing roles which could hinder the group. And although Jan has a row total of only 12, that's the highest total possible for the task and maintenance roles combined—everyone sees her as contributing functional role activities to the team's work. In the case of row totals, "the biggest ain't necessarily the best." The breakdowns will tell the story.

The column totals, summed down through all group members, are perhaps a little more meaningful by themselves. The maximum total possible for any column will be the number of team members times the number of raters for each person (again, group size minus one). So for this seven member team, the highest possible column total is 42 (7 x 6). As the bottom matrix of Figure 8.2 shows, there appears to be quite a bit of both "task" and "maintenance" role activity going on in the group, contributed almost exclusively by five members, and some "individual" role activity, provided mostly, it seems, by Ron. Also, there's approximate balance between task and maintenance activity, showing that the team—or five of them anyway—are actively working on both the task and the team itself.

Keep in mind that all of the composite cell data in the "Team Role Matrix" are "coarse." The original instruction to raters was to put a check if the person showed *any* activity within a role category. So no single rater's completed matrix shows either the number of different roles or which specific roles within categories were enacted by different team members. Consequently, the composite matrix on the entire team won't reveal that information either. A skilled facilitator can get the team talking about these specifics, to ensure the most individual and team learning from the exercise.

Of course a method of designing this specificity into the exercise up front could be to list all of the specific roles across the top of a matrix, and then proceed in the same way. The large number of roles, however, would make this an absolutely mind-boggling and extremely time consuming task. With facilitation, team members can readily pull out specific roles and apply them to each other in a discussion of the composite matrix built around just the three role categories.

Approach 2: Role review and dialogue. The second approach that I have found useful in stimulating team communication about roles is very versatile, in that it focuses team discussion on members' roles in general, not just those performed in problem-solving deliberations. This approach works best with a facilitator who is not a member of the team, to allow team members to concentrate on the dialogue rather than its process. It is also important for any formal team leader(s) to be present. Depending on team size, this team activity takes anywhere from one-half to one full day. Teams as large as ten people or so can use it in a one day session. The activity requires a comfortable, informal setting for team members to talk, protected from interruptions. The facility should have document-copying equipment nearby, the need for which will be clear momentarily.

The basic approach used is grounded in the kind of "role analysis" developed by Dayal and Thomas (1968), but modified to examine the roles of all team members in one session—rather than several sessions—and to produce a written team product from that session. The session consists of two phases, "data generation" and "data sharing," much like the problem solving role matrices discussed previously. Table 8.3 summarizes the steps involved within each of these phases.

The data generation phase should be completed in about 45–60 minutes. During this time, members work alone, writing out as legibly as possible on paper provided, *key words and phrases* describing their perceptions of: (1) the purposes and fit of their roles in the team (about 15 minutes); (2) key "prescribed" and "discretionary" activities of their roles (about 15 minutes); and (3) key expectations they have of other roles in the team which most directly affect their roles (about 30 minutes). After team members have composed these role worksheets, the facilitator collects them and photocopies them for everyone. *Every* team member receives a copy of *every* member's "role packet," for use in the data sharing phase. The latter occupies the remainder of the session.

The data sharing phase makes the role of one person at a time the center of team dialogue. About 30–45 minutes are spent on each person or "focal role," before taking up the next role. With skillful facilitation, this pace can be kept,

Table 8.3
Role Review and Dialogue Procedures

Data Generation (on worksheets):
1. List key words or phrases describing what you see as the purpose and fit of your role in the team.
2. Using key words or phrases, list the activities which you feel make up your role in the team. Which ones are "prescribed" ("P") and which ones "discretionary" ("D")?
3. List up to 3 "key" expectations you have (or more, if you have them) of those other roles in the team which *most directly* affect your role.

Data Sharing (using data generated, complete steps 1-4 for each focal role):
1. Focal role reviews role purposes and fits (number 1 from role worksheets). Questions/discussion.
2. Focal role reviews prescribed and discretionary role activities (number 2 from role worksheets). Questions/discussion.
3. Focal role reviews his or her expectations of related roles in the team (number 3 from role worksheets). Questions/discussion.
4. Others in team review their expectations of focal role (number 3 from role worksheets). Questions/discussion.
5. Next role, repeat 1-4.

Source: Adapted from Dayal and Thomas (1968).

allowing for breaks as needed. For these 30–45 minutes, two types of information are shared. First, the "focal role" helps the group review and interpret his or her role worksheets, taking them through: (1) purposes and fits the person sees for his or her role in the team; (2) the "prescribed" and "discretionary" role activities seen by the person; and (3) the person's key expectations of related roles in the team. Second, other members of the team share: (4) their key expectations of the focal role, working from item number 3 of their own role worksheets, where they specified expectations of other roles. Throughout all of this, people seek clarification and offer qualifications or even revisions on any of points 1–4 as needed. The facilitator keeps the whole process focused and moving, and urges the focal person and team members to pay special attention to the written role expectations they have shared, and to publicly amend them right there as needed.

That basic sequence is followed for each member until the roles of all members have been discussed. The process of specifically sharing role expectations moves the slowest through the first few roles discussed, when points 3 and 4 above require just about "everyone" to spend time talking through any relevant expectations. But with each successive role reviewed, exchanges of expectations in connection with points 3 and 4 automatically dwindle, because they get covered in earlier discussions. So by the time the last role is discussed, points 1 and 2 above—purposes, fits, prescribed and discretionary role activities—almost always occupy more attention than points 3 and 4.

This team activity does many things for the team. First, it gets people talking about what they *think* their most important team roles are. Making this information public in itself does the group much good, because people hardly ever see their own roles as others see them. Addressing the discrepancies can be more than "worth the price of admission" by itself, so to speak. Second, it requires that team members make their role expectations for each other explicit. Also, doing this shows the team very graphically which roles interlock, and in what ways they are and are not integrated. Fourth, the activity produces written documentation of what team members feel are their most important roles and expectations at a given point in time. This document is a valuable "living" reference for team members to know who expects what of whom. And finally, the activity is just an excellent, nonthreatening way to promote team communication about an essential topic of team functioning. Teams that clarify the roles of their members through this or another structured, communication-intensive activity do themselves a huge favor that will repay the team many times over in performance and in *prevented* role problems.

Awareness of Norms

All teams develop norms over time. Norms are simply prescriptions and proscriptions for team members—dos and don'ts. In a way, they're an evolved rule book of what it takes to survive and succeed in a team. Some of the rules are formal and explicit, like codes of conduct, decision rules, and the like. Some of the rules are informal and implicit, yet nevertheless—in fact, all the more—influential in determining individual and team behavior. With regard to norms, the difference between effective and ineffective teams is that the former are more aware of theirs than the latter, and so are able to assess and work at changing theirs if need be. The most powerful team norms, constructive or destructive, are the norms that "organize" people's behavior, but that have long since faded into "just the way things are," too habitual or routine for anyone to notice them. Teams "just do" some things a certain way, because they've always done them that way. Often it takes a newcomer "tripping" over an implicit norm—violating it or asking about some anomaly—to expose it as a do or a don't. The team and the newcomer may both have their consciousness "tweaked" momentarily, but typically the team will try to find a way, behaviorally or with words, to enforce the norm.

Teams develop norms around almost anything imaginable: performance (amount, quality, etc.); conflict (handling it head-on, avoiding it, punishing it, etc.); communication (open, closed, superficial, deep, etc.); time (legitimate uses of, value of, punctuality, delay of gratification, etc.); leadership (shared influence, unshared influence, etc.); decision making (consensus, majority vote, one-person, etc.); problem solving (methods of inquiry, orientation toward innovation, etc.); and orientation toward self-examination and team learning (head-in-sand, inquisitive, action oriented, etc.). Not coincidentally, most of these subjects are elements from Table 8.1, elements that can make or break a team. Teams develop norms around all of these subjects and more. Awareness of this alone can be helpful to a team. Knowing of a norm's existence implies that there are *other* choices. Making an implicit norm explicit gives a team much greater power to examine its viability in serving the group and to change it. How does a team expose its norms?

A questioning process not unlike that of Chapter 7, on ascertaining "culture," will help. Examining artifacts and patterns of behavior will help reveal norms. Asking, out loud, "why" these things exist will get at values and supporting rationales. Along these lines, newcomers can be especially illuminating, since their vision and experiences have less likely been "de-sensitized" to norms than veteran team members. In a team setting, leaders or outside facilitators can ask newcomers to talk about some of the "interesting" or odd patterns of behavior or artifacts that they've seen.

Another technique that can assist in this comes from Cummings and Worley (1993). They suggest having team members complete these two sentences with lists of behaviors: "A good group member should____" or "It's okay to____" (p. 101). Patterns in the answers will help reveal key dos and don'ts in the team, and heighten members' awareness.

In a team forum, best facilitated by an outsider, implicit norms should be exposed—put in writing—and evaluated by the team as to what each norm does *for* the team. A discussion of this will help sharpen for the team what it *wants* as norms for different dimensions of behavior versus what it presently *has* as norms. The team should articulate replacement norms for any dysfunctional existing norms, and put the new ones and the functional existing ones in writing.

The lists of desired norms and the undesirable old norms should be printed and kept public before the team. Every team member should be appointed as a member of the "norm police," and made responsible for publicly pointing out in team meetings and elsewhere when the group or members are displaying old dysfunctional norms. Notice should also be taken and publicized when the new desirable norms are followed.

Appreciation and Management of Conflict

Probably the single biggest liability of teams with skilled, diverse, empowered members is the *conflict* that inevitably results. Probably the single biggest asset of teams with skilled, diverse, empowered members is the *conflict* that inevitably results. Both of these statements are true, depending on different circumstances.

Conflict has always been on managers' "public enemy" list, it seems. A large part of this stems from the dominance of the "machine" metaphor in framing our thinking and deepest assumptions about what makes for "good" organizations. One of the central values underlying mechanism is that component parts should function in "harmony." We even see linguistic evidence of the machine metaphor all the time in business, often expressed as variations on themes of "harmony" and the importance of "frictionless" functioning: "He just rubs me the wrong way." "There's surprisingly little friction within this group." "It's a pretty good proposal, but here's the rub." "I'll try to smooth things out for you."

"She's got a few rough edges, but she'll work out." "Man, the sparks really flew between them." "The whole project just came grinding to a halt." "Look, we'd better get in sync here." "He's just a square peg in a round hole." "This'll help grease the skids for us."

Mechanistic images of organization—and our language—have helped managers assume that conflict is unnatural and unwanted in organizations, that it produces unhappy consequences. The last part of this is often true, but an important reason behind it is the operation of a self-fulfilling prophecy as much as anything else. A natural human response to assuming that conflict is unnatural and "bad" is to do everything possible to avoid it. Which is exactly what many if not most of the managers I've worked with do. Common sense and experience tell us that if the "causes" of a conflict are substantive enough, they're still there even when we avert or close our eyes. And the next time we look, or they *force* us to look, they often loom larger and more consequential—unhappier—than before. Full circle, from assumption of "bad," to avoidance, to unhappy results, to verification of assumption of "bad." And so it goes.

Even our omnipresent companion, the conduit metaphor, reinforces the value of "harmony" and other fundamental tenets of mechanism. What is "harmony," if not a form of perfect correspondence between two elements, such as the conduit metaphor teaches us about messages as "sent" and "received?" In the communicative world of the conduit metaphor, "difference"—between "sent" and "received" meaning—is assumed to be an *unnatural* outcome of communication. Disharmony means that communication isn't working, that it's somehow flawed. In this view, "disharmony" can and should be eliminated. But in the communicative world of the alternative view of communication developed in Chapter 3, "disharmony" is assumed to be a natural, inevitable outcome of communication. Disharmony means that communication *is* working, that that's the way it *is* and will be. In this alternative view, we're better off facing the inevitability of "disharmony" than mistakenly believing we can eliminate it. And appreciation and management of disharmony holds the key to our competence as communicators.

The same holds true for conflict. Without question, few people truly delight in the experience of conflict. Part of that is a learned value perspective, as noted above. Another part of it is misgivings that many people have in their ability to deal constructively with conflict. And a third part is that, at its core, conflict portends *change* more than anything else. In reality, conflict is another of those inevitable challenges in life that bring about growth or destruction, maturity or immaturity, vitality or stagnation, depending on how we work with it. It's not the absence of conflict that makes a team or an organization effective, any more than the absence of death makes a life effective. It's what we do with conflict. It's the appreciation and management—and the *uses* made—of conflict that separate effectiveness from ineffectiveness.

Teams that embrace the value-neutrality and inevitability of conflict and that recognize the adaptiveness—the variety—of "differences" are likely to work at managing conflict. Teams that embrace the inherent "badness" and preventability of conflict, and which abhor the inconvenience of "differences" are likely to be "worked over" by conflict.

The "work" of managing conflict is communication work. Part of this "work" will require supportive team norms which promote the open expression of issues, especially tough ones. But a norm doesn't just materialize from high hopes. It must come from somewhere else. Team leaders will play critical roles in "setting" conflict management norms, by the way they handle critical conflict episodes in the team. Leaders who squelch the expression of conflict, or who take all sorts of evasive action when it manifests publicly, will show the group how they think it should handle conflict. The germ of a norm will be implanted: "duck your heads—I'm ducking mine." Recurrences will embed the norm, until finally conflict itself can become an "undiscussable." Like trust, conflict management norms come from experiences with managing—or being managed by—conflict.

The key to managing team conflict is to address it head-on, to prevent it from becoming an undiscussable—basically, to talk about it, specifically the issues that are at conflict, and how disputants feel about them. Much easier said than done. The most productive approach to addressing conflict between two parties (people, factions, etc.) is *structured dialogue*, which almost always requires a skilled third-party facilitator. The facilitator can be an impartial insider or an outsider. Skill level is most important, although there are critical issues connected with the "insider-outsider" question.

"Dialogue" means that the two parties will talk. "Structured" means that the disputants will talk about certain things, in a certain sequence of dialogue. The issues of special facilitator and disputant qualities needed, along with the detailed reasoning behind different structural approaches, are too space-consuming to go into at length in this section, but following are some specific, usable suggestions, based on my experiences with this broad subject. These are summarized in Table 8.4. Also, anyone interested in facilitated conflict dialogue should start with Richard Walton's (1987) *Managing Conflict: Interpersonal Dialogue and Third-Party Roles*, in my view the very best theoretical and applied source for understanding and resolving conflict.

The image of an effective team as "smooth running, noiseless machine" is the fanciful product, the wildest dream, of some social engineer's overlubed imagination. And, it's dangerous. *In*effective teams run silently. Ineffective teams suppress and dodge issues that almost always resurface as hidden agendas, duplicity, divisive forces, side-choosing, ulcers, and worse. Effective teams are noisy places, filled with open expression of inevitable differences. They relish in and then exploit their differences, to the team's betterment. They thrive on the stimulation and the new ways of seeing and doing things that come when different ideas collide. Earlier in this book it was said that innovations in all forms of human accomplishment—science, medicine, technology, and virtually everthing else—have been pushed along by metaphors. Metaphors, those catalysts

Table 8.4
Issues in Structuring Dialogue

<u>Facilitator qualities</u>
•Impartial (as seen by both parties)
•Good listener (content and relational)
•Skillful communicator (good questioner; can frame difficult, personal issues
  nonthreateningly; good summarizer/synthesizer—can pull core elements from mass of
  data generated by dialogue; assertive, to keep dialogue focused, to confront issues)
•Credible (credentials, background, etc., are accepted by both parties)
•Knowledgeable (especially of human psychology and conflict processes)
<u>Disputants' qualities</u>
•Motivated (to address issues; to really work at resolving issues)
•Good listening skills (willingness to hear what others say, to work at understanding
  others' views)
•Good communication skills (openness, expressing issues honestly)
•Ownership (willingness to "own" the problems and solutions)
<u>Setting qualities</u>
•Private (no interruptions)
•Comfortable (encourages "close" exchanges; room for "data display")
•Seen as "neutral turf" by both parties
•Time (to talk in-depth)
<u>Ground rules for dialogue</u>
•No interrupting each other (each gets "air time")
•Honesty (by disputants and by facilitator)
•Dialogue is kept issue focused
<u>Structure of dialogue</u>
(Disputants write answers to questions 1-2 on newsprint, for later display, and then
proceed through steps 3-7, with facilitator.)
1. How do I contribute to the problem? What do I *do* (behaviors) to help create the
    problem? List as many as possible.
2. How does _____ (other) contribute to the problem? What does _____ *do*
    (behaviors) to help create the problem? List as many as possible. After listing, rank
    them (1 = most important, 2 = next, etc.).
3. *My contribution* to the problem: Each party reviews Question 1 list for facilitator and
    other disputant(s). Questions/clarifying comments. Does the other party agree/
    disagree that these behaviors contribute to the problem? (Answers should be noted
    "A" or "D" on newsprint as reviewed.)
4. *Your contribution* to the problem: Each party reviews Question 2 list for facilitator
    and other disputant(s). Questions/clarifying comments.
5. *Issues summary/synthesis*: Facilitator and disputants tease out and prioritize issues
    from dialogue data; jointly define which issues are controllable and which aren't.
    Listed on newsprint.
6. *Joint problem solving*: From list of controllable issues, disputants address "who" will
    do "what," "when," etc. Negotiation for the behaviors needed from each party by the
    other. These agreements are *written* up, signed by both parties, with copies given to
    disputants *and* to affected others.
7. *Follow up* built into agreements to monitor compliance. Adjustments as needed.

of creativity and innovation, are nothing more than the collision of different ideas. Effective teams are enacted metaphors in motion, creating the sweet music of *dis*harmony.

Resource-full Decision Making and Problem Solving

Although decision making and problem solving can legitimately be separated as different activities, they are similar enough in certain key processes and in what I want to note about them to combine them for consideration here. The thread connecting decision making with problem solving in teams, and both of these with team effectiveness, is the notion of *sufficiently* tapping the team's resources to meet the following demands of the decision or problem before the team: its complexity, the need for quality in the outcome, the need for commitment to the outcome by the team, and the available time to make the decision or solve the problem.

All of these raise the issue of "variety" again. The more complex the decision or problem task, the more complicated the decision maker(s) or problem solver(s) had better be. There are any number of ways of thinking of what makes a decision or problem complicated. For each of the following questions, a "yes" answer *simplifies* and a "no" answer *complicates*, making a task lower or higher in variety, respectively: Is the necessary information readily available to one person? Is it understandable by one person? Are the necessary skills available in one person? Is there one "best" solution or decision? Will the quality of the outcome be highest with just one person deciding or solving the issue? Is commitment to the decision or solution inconsequential? Does the decision or problem have a time demand?

The main ways of complicating decision makers or problem solvers are through the mix of content skills and the processes used to employ those skills. We've already discussed increasing team variety through diversity of skill and of people. The way to increase variety through process is essentially by using participative or consensus decision making or problem solving methods—processes that allow the team to use all of its resources as needed. And, it is well known and documented what participation means for enhancing commitment.

A major issue with deciding and with solving problems participatively is for the team to evolve a system for ensuring that *everyone* participates. In any team, there will be members who are more actively vocal than others. Team leaders must make sure that everyone has a voice in team deliberations, and that if people occasionally remain silent, they do so by choice and not by lack of "a voice" with the team. As needed, team leaders should actively draw the more quiet members out. Like so many other things, vigorous participation can become a norm.

With consensus, the issues are usually two. First, many managers equate consensus with unanimity of thinking or decision among team members. This view almost guarantees problems for teams, because it gets them "stuck" on their definition. Consensus is not unanimity of thinking or decision. Consensus is *unanimity of support* for whatever decision has been reached by the team. Big difference! A team reaching consensus has thoroughly aired everyone's views, and through that dialogue, has forged a view that maybe not everyone can agree on, but that everyone in the team can and does *commit* to support. This takes skill, persistence, and time. Participative or consensus methods are more difficult to manage than simple majority rule or one-person calls, but they pay back in team "variety," quality of outcomes, and commitment, what they cost in time and effort.

The second issue with consensus relates to the first. I have known many managers and formal team leaders who have occasionally allowed "consensus"—or their definition of it, really—to paralyze their teams. Confusing the need for *consensual support* with *unanimous agreement* on an issue, they've insisted on the latter before moving on an important question. Consequently, their teams got stuck all of the time, as would any teams of smart, independent-minded, and diverse people. It ought to be nearly impossible for such people to all agree on complex issues. If not, something is terribly wrong. But on the other hand, it should be quite possible for all people to commit their support to a group-discussed and determined course of action. Effective teams make decisions and solve problems consensually, getting the full measure of their resources.

Shared Leadership

In an effective team, everyone is expected to influence the work of the team. That is, everyone is expected to share leadership responsibilities as needs and expertise dictate. It is *not* true that a group can have only one leader. An effective team can have as many leaders as there are members, and they all bring their resources into play as needed. A team with only one leader is much lower in variety than one with shared leadership.

Performance Challenge

In a way, this ties in with what was said earlier concerning "goals" and effective teams. But here, we are referring specifically to stiff performance challenges rather than any particular goals. Katzenbach and Smith's (1993) work with successful teams showed that "performance is both the cause and effect of teams" (p. 107). Demanding performance challenges congeal serious team efforts, and of course, serious efforts are a necessary ingredient of team performance. Performance challenges promote efforts, which promote team successes, which attract capable people and resources to the team, which promote more performance challenges, and so on. It's the best kind of circular logic. And it works.

Self-Analysis, Correction, and Learning

Because of the preceding qualities of effective teams (Table 8.1), all of which are communication-intensive, effective teams distinguish themselves from ineffective teams by being more self-analytic, self-correcting, and learned. They know how effective teams should function, and develop norms of self-consciously minding their own workings. The team assumes ultimate responsibility for its own self-development, and members realize that that proposition means vigilance and constant change. Self-analysis, correction, and learning by definition imply communication. Effective teams are more self-aware, and they use that self-awareness to develop their own capabilities through learning.

Team action research. One of the most reliable methods for building self-examining and self-developing teams is an "action research" framework applied to the ongoing activities of any team. This is a form of inquiry into team functioning that has definite action implications for the team. In its simplest form, team action research will follow these steps:

1. Planning: The team plans to gather data about itself, using an insider or/and an outsider. Planning includes the development of questions to be answered by the effort (on subjects such as purpose, communication, norms, roles, leadership, conflict, etc.), how the information will be gathered (by interviews, surveys, in a team meeting, etc.), when it will be gathered, and so on.
2. Data gathering, according to plan.
3. Data sharing: The team faces the data, interprets it, identifies, and prioritizes issues the team should address.
4. Action planning: On the basis of issues raised by the data, the team works out a written agenda of "who" will do "what," "when," and so on, to address the issues.
5. Follow up: The team follows up on issues targeted in previous action planning to see if they've been addressed to the team's satisfaction. Additional action planning may take place at this point.
6. Re-cycle: Periodically, regularly, the team undertakes new action research, re-newing the process each time.

Regular team action research will keep teams aware of their functioning and, with diligence, will help instill norms of self-analysis, self-correction, and team learning.

Productive team meetings. One of the major vehicles through which teams come to be themselves, to know themselves, and to learn together is the team meeting. A great deal of what has preceded this section on team self-awareness has concerned phenomena that occur in team meetings. There is really only one thing to add to all of these comments on effective teams, something that again comes from the experiences of seasoned managers. A few years back, a couple of hundred managers and supervisors shared with me the features of team meetings that, based on their experiences, either "helped" or "hindered" the productivity of meetings. The most frequently mentioned answers were published in a little article entitled, "Toward Productive Meetings: Advice from the Firing Line" (Axley, 1987a). Those results contain some sound advice on managing team meetings effectively. Table 8.5 lists some of the most important things that "help" and "hinder" the productivity of team meetings.

LEADERSHIP, COMMUNICATION, CHANGE

Effective teams don't just happen. Someone builds them—builds into teams the qualities covered in this chapter. Effective team builders do what they do by virtue of communication more than anything else.

Today's leaders face unprecedented communication challenges, challenges more complicated than those of even a few years back. Those challenges take many shapes—communicating with diverse employees, communicating with diverse customers all over the world, communicating within new organizational structures and role relationships mandated by competitive pressures and environmental exigencies, communicating to exploit the new possibilities but avoid the new problems posed by increasing reliance on communications technologies. All of these have one thing in common: they're all manifestations of accelerating *change*. Today's organizational leaders are having to build proactive and adaptive organizations that can compete globally and satisfy ever-more-demanding customers, communities, and employees, and ever-more-volatile environments. Hence the widespread move toward the exploitation of empowerment, culture, and teams in organizations. These qualities equip organizations for flexibility, stability, speed, and human commitment to common purposes.

Communication is what makes it all possible, what makes or breaks the effort. Change, and managing change, is perhaps the most important test of a manager's communication perspective and skills. It invokes virtually every dimension of communication competence covered in this book—appreciating what communication is and isn't, using that understanding to communicate with enhanced accuracy and to promote strong relationships, communicating so as to influence and lead, empowering others, shaping and assessing culture, and building effective teams. The implications of failure to change and manage change are very far reaching and unquestionably the most serious of any consequences considered in this book. In these quicksilver times, failure to manage change means being managed *by* change. It was mentioned at the end of Chapter 1 that organizations these days are and will be shooting the most dramatic stretch of "white water" in history. An organization that doesn't manage change perches right at the precipice, just above the raging swirl, with nothing but luck as a paddle. Managing change sees the same organization at the same precipice, but with the ultimate high-variety tool to help it navigate the white water so as to not just survive the ride, but to learn and benefit from it. Change is most effectively navigated by managing communication. That's our next, last chapter.

Table 8.5
Things That "Help" and "Hinder" Team Meetings

<u>These Things "Help"</u>
•An agenda, prepared and handed out
  in advance.
•The formal leader is prepared and
  manages the meeting.
•Team members prepare to participate,
  and then actively, vocally participate.
•Team members listen to each other.
•Supporting materials (visuals,
  handouts, minutes) document
  accomplishments.
•Meetings start/end on time, and
  members are on time.
•No outside interruptions.
•Meetings produce decisions,
  resolutions, closure.

<u>These Things "Hinder"</u>
•No agenda.
•Key members aren't there.
•Members aren't prepared.
•Domineering formal leader.
•"Soliloquies" by one or a few
  members.
•Personal attacks, competition.
•Unaccommodating facilities;
  furnishings inhibit team interaction.
•Scheduling of meetings which
  prevents sufficient member
  preparation, and which costs
  members their "personal" time.
•Outside interruptions; people in and
  out of meetings.
•No decisions reached, except to meet
  again.

Source: Adapted from Axley (1987a).

Chapter 9

Managing Change through Communication

It's like moving a cemetery.

Arjay Miller

[Information] Technology will not necessarily make things better or worse. It provides an opportunity to do either profoundly, dramatically, and really fast.

Don Tapscott

I'm concerned that this global cacophony will in fact be garbage at the speed of light.

Tom Peters

The future isn't what it used to be.

Steve Axley and many others

AND THE TIMES, THEY ARE . . .

A changing world provides the ideal proving ground for an idea stressed throughout this book, that *it takes complication to manage complication.* A changing world introduces new demands on our adaptiveness, new possibilities to exploit, new choices, new ways to succeed and to fail, new hopes, new worries, new language, new metaphors, new ways to see and do, new issues for us all. With a rapidly changing world, there's just more "out there"—and consequently, more in our heads—that must be managed. That's complexity.

Complicated people and organizations will be better able to prosper in a complicated world. Much of this book has been devoted to principles and skills that will "complicate" ourselves and our organizations, producing a better fit with the changing demands of today. The perspective on communication that best "matches" the complexity of the phenomenon assumes "uncertainty" as the rule, not the exception. People who fully understand and "live" that assumption will be, on the whole, better off communicating in a changing world than those who don't. Leaders who "diversify" people's skills, who strive for diversity among people, who can manage that diversity, and who empower people will do better at leading in a changing world than leaders who don't. Empowerment complicates an organization. So do teams, managed effectively. Effective teams operationalize empowerment and harness diversity of talent, making "variety" their competitive advantage.

At the root of what causes lots of people (and organizations) so much grief with change are the demands it places on information processing. For most of us, just keeping up with all the "bloomin' and buzzin'" is tough enough, and integrating even the tiniest part of it usefully with our personal and organizational lives, harder still. The "keeping up" poses problems of *getting* relevant information, enough of it, and in a timely way. The "integrating" poses problems of *using* the information we get. More than anything else, change taxes the information processing capacities of people and of organizations. Paradoxically, many of the most significant information processing problems facing people and organizations nowadays—fundamentally problems of change—are both caused *and* solved by the same thing. To help understand, let's take two slices of time.

It's 1971

You're a junior research associate in the planning department of XYZ Corporation, a vertically integrated competitor in the petroleum products industry. Your company has been contemplating a diversification move into industrial and agricultural chemicals. You've been personally charged with providing senior management the information it needs to examine the feasibility of such a move. Due to a sense of urgency "upstairs," you've been given one month to prepare a full report for top management.

Here's the mountain you're climbing: (1) You must profile XYZ's financial, marketing, human resources, operations, and technological strengths and weaknesses. (2) You must profile the industry dynamics for industrial chemicals and agricultural chemicals, including major competitors and customer groups in each industry. (3) You must profile the most significant opportunities and threats in the external environments of industrial chemicals, agricultural chemicals, and petroleum products. This includes key sociocultural, economic, political-legal, and technological forces, as well as issues involving suppliers, creditors, communities, government, unions, stockholders, and several other groups. (4) Finally, you must forecast investment, sales, and earnings figures five years out, as well as the most significant external environmental trends which will affect XYZ's existing and new businesses 5, 10, and 15 years into the future. In *one month*.

It's not that this job can't be done in some fashion. There will be endless hours digging through the company's reference books in its small library, and countless trips to other reference libraries nearby. All this first, just to locate titles of things you need to read. But then some of the titles you need will be checked out. Others, you'll have to read in the library. For others, you'll have to make oily photocopies to take with you—libraries don't stay open all night, like your eyes are increasingly being forced to. Whatever the case, you'll be limited by the local libraries' holdings and by what you can purchase. After 'round-the-clock reading and note-taking sessions, you'll handwrite a draft of the report or plink it out on your electric typewriter. Whomever types the final draft will also plink it out on a typewriter. Any complex charts and graphs will have to be done by hand or by a graphic artist. If, after the final draft is typed, you discover something important that you *must* add or delete from the report, someone is looking at retyping the entire document or at a sizable "cut and paste" job.

As previously mentioned, it's not that this job can't be done in some fashion—just not very well, very thoroughly, very efficiently, or very stress-free. In effect, the mountain you're trying to scale is Mount Everest. But the resources you've got to do it with amount to an okay pair of hiking boots, a serviceable walking stick, and your own intelligence. Your intelligence is up to it, but the other necessary tools—information-getting ones and information-using ones—aren't complicated enough for the demands of the situation. Now let's update.

Back to the Present

You're the same researcher, facing the same job assignment and the same deadline. There's only one difference, but what a difference! You're wired.

You login to the "net." Your desktop personal computer by itself has more raw computing—information processing—power than *all* of those big clunky machines used by NASA mission controllers in Houston for the Apollo moon landings (by the way, that's true). And the net links you communicatively not just to everyone in your own organization, but literally to the *whole world*. Very selectively, using keywords and other screening parameters of your specification, your computer methodically, tirelessly scours databases maintained internally and by every major research institution worldwide. In hardly any time at all, it locates more sources than you could possibly read in a year, let alone in the limited real time you have before your deadline. You download the text of a sizable number of relevant sources directly to your computer, and get several others faxed to you. Although you still have to read what you find, at least you can access it all right from the seat of your pants, sitting wherever you work—and even wherever you live.

Like in 1971, you still have to organize your notes and write the draft. But your computer has already done more for you than your feet, those libraries you had to visit, and that old typewriter ever could, by first putting you in touch with what's "out there"—getting you information that you need, almost instantaneously. And if that's not enough, its information-using powers have only begun to assist you. First, because of the machine's versatility, you can compose without inhibition right at the keyboard, knowing that you can instantly change anything you've said at anytime, without missing a step. You can also create the necessary supporting graphics right at the computer. And what about when you think you're done, but then find things you have to move around, revise, expand, and/or delete? You'll just do it with the necessary keystrokes, then reprint the report. Still don't like what you see? Experiment with more changes. Your options are basically unlimited.

The mountain you're climbing now? It's still Mount Everest, but what a difference a few years makes in "climbing" and "climbing gear." It's almost like having your own personal tram to the top. But watch out. Parts of the challenge are now much easier, but also *more dangerous*, than ever before.

FIRE AND WATER

We're *all* researchers really, as managers, scientists, assemblers, educators, parents, welders, lawyers, doctors, secretaries, engineers, "assistants-to," whatever. We all have projects due, research to do, information to get and use, and we must learn and continue learning. It takes intelligence and effort for us to meet these challenges nowadays, just as it did in 1971. That hasn't changed, and no one's likely to find a viable substitute for human intelligence. But a new generation of tools has come along to augment our intelligence—to change both the reach of our brains and the nature and amount of work that we do with our brains, which, of course, means just about everything we do. The world is getting more complicated, and our survival and success in any role depends on our adaptiveness to complication in the world around us and our ability to alter the world around us.

Nothing in the human-made world is changing more, and consequently challenging our adaptiveness more, than information technology. And nothing in the human-made world is enhancing our ability to change the world more than information technology. Information technology is both fire-starter *and* fire department—the major impetus behind so much environmental complication, but paradoxically, itself the greatest equalizer in helping us complicate ourselves enough to meet the information processing demands of change. Problem *and* solution.

Which, of course, is not uncommon for technology. All technologies, low or high, are basically problem-solvers. And many themselves become problem-*causers*, requiring more technological solutions, which then trigger more problems, and so on, in a seemingly infinite regress. Two common examples: the need for mobility spawned a technological solution in the form of gasoline powered automobiles that, along with their numerous benefits, have themselves caused significant problems of pollution, highway congestion, safety and health, and depletion of finite resources, among other problems. Ironically, the very technology that has afforded us more mobility over the short run has the potential of making us *less* mobile over the long. Until, that is, another technological solution repeats the cycle. Or consider that ubiquitous techno-logical fact of modern living, chemicals. Industrialized, developed societies use chemicals to help solve innumerable problems, ranging from health care to manufacturing, from transportation to agriculture, from food processing to entertainment, and everything in between. But of course chemicals also belch and spew from our factories, run off our fields into the water supplies, and mutate resistant superbacteria and superbugs to invade us, our homes, and our farmlands. Technological solutions become related problems to solve, techno-logically. More technological solutions, more related problems to solve—technologically, of course.

The New Freedom?

We're right on the front edge of an information technology revolution, one that's going to shake the worlds of work and of organizations right down to their most fundamental definitions. Today's "researcher" profiled above—which is all of us, really—has an amazing collection of new information gadgetry to work with. All of these are changing our access to and uses of information, the lifeblood of both organizational adaptability and, not coincidentally, communication in organizations.

Consider just a few of today's innovations: computer networks within organizations, linking virtually everyone in-house with everyone else in-house, communicatively; organizational computer networks connected to national and international networks, linking thousands of organizations with each other, with gigantic databases all over the globe, and with dynamic political, economic, legal, ecological, and customer events everywhere, right as they develop; electronic "agents" that work around the clock to sniff out information of relevance and deliver it to particular users; electronic and voice mail systems, keeping people ever in touch with what's going on in-house, and externally, with those next door and in next hemisphere; faster, smaller, cheaper personal computers that let people put their *jobs* in a briefcase, do them on a plane, on the commute, at home, or on the beach, and transmit their work wirelessly to the office; software which does every information search and word/data processing chore imaginable; interactive, multimedia TV for self-paced instruction and assessment, video conferencing, and all sorts of many-to-many communication; groupware that automatically routes messages throughout teams, streamlines and redesigns teamwork processes, facilitates electronic team conferencing and consensus building, and coordinates team members' meeting schedules (Kirkpatrick, 1993); palm-sized personal data assistants that collect and organize unbelievable amounts of information on all sorts of useful topics. This is today.

Tomorrow promises to take the technological wherewithal presently found mostly in organizations and bring it affordably, along with any interim gadgets, right into the home of John and Jane Q. Public. The National Information Infrastructure—the so-called Information Superhighway—hopes to do for the average person on the street what all those things in the preceding paragraph can currently do for organizations: connect everyone in the United States with everyone and everything else, in a multimedia, interactive cornucopia of information. We'll see.

Back in the organizational world of today, businesses are taking the exigency of information technologies dead seriously. Virtually every business periodical and trade publication has been devoting significant space and entire issues to the various themes of managing with information technology. And with good reason. Before the dust settles, information technology promises to re-create the very ideas of "work" and "organization." And what are some of the issues before us?

The New Boss?

At this stage of events, anticipating the most important issues connected with information technologies and change is difficult at best, because so much is happening, on so many fronts, so fast. Because the possibilities are so numerous, let's stick with the ones that seem most probable and impactful. The issues fall within three categories: (1) work redesign, (2) organization redesign, and (3) communication. My working definition of communication is broad enough to overlap the first two categories in several places. The issues connected with all three categories are summarized in Table 9.1.

Work redesign. The natural symbiosis between information and teams will flourish with information technology. Information is power, and networked teams will have the potential to magnify their power in as yet unimagined ways. Because team designs are moving toward multidisciplinary structures rather than one-function schemes, high tech communication networks will allow teams to exploit their diversity like never before. Also, networks will effectively lower many of the obstacles and costs posed by distance. When teams can video conference, share information via networks, and coordinate their efforts by way of various networked "groupware," travel costs go down, information-based delays shrink, and the overall "in-the-know-ness" of the team and speed of team activities can increase dramatically.

The new design features of work carry some potential costs, which at this point are indeterminate, but possibly significant. Communication "on the net" still ultimately depends on the message creation skills of communicators—which, as you know, from my perspective, include writing and speaking *and* reading and listening. It is well known that the reading and, worse yet, writing skills of many of the people who will populate tomorrow's networks—today's students—are not what they need to be. Tables 1.1 and 1.2 from Chapter 1 show that managers far and wide decry the sorry writing skills of today's business school graduates, and press the critical need for such skills. More generally, in survey after survey, today's managers and educators highlight writing skills as something we should worry about. Granted, the "net" will send messages everywhere at the speed of light, but if what's written is unintelligible, is that so good? Writing skills in particular will be important for team members on the net.

Table 9.1
Issues of Managing Information Technologies

<u>Work Redesign</u>
•Networked: information is power to all.
•Multidisciplinary teams designed around core processes.
•Writing skills become more essential, to exploit networks.
•Issues of morale and stress associated with computer-tracked performance.
•Electronic "schmoozing" issues.
<u>Organization Redesign</u>
•Flatter.
•Networked; broad access to information and people, throughout.
•Greater responsibilities of workforce.
•Empowered workforce, to use information in decision making.
•Accountability of workforce to use information.
<u>Communication</u>
•"Overpowered" by information: overload.
•High-speed "communication crashes."
•High tech/low touch impact on speaking and interpersonal skills.
•High tech/low touch impact on "community."
•High tech/low touch impact on morale and use of systems.
•Privacy, when everyone is "netted?"
•Information technology and the assumptions of the "conduit metaphor."

A second potentially serious issue concerns the impact on morale and stress levels when, increasingly, people's performance becomes computer tracked, very precisely, and analyzed in heretofore unheard of ways.   When people are networked and so much of their work requires being "logged on," there's an automatic control system that can be used to show members' contribution to team performance, with great precision. For many people, the always-open "eye" of the computer adds another big twist of the tuning peg to jobs that are already tuned too high. Without question, many people will view computer monitoring as just one more step in the direction of organizational "Big-Brotherism," and will resist it tooth and nail. An important way of possibly helping to "soften" these concerns is for organizations to use the enhanced performance feedback to coach employees on their performance *and* to explicitly link stronger individual contributions to "team" performance with higher individual and team rewards.

A third potential issue of networked team work is the "schmoozing" issue. To the uninitiated, schmoozing is that wonderfully low tech and comfortable form of interpersonal communication based on two main questions: "howyadoin'?" and "whatsgoinon?" As any experienced schmoozer knows, the activity not only makes you feel good, but it often produces abundant "intelligence" about how others are "doin'" and what, in fact, *is* "goin'" on. People in teams need very much to know the answers to these questions. Regular schmoozing thus certainly performs a valuable service in team communication. But the power and the reach of networks is seductive to any natural schmoozing proclivities we might already have. This is amply demonstrated by the explosion of discussion groups on the biggest "net" of all, Internet. If the face-to-face kind of schmoozing is fun and informative, the interface-to-interface kind can be downright addictive. I've never seen a new network installation that, at first anyway, *didn't* provoke something like a cross between an ongoing electronic "happy hour" and the "Three Stooges Get Wired." For some teams, this can become habit-forming and a norm, which isn't necessarily bad, unless that's all that gets done. Team play needs to be balanced by team work.

Organization redesign. The issues of "work redesign" discussed above apply as well to "organization redesign." And there are some separate issues of a general nature that can be mentioned here. Managers who expect to fully exploit the power of information and of information technologies had better get used to ideas of empowerment. Networked organizations will by necessity become flatter, because the "costs" of tall structures will be intolerable. Decision "action," responsibility, and accountability will need to be shared everywhere, mainly because the information bearing critically on key decisions will *be* everywhere. Communication systems will virtually mandate broad access to information and people throughout an organization. This is not a comforting thought to many managers, who have been steeped in elitest traditions of "management's prerogative" and even secrecy when it comes to information sharing. But those views and actions won't cut it in communication-intensive organizations. Information and decision hoarding will be rewarded by the doors of offending organizations—and managers—being blown off as their fully empowered competitors zoom right past them on the information superhighway.

Communication. There are a number of communication issues here, a few of them related to the work and organization redesign issues described above, and several unique ones. The first one concerns information processing—the human kind. While limits on the technological kind seem to be expanding exponentially, limits on the human kind haven't changed much in a few thousand years, and aren't likely to, either. (Although there are many people who feel that humans are getting progressively "dumber," aided in no small way *by* technology.) If information is power, then most certainly we're facing potentially an ironical and exceedingly dangerous situation of being "overpowered" by it. Information overload addles things—thinking, decisions, problem solving, actions, lives, organizations, and the like. While we're opening the floodgates of information, we'd better keep this caveat in mind: *everyone* will need ongoing "swimming" lessons in how to manage and control information and information technology. This means not just the standard training in hardware, software, and networking applications, but also training in time management, stress management, creative problem solving, and choosing between what's truly relevant and what's "electrobabble," and so on. These latter skills will be "survival skills" in the Information Age.

A related "Frankensteinian" potential of information technologies is that they will simply hasten and magnify communication screw-ups that, even at the pre-tech slo-mo speed of sound, are already messy and frequent enough. Combining the reach and speed of information technology with the "natural" and inevitable *mis*communication between humans may be—borrowing on P. J. O'Rourke's (1991) elegant lampooning of money and power in U.S. government—"like giving whiskey and car keys to teenage boys" (1991, p. xviii). The possibilities for high-speed, far-reaching "communication crashes" are scary.

On another front, the "low touch"—impersonal—quality of much information technology may carry associated communication and "human" costs. One common concern is that in an organizational world dominated by human-machine interfaces, spoken language and interpersonal skills will be devalued and consequently harder to develop and maintain. This is one of the worries linked with multimedia instruction of children—that speaking and social skills may suffer when "teachers" and friends whom kids spend the most time with are in "the box." Few hardware and software designers are optimistic that any machine will ever fully communicate *relationally*, in the sense of rich nonverbal cues, ↑, ↓, →, and the like. These are human attributes—and needs, which won't be met by machines. More broadly, these questions about the "human-machine" interface center on the question of "community," and whether "human community" will be altered for better or worse by electronic communities—far-flung communities on "the net," more or less affiliated by people's common interests and needs. At this point, who knows? But whatever the answer is, asking the question repeatedly in the coming years will be warranted.

"Low touch" high tech exacts another form of "cost"—it simply offends many people, demoralizing them with what they see as its dehumanizing features and demands. As a result, a number of people viscerally shun the high tech systems that the rest of their world is coming to use ever more extensively. I have an organizational colleague whose hostility to networks and e-mail was such that he simply decided not to use his connection, which included never even checking his "mailbox" the first few months everyone was on-line. To compound things, after events finally persuaded him that his actions were proving costly—keeping him ignorant of several items of personal and professional importance—he then had to dig out from under a heap of "stuff" that had been piling up all those months in his e-mail. An added bite by the byte. And although he eventually "logged on" for good, ever so reluctantly, his acrimony toward the technological imperative has never really wavered.

Another communication issue that troubles many about the growth of information technology is "privacy." To an extent, this relates to the "morale/stress" issue raised above. But it goes farther, in that tough questions are being raised about that day when in fact most of the citizenry, in and out of organizations, are "networked." How easy will it be for government, organizational, and individual intruders to "watch" our private activities, our purchasing decisions and patterns, our conversations with others on personal subjects, our political leanings, our idiosyncracies revealed in words and choices that we exercise on-line? When everything about us exists in various "files" somewhere on "the net"—credit history, medical records, legal and financial dealings, and the like—how easy will it be for information thieves to burglarize our "lives," no matter how secure we're told we are? Does information technology on the scale of the Internet and the Information Superhighway further the purposes of democracy, or provide a perfect vehicle—especially in its scope and subtlety—for insinuating info-totalitarianism? Of course at this early stage no one can answer these questions with certainty, but for sure the debate will be heated, and we know that time will tell us. One of the most thought-provoking sources on these subjects is Howard Rheingold's book, *The Virtual Community: Homesteading on the Electronic Frontier* (1993), particularly the last chapter, which he entitles "Disinformocracy." Although Rheingold is unabashedly a cyberspace traveler and advocate, his review of these types of issues is balanced and very insightful, concluding that "we need to look closely at new technologies and ask how they can help build stronger, more humane communities—and ask how they might be obstacles to that goal. The late 1990s may eventually be seen in retrospect as a narrow window of historical opportunity, when people either acted or failed to act effectively to regain control over communication technologies" (p. 300). His words are worth pondering.

For the purposes in this book, possibly the most ominous communication issue concerns the "state-of-mind" that information technology may well reinforce regarding the subject of "communication" itself. In a 1974 lecture published several years later, Kenneth Burke spoke of "man's" technology: "His machines are not just the *fruits* of human rationality. They are in a sense the *caricature* of his rationality" (Burke, 1978, p. 33; emphasis in the original). If ever there was the physical caricature of the conduit metaphor, it is information technology. The imagery and terms associated with communication networks, transferral of information, sent and received messages, plus the speed and precision with which the hardware work, all reinforce the underlying assumptions of the conduit metaphor. Unassisted, there's plenty in the structure of the English language to keep the conduit metaphor ever in our consciousness about the communicative world. And now it seems information technology, increasingly pervading our lives, will work even more deeply "undercover" to validate those assumptions. In a four-sentence paragraph concluding his seminal *1979* article on the conduit metaphor, Michael Reddy made a statement, positively dripping with dark portent:

The conduit metaphor is leading us down a technological and social blind alley. That blind alley is mass communications systems coupled with mass neglect of the internal, human systems responsible for nine-tenths of the work in communicating. We think we are "capturing ideas in words," and funneling them out to the greatest public in the history of the world. But if there are no ideas "within" this endless flood of words, then all we are doing is replaying the myth of Babel—centering it, this time, around a broadcasting tower. (Reddy, 1979, p. 310)

And even before that, when most any "info-tech" issues would surely have seemed like just so much science fiction, again Kenneth Burke offered an observation, in an essay about moral issues, which prophesied in important ways the very issue raised here. In a statement that I've always felt packed as much inimitable weighty economy as "e = mc²," Burke assailed what he viewed as a basic moral problem: "Such thoughts concern man's *identification* with his machines in ways whereby he mistakes *their* powers for *his,* and loves himself accordingly" (Burke, 1973, p. 270; emphasis in the original). The fundamental moral problem stems from what Burke eloquently described as the "brutal disproportion between decision and the consequences" that arises from technology (p. 270). Although he was not writing about *information* technology, the "brutal disproportion" today is wider and more meaningful than when he wrote it, largely *due* to information technology. In the latter's case, I fear that the self-love of which Burke speaks will "fit" ever so comfortably with the complacency, laziness, ill-founded confidence, and just plain wrong-headedness that too many people presently exhibit in matters of communication and communicating. And that our "machines" will often just hasten and magnify the consequences of these delusions.

THE OLD BOSS:
TRADITIONAL ISSUES OF COMMUNICATION AND CHANGE

What happens will happen. Through all of the excitement of the new "Information Age," some things will not change. Among them, organizations will continue to rely on communication of all forms to accomplish anything they do. Several years ago I surveyed 164 experienced "communication consultants," asking them all sorts of questions about what they do, how they do it, for whom they do it, resources they find helpful, training and credentials they consider essential, and so forth (Axley, 1987b). Among my questions to them was one that asked about the future "hot" areas for communication consulting for the next ten years.   This should help show us what some of the issues are for communication and change. Let's see what they said.

Here's the breakdown of the top six "hot" areas: 32% said that "basic communication skills—speaking and writing"—would *always* be hot; 29% identified "computers and information processing"; 11% made up an "Other" category, a broad variety of single mentions; 8% said "office automation"; 7% specified "telecommunications and teleconferencing"; and 6% mentioned "human adaptation to technology" (pp. 11–12). It's interesting and important that the largest single percentage focused on the plain old communication skills of tradition, speaking and writing. Nobody mentioned "listening" or "reading" or "interpreting," however—no surprise to me. But these communication consultants also foresaw the writing on the wall—or the screen, really: by summing across all remaining categories except "Other," we see that 50% of this sample of consultants centered the future of communication consulting—meaning, much of managerial and organizational communication—around information technology. No surprise there, either. I'd bet the estimate would be even higher today.

Communicating About Change

Without question, every organization will face change in the future, and the communication basics will share center stage with information technology as areas for which organizations request and need help. Because change will be so prevalent as organizations try to maintain their adaptiveness in a fast-changing world, an especially important question facing virtually every organization will be "how to communicate effectively *about* change?" Organizations that can communicate effectively about change increase the odds that changes they undertake will be successful, and that environmental changes they encounter will be understood. Organizations that mismanage communication about change or simply ignore the need for it when change is eminent, help guarantee their own struggles and failure to change.

From my experience, managers and organizations facing change need to address a number of broad questions, the answers to which should help determine just "how" to communicate about organizational changes. Although there is nothing about these questions beyond common sense, it's astonishing to see how little attention they get from managers confronting change. Perhaps that's because the "common sense" to which I refer is "common" mostly within the perspective on communication advocated in this book (Chapter 3 and 4), while the "sense" that many managers commonly work from regarding matters communicative is that of the conduit metaphor (Chapter 2).

More often than not, managers zero in on so-called "sending" concerns to the neglect of "perceiving" concerns, assuming that if "sending" is done adequately, then the rest of the process will somehow take care of itself and serve the best interests of "senders." "Sending" concerns revolve almost exclusively around "the message" and its source, construction, and delivery, apart from the myriad contextual factors that affect how others *perceive* it. Concern mainly for "the message" creates questions like these: How, exactly, should messages about change be worded, to best convey management's intentions unambiguously? From whom, or what message source(s), should messages about change come? What channels or communication media will convey messages about change most efficiently? When should messages about change be communicated?

Now there's really nothing wrong with these questions. In fact, they would offer a petty good start toward generating some useful "particulars" in an initiative to communicate about change—apart from the unrealistic hope of communicating "unambiguously," and the trade-offs attendant to communicating "most efficiently." Their limitations are mainly ones of scope or breadth. What ultimately determines the success of an attempted organizational change is not so much what the "agents" of change, or so-called "senders" of change messages—usually managers—want or intend, but rather the meanings that perceivers *make* of change agents' actions and messages. In my experiences, perceivers of these actions and messages almost always want answers to these five broad questions: *Why? What? Who? How?* and *When?* In turn, each general question relates to specific issues of relevance to the people affected by change.

Figure 9.1 shows that one ultimate objective of any attempted organizational change is simply "successful change," whatever that may mean for a given situation. It assumes that how communicators—usually managers—answer those questions will impact perceivers' "accurate understanding" of the relevant change issues, as well as the "relational strength" that exists between change agents and those affected by the changes. Accurate understanding of the change issues and relational strength then affect the likelihood of successful change. Of course this figure is oversimplified. As a small consolation, I've inserted a catch-all "resistance" filter at each connection to suggest that any number of dispositional, perceptual, motivational, and other factors can alter the connections. But I don't think this compromises the main points of the model, those being that: (1) as a communicator about change, answering these questions will further the purposes of "accurate understanding" of the change issues and "relational strength" between change agents and people affected by changes; and that (2) accurate understanding and relational strength are the allies of change agents in facilitating successful change. Let's look at these basic questions more closely.

Why . . . ? The "why" part of communicating about change means a couple of things. The first one relates to change agents themselves. If I as a manager can't clarify to my own satisfaction all of the reasons "why" a change is occurring and should occur, how can I possibly hope to explain it to your satisfaction? Nothing will discredit a change initiative faster than the public fumbling of an explanation of "why the change." It will feed every germ of angst that exists in people affected by the change, and fan any embers of resistance that might be glowing. Taken as a whole, this first rationale for communicating "why" can be focused in these questions directed to change agents:

Figure 9.1
Questions for Communicating About Change

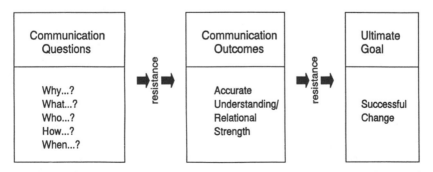

Can you itemize all of the reasons supporting a given change? How would you explain them to the people affected by the change?

The second reason for wrestling with "why" is no less utilitarian, but also has the added benefit of being decent. When something important will be changing or needs to change, the people affected by it almost always want to know "why." I've seen many a manager seriously underestimate people's interest in knowing "why" a change was occurring or was needed, believing instead that employees cared only about "how" the outcomes would affect them, their routines, or paychecks, and the like. This attitude invites *major* resistance, because of its message value, both informational and relational: informationally, it thwarts most people's fundamental need for a clear "purpose" in what they do; and relationally, the "self-superiority" and audacity implied by someone denying others the simple courtesy of an explanation insults people's need to be treated like equals and like adults. Double whammy. And the resulting resistance will be double trouble. The questions here for change agents are:

Do the people affected most by a change know why it's needed or being made? Do they accept the reasons as valid justification? If they do not, what are the implications for their commitment to the change?

What . . . ? The "what" component of communicating about change means many things. One of them concerns the obvious informational question of "what" the message is, or what change agents want it to be. As said earlier, this tends to focus attention on phrasing matters and specific word choices, which of course is a good idea. So here, change agents should make sure that communication about change accomplishes the following:

What is the essential message about change that those affected by it need to know? What are the key ideas and words about the change that must be clearly understood by perceivers?

A related issue of the informational message about change concerns how far a change departs from the way things presently are and have been. Dramatic changes place many more demands on communication about them than do minor changes. Dramatic changes almost always mean *more*: more controversy, more uncertainty and insecurity about them, more disruption of "routines" and people's work lives, more likelihood of tromping on the "culture," more time involved in establishing changes, more people affected by them. All of which means more resistance. The challenge of dramatic change is higher in variety than that of minor change. So as a tool for managing variety, communication itself must match that variety—meaning that the more human issues that surface due to the magnitude of change, the more intensely that change agents' communication must speak directly and explicitly to those issues. Without direct and explicit communication attention, dramatic change very often produces dramatic failure.

Questions that should shape change agents' communication along these lines include:

How far does a change depart from the way things are and have been? What does the change mean to those affected by it? How controversial is the change? Why? For whom? What issues stemming from the magnitude of change must you address in your communication about change?

A third issue connected with the informational element of communication about change pertains to "what's in it" for those affected by a change. Part of the information here reflects back to the question of "why the change?" Almost certainly, some of the reasons for "why the change" should relate to "what's in it" for those who are affected by the change—from *their* point of view. Only by helping to provide things that people value will a change be embraced. Sometimes people affected by a change will react reflexively and negatively, without really going into all of the possible "pros" and "cons" associated with it for them personally. This doesn't mean change agents should try to tell people what they should value or how they should feel about a change. The relational "↑" of telling others, in effect, what they *should* value or feel, is a quick way to get yourself "↑ed" right back. Better to lay what's in the offing, as best anyone can objectively tell, out on the table, and talk about—find out—what's good and not good, from the perspective of the people affected. Only that way will everyone share an understanding of "what's in" a change.

Sometimes the outcomes of a change aren't immediately "rewarding" to anyone, but rather serve to eliminate or reduce the threat of something worse than the change, at least temporarily. This situation characterizes many change initiatives, in that quite often, much direr consequences than disruption, uncertainty, and inconvenience await the organization that *won't* change. When this is in fact the case, communication that can clearly reveal "big picture" issues and the contrasts between "short-term" and "long-term" outcomes is essential. A classic example of this was when former Chrysler CEO Lee Iacocca bluntly explained to labor leaders what was "in it" for them without their concessions in his eleventh-hour attempts to save Chrysler from bankruptcy: all told, the loss of several hundred thousand jobs when the company went under. This is not to advocate "threats" or "promises," as much as it is to advocate *honesty* in communicating about what people can expect from a change, taking into account the good and bad, the short and long term, the small and big picture. The long-term relational payoffs from realistically presenting people with *all* of the expected outcomes up front will far surpass any short-term gains from discussing only pleasant consequences, particularly when time reveals the rest of the story. The questions that change agents need to consider here include:

What's in it, good and bad, short and long term, small and big picture, for those affected by a change? What do they see "in it" for themselves, along these dimensions?

Beyond the realm of pure information—the wording of messages, the magnitude of change, the expected outcomes of change—the relational dimension of communication plays an especially significant role in determining for perceivers "what" the message about change really is. One instance of this is the consistency that perceivers see between words about change and deeds about change. A manager colleague of mine complained to me about the change his company was undergoing, and what he said was top management's role in his and others' confusion. The problem, he said, wasn't really the change itself, but rather the fact that the same top manager who verbally "tried to work us into a frenzy to change" contradicted the importance of the change with his own actions, by not even attending key events in the change process, among other perceived inconsistencies.

In another instance, while helping a 400-employee firm assess its climate and culture, I had occasion to survey the entire organization and to interview a large number of employees. Somewhere in such efforts, I almost always like to ask employees a question like this: "Do you think management will make constructive use of this information?"   The answers from almost everyone, interviews and surveys, were either "No!" or "Who knows?" Upon further inquiry, the reason for doubt emerged: a similar type project had been undertaken several years prior, with great fanfare and promises of change. But then the results of the surveys that people had so painstakingly completed—exposing their real frustrations and dreams, so they said—were never even shared with employees. And according to employees, all the hoopla and optimism just faded into "the same old same old," along with any hopes for change. So should it have been surprising that when I came along with my questions about their frustrations and dreams, more than a few employees had trouble taking me seriously? They had been lied to before—management's actions betrayed management's words. In the eyes of many employees, that single inconsistency was enough to discredit other management attempts at change.

Along these lines of consistency, change agents should consider this question:

Are your actions regarding a change consistent with your words about the change—its importance, benefits, urgency, and the like? (Ask others affected by the change what they think about your consistency.)

Consistency between words and events plays another role in determining the effectiveness of communication about change. In a sense, this is similar to the agreement between words and deeds mentioned above, except that here let's "particularize" both the words and deeds in question.

Repeatedly in this book metaphor has been noted as being throughout history a catalyst of invention, which means that it has been a catalyst of change itself. Taking this thinking a step farther, or at least on an interesting tangent, Robert Marshak (1993) shows us that metaphors not only drive change, but also *structure* and *reveal* our thinking about it. This is right in step with what I've argued, here and elsewhere (Axley, 1984), about metaphor's relation to our world in general. Marshak's work identifies four main metaphors for change: "Fix and Maintain" metaphors; "Build and Develop" metaphors; "Move and Relocate" metaphors; and "Liberate and Recreate" metaphors (pp. 47–49). Note that these seem to span a continuum describing whether change alters the fundamental nature of that which is changed. Marshak says that our metaphors will affect both how we approach change—for example, such as "fixing" what's there, versus dismantling what's there and "recreating" something in its place, and so on—and how we communicate about change. Among a number of fascinating and highly practical conclusions, Marshak offers these gems of advice: (1) know your metaphors—they tell others how you view a change, as well as something about the nature of the change; (2) mind your metaphors—keep your spoken metaphors consistent with each other, and consistent with what you see as the nature of the change; and (3) consciously use self- and change-consistent metaphors to frame people's thinking about change in the ways you want—and encourage others to discuss the change in those same metaphorical terms.

More generally, we might put questions like the following to change agents who need to communicate about change:

What are the prevailing metaphors for a change—yours and others—as evidenced by the language about it? Do people seem to conceive of a given change with fundamentally *different* metaphors? What are the behavioral implications of different metaphors for how people will approach a change, for what they expect of it? How do people's metaphors square with the realities of a pending change? Are your spoken metaphors self- and change-consistent?

Who . . . ? In communicating about change, the question of "who" means, most basically, "who from?" and "who to?" "Who from" is the source of the main messages about change. In most situations involving important organizational change, the top-most officer and officers are the people employees expect to hear from. Anything or anyone less can have all sorts of negative and unintended message value, including: the top leaders don't really care enough about the change or the people affected to get involved first-hand; they're not supportive of the change; they don't want to take any responsibility or fire by being the messengers; and they don't know enough about the change to communicate about it clearly. In the absence of "an explanation" as to why the "appropriate" messenger(s) didn't deliver the message, people are free to create any explanation—and will. As a rule, the stature of the messenger(s) of change should be up to the stature of the change. Important change? The most important messenger(s) in the organization should communicate about it. If more than one person serves as messenger, it is essential that these people coordinate their efforts *and* their language about change, including their metaphors. In view of these things, the obvious questions here for change agents are:

Is the stature of the messenger(s) of change up to the stature of the change? If there are
two or more messengers of change, how are their efforts and language coordinated?

"Who to" refers to the different "audiences" for messages of change. This book
has pushed "vigilance" and effort in communicating. In this regard, a "given"
of communicating effectively is knowing your audience—any special qualities
they have that may affect what they "make" of your words and deeds. And then
working—tailoring words and deeds—to accommodate those qualities.

In large-scale, important change, probably the biggest single "audience" for
communication about change is the whole organization, along with relevant
external stakeholders. There no doubt will be messages that all members of this
broad "audience" should get. But within the general audience, and particularly
in organizations emphasizing employee diversity, there also will be any number
of different "audiences," with each having possibly unique concerns, language
and interpretive qualities, ways in which change will affect them, and so forth.
For instance, some of the features that could "partition" different audiences,
depending on the type of change, might include gender, ethnicity, education, age,
seniority, function, and more—too many to possibly mention. The point is that
change agents must determine "who" the relevant audiences are, what issues are
likely to differentiate them for a given change, and then speak directly to their
individualized concerns and needs relative to the change. A "one-size-fits-all"
approach to communicating with "different" audiences won't fully address the
needs of any of them.

This is "Marketing 101," admittedly. But it's also "Effectiveness 101." A
perfect example comes from a company whose name is almost synonymous with
"blue jeans," and is becoming synonymous with progressive, value-based human
resource practices, diversity being among them: Levi Strauss & Company. In
a recent profile (Mitchell and Oneal, 1994), an example is recounted in which
the company's Hispanic employees and customers criticized Levi's "501 Blues"
TV ads directed at the Hispanic market as being out of step with Hispanic
culture. The ads, featuring people by themselves, seemed to play up "individ-
uality" while downplaying togetherness, the latter connecting more with Hispanic
culture, so the critics said. Changing the ads to accommodate this important
cultural qualification sent sales in the Hispanic segment soaring (p. 49). So for
different audiences? Fine-tuned differences in messages.

The questions for change agents along the lines of "who to" communicate with
include:

Who is the largest audience for messages about a given change? What are the messages
everyone in it should get? Along what lines are there different audiences for messages
about a given change? Should messages about change be tailored to different audiences?
How should messages to different audiences be constructed so as to speak to the most
important differences and different issues, yet remain integrated?

How . . . ? The "how" element of communicating about change relates most importantly to questions of which particular "channels" to use and what kind of approach or manner will most effectively accomplish the goals at hand.

There are numerous channels or media available for communicating about change. Information technology has dramatically expanded the options, too. The most likely channels would include face-to-face (one-to-one or one-to-many), voice mail, e-mail, bulletin boards, pay inserts, newsletters, video conferencing, network conferencing, one-way TV, and teleconferencing. Four of the most important evaluative criteria for selecting any channel of communication are (1) time to coverage, (2) reach, (3) interactivity, and (4) cue variety. "Time to coverage" refers to the time it takes to achieve full delivery of relevant messages to an entire target audience. "Reach" means the breadth of exposure possible each time a message is communicated. "Interactivity" pertains to the extent to which the channel enables instantaneous and ongoing interaction between everyone involved. And "cue variety" refers to the richness and variety of cues to interpretation the channel provides. For instance, a one-on-one face-to-face channel is slow in time to coverage if more than a few people are involved, limited in reach due to human limits, time limits, and so on; highly interactive and high in cue variety; providing an abundance of interpretive cues for everyone concerned. At another extreme, pay inserts are moderately fast in coverage and broad in reach, but low in interactivity and cue variety. As a third example, video conferencing offers a blend of speed, reach, interactivity, and cue variety. So trade-offs are the rule with different channels for communicating about change. Figure 9.2 summarizes them.

There are a number of suggestions for change agents to consider in the selection of channels to communicate about change. First, "human" needs should be balanced against speed and reach, especially in times of high uncertainty and anxiety for people affected by a change. People will see many of the purely visual channels, and especially ones with just printed words to be read, as sterile and uncaring—big relational costs that usually come back to haunt managers when they can least afford them. Plus, low interactivity and cue variety increases the potential for huge misunderstandings and misattributions at precisely those times of greatest personal and organizational stress. Second, change agents should consider organizational culture constraints on the media chosen. An organization with a tradition for the "personal" touch had better be careful about relying on too many "impersonal" media to communicate about important change. It just rankles cultural forces. Or on the other hand, an organization with a tradition of exploiting state-of-the-art information technology probably can do well with a strong emphasis on speed and reach, because its culture is likely to be more open to the use of those channels. Third—and overarching the first two suggestions—change agents should think *redundancy* of channels, to increase exposure, to help promote convergence of "meanings" through different channels, and to allow "tech" and "touch" to complement one another. The "relational" benefits from using interactive channels high in cue variety won't hurt, either. Using multiple channels that "backstop" each other will work best under most important circumstances.

The questions to change agents contemplating different channels to communicate about change include:

Using Figure 9.2, which channels are available to you to communicate about a given change? Is the change highly important, the situation highly charged, or highly uncertain? What are your communication needs concerning time, reach, interactivity, and cue variety? What are the communication needs of those affected by the change concerning time, reach, interactivity, and cue variety?

The approach or manner of communicating about change will also affect the likelihood of successful change. Several factors enter into determining approach. Again, an important one is an organization's culture. If an organization has functioned successfully with a culture of unilateral decision making by a few managers, then for many types of changes it probably will be relatively easy for the appropriate authority figure(s) to just issue the relevant directives as to how things will be changing. No questions needed, invited, or maybe even allowed. Same for participative cultures: for almost any form of change, the *question* of changing will be run up the flagpole to test the prevailing winds and see what people think. In each case, "fit" between culture and approach is key. The managers of an autocratic culture suddenly attempting a participative approach will have just as much difficulty being successful as the managers of a participative culture suddenly turning to autocratic methods, for different reasons of course. Change agents need to assess the cultural constraints on their approach. Managers whose approaches flout the critical cultural constraints often get to experience change themselves: from being employed to being un-employed. It's not that challenging a culture shouldn't or can't be done. Sometimes *that's* exactly what's needed to save an organization. But the change agents looking to do it had better plan very carefully, and be prepared for a long, slow process of incremental change, a few steps forward and backward and forward, and so on, at a time—*if* they last in their positions long enough to pull it off.

A second factor relating to approach is the time available to communicate about change. Directive approaches generally take less time than consultative and participative—interactive—approaches. The trade-off, however, is often time saved at the expense of people's commitment to a change. We've addressed this at several other points in the book. I've yet to meet people who don't appreciate the opportunity to be heard and especially to influence their own destiny in times of change.

A third factor relates to the first two, and is the extent to which resistance to a change is anticipated. In such a situation, directive, "telling" approaches will almost undoubtedly fuel more antagonism. A certain amount of resistance usually stems from people not knowing such essentials as what a change is about, why it's needed or happening, where it will lead, and so on. Another part of resistance comes from the need for a voice in the change processes. Some of it surely comes from what is often seen as the "punishment" of new ways, new policies, new expectations. And probably some resistance can just be chalked up to orneriness. Interactive, consultative, and participative approaches are much more likely to address the ignorance, the ownership, and the punishment issues than directive approaches, and their relational appeal to reciprocity might even soften some hard-core nay-sayers. But don't do it just because it's nice. A better reason is that it's necessary, for the long-run adaptability to change.

Questions for change agents regarding approaches to communicating about change include:

What are the cultural constraints that would make one approach to communicating more advisable than another, particularly as regards decision making? Does your approach fit the most important cultural values or expectations? If not, is that your intention and how have you planned around it? How should time figure into your approach? Is people's commitment to change an important issue? Do you anticipate resistance to change? From whom? Why? How is your approach likely to affect resistance?

Figure 9.2
Features of Communication Channels

Channels	Time	Reach	Interactivity	Cue Var.
Face-to-face 1-1 1-many	Slow Mod.	Limited Mod.	High Mod.-High	High Mod.-High
Voice mail	Fast	Broad	Low (delay)	Mod.
E-mail	Fast	Broad	Low (delay)	Low
Bull. boards	Mod.	Broad	Low	Low
Pay inserts	Mod.	Broad	Low	Low
Newsletters	Mod.	Broad	Low	Low
Video conf.	Fast	Broad	High	Mod.-High
Network conf.	Fast	Broad	High	Low-Mod.
One-way TV	Fast	Broad	Low	Mod.
Teleconfer.	Fast	Broad	High	Mod.

When . . . ? This question for communicating about change is just as it appears: it concerns "timing" and "when" information about change is communicated. If ever there was a "gimme" of communicating about change, this is one. When was the last time you learned some essential, possibly life-altering piece of information from someone other than the source you think it *should* have come from? How did it make you feel? I know a manager who learned that the unit he headed was to be merged with another unit. Trouble was, he learned it from a friend some 300 miles away, who had read about it in a local newspaper, and who just wanted to see if the manager was "excited" about the new "opportunity." He was. He'd heard not a peep through official channels inside his own company, but was "blindsided" by a newspaper blurb. It's true: timing very often is everything. People don't like to be kept in the dark. And they like even less finding out what's going on by virtue of dumb luck and any sources other than those who should have been forthcoming from the very beginning. Bad timing of this sort is a dart to the heart of trust. Get your own "word" out *before* any other "word" gets out. There's always some relational cost to those who don't, and some relational payoff to those who do. The questions to change agents on matters of timing include:

What are the possibilities of your being "scooped" by unofficial sources on a given change? What are the likely relational consequences of this and, if any, can you afford them? When is the earliest *you* would want to know about a change that affected you importantly?

A Little Research, If You Please

Along the general lines of communicating about change, there is much anecdotal evidence and just a little evidence of a more systematic or "scholarly" nature. One of the more interesting of the latter is a recent study by Larry Smeltzer (1991). Smeltzer looked at the strategies for announcing organization-wide change in 43 large organizations. His results contain the seeds of some very useful advice (pp. 18–21): (1) only 4 of 43 companies had developed formal strategies for announcing change; (2) 80% of the announced changes showed some sign of major failure—with management unaware of it—evidenced mainly by either rampant, inaccurate, negative rumors, or/and by people learning of change from someone other than management; (3) people resented the use of what Smeltzer calls "lean" channels (e.g., memos) to convey emotionally weighted messages; (4) managers communicated essentially the same message to all groups of people affected by the change; (5) people especially disliked euphemistic, sugar-coated announcements; and (6) managers didn't see announcing change as particularly difficult, equating just "telling them" with adequate communication. The blindered, easy confidence manifested here in these attitudes and outcomes reminds me of the smug driver who has never been personally involved in an accident, but has caused scores of them for others. Does it all look familiar? It should.

Another recent study on large-scale change offers change agents additional advice worth considering. Teresa Covin and Ralph Kilmann (1990) surveyed 108 managers, 53 internal organizational consultants, 40 external consultants, and 39 researchers/faculty, almost all of whom were experienced with large-scale change, about what respondents felt were issues having either an extremely positive or negative impact on large-scale organizational improvement programs. The questions produced more than 900 issues that content analysis boiled down to fourteen categories, six "positive" and eight "negative." The category labels themselves are intriguing, and highly suggestive that communication has a bearing on virtually all of them. From the "positive-impact" category, things that help the chances of change: "Visible Management Support and Commitment"; "Preparing for a Successful Change"; "Encourage Employee Participation"; "A High Degree of Communication"; "Recognition of a Strong Business-Related Need for Change;" and "A Reward System That Supports Necessary Changes" (pp. 244–245). And from the "negative-impact" category, things that hurt the chances of change: "A Lack of Management Support"; "Top Managers Forcing Change"; "Inconsistent Actions by Key Managers"; "Unrealistic Expectations"; "A Lack of Meaningful Participation"; "Poor Communication"; "Purpose of Program is Not Clear"; and "There is No Placement or a Misplacement of Responsibility" (pp. 245–246). The question warrants asking: how could any of these fourteen activities take place *without* communication? Indeed, every single positive- and negative-impact category contains behavioral elements that are pure communication activities as discussed in this book. And several of them, I argue, are more "communication" than anything else. But the most direct, albeit narrowly focused, communication advice comes from looking at the items that operationalized the two categories explicitly labeled as "communication," one positive and one negative. Table 9.2 shows these items; good advice from Covin and Kilmann.

The Tools of Change: Communication and Communications

This chapter has been about what *was*, what *is*, and what *will be*. Change is not just something that creeps up on us from time to time, to be reckoned with only as we sense its proximity and urgency. Change is the "rule" of organic, living, and open systems. A microscopic organism survives and thrives by interacting with its environment, by changing to meet environmental demands and to exploit opportunities, and by modifying its environment as possible. A person survives and thrives by interacting with her or his environment, by changing to meet environmental demands and to exploit opportunities, and by modifying the environment as possible. So do organizations. And societies. And humanity.

But by "what was, is, and will be," I really don't mean change itself—although that applies—as much as I mean *communication* in relation with change. Anyone of experience has lived firsthand with at least some of the facts of increasing change: in population shifts, in changing forms of "family," in new

Table 9.2
Communication Factors That Help and Hurt Change Initiatives

<u>These Help</u>
•Getting key middle managers talking
 to each other.
•Communication of success stories
 from the change.
•Communication of goals both to
 employees and customers.
•Coordination of groups working on
 different aspects of the program.
•Maintaining substantial
 communication with all levels of the
 organization involved in planning and
 implementation.
•Clear objectives positively
 communicated to all organizational
 members.
•Frequent meetings for evaluation of
 the program.

<u>These Hurt</u>
•Failure to communicate reasons for
 change.
•Not being honest with all involved.
•Not disclosing information to
 managers who must implement.
•Lack of effective feedback
 mechanisms to let management know
 when behavior is inconsistent.
•Failure to create a climate for open
 dialogue.
•Too great a time period between
 meetings/communications.

Source: Table entries quoted from Covin and Kilmann (1990, pp. 245–246).

faces of the workforce, in downsized organizations, in defunct organizations, in planned organizational change initiatives, in technologies that bring us nose-to-nose with questions like "when does life begin?" "when does it end?" and "what's the quality of it in between?" We're neither sufficiently aware nor skillful in the role that our communication plays in managing change. What was, is, and will be, is communication, the tool of humanity which enables the creation of every other tool of humanity. For practical purposes, plain old speaking, listening, writing, and reading have always been with us and will always be essential to our ability to manage change. These are forms of "communication," without the s, from one person(s) to another person(s).

But "communication*s*" interpose information technology between people, and are increasingly shaping both "what is" and "what will be," even "what can be," in the realm of human communication. What makes the modern relationship between communication, communications, and change unprecedented in importance is that while the essential tool of humanity, communication, will almost certainly be enhanced in many ways, quite probably it also will be subverted and impoverished in unknowable ways, all by the very tool *it* created, communication*s*. While most everyone recognizes that "necessity is the mother of invention," it's equally also true that "invention is the mother of necessity." Certain inventions have, without question, created "necessities" that probably their inventors never anticipated, or wanted. The inventors of TV no doubt envisioned an informed and educated populace, partly indebted to their invention.

And maybe they were a little bit right. But in the deal they also got an alarmingly large TV subculture of happy idiots who would much rather "tune in and tune out" than read or write or talk or think—mainly because "watching" the world is so much less demanding and complicated than reading, writing, talking, or thinking about it.

Nobody knows just how communication and communications will change in the years to come, only that they will—dramatically—and that change will always be the ultimate test of an organization's capability. One way or another, communication and communications both will play *the* defining role in managing change. Earlier in the chapter, I suggested 17 issues that will be important in managing information technologies (Table 9.1), several with a few subissues each. A number of them speak directly to questions of which "tool" will "rule." My hope there was admittedly to tip the odds just a little, if that's even possible at this point, in favor of human communication, while still encouraging the measured exploitation of communications technologies. It will be an ongoing uphill struggle to use communications in ways that promote effective communication, and all that the latter term implies. But because communications technologies are as certain as time, we'd better do the best we can to accommodate their demands without compromising our skills, along with the potential for good, in human communication.

Change is complicated, and complicated change agents will do better at managing it than uncomplicated ones. All told, more than 40 specific questions grew from those five general ones of Figure 9.1, *why, what, who, how,* and *when,* and I am convinced that each one can help change agents develop greater awareness and skill with regard to the considerable communication responsibilities accompanying change. Additionally, Smeltzer's (1991) findings and those of Covin and Kilmann (1990) give organizational change agents both something more to consider and something more to *do* in their roles. It will take increasing "variety" to manage the increasing "variety" of change in the future. Communication, enriched by communications, will be the best we can do to manage the complications of change.

Epilogue

THE FABLE OF THE WIZARD OF CON

There once was a land where a powerful and malevolent wizard dwelt. All his life he dreamt of subjugating the people who inhabited the land, wanting nothing less than absolute dominion over them. One day, in a flash of evil brilliance, he devised the most insidiously perfect way to disempower the populace: invisibly, with the help of the people themselves. He would create conditions in which people would unknowingly yet cheerfully exile themselves in a swamp of their own making.

He did this: One night while the people of the land slept, he cast a spell that ever-so-subtly altered the structure of their language. Thereafter, whenever people thought and talked about human communication, their language gave them limited options with which to portray it. The expressions most abundantly and easily available to them in their language made it seem as though meanings existed outside of themselves and that communication somehow involved the transfer of meanings from person to person. So what the wizard had done was give the people a simple, concrete, and comfortable way of describing that most common of human activities, communication. But in effect, he gave them much more.

At first, nothing much resulted, other than an uneasiness among people that in some ineffable way, the world had changed. Over time, though, the magic began to work on most people: the structures and images of the language people used to "talk about things," particularly human communication, insinuated lessons about what they *should* take for granted in human affairs. The lessons became the underlying justification for people's communication practices and for the way they treated one another. The foundation on which people had lived and toiled in the world began to soften *from within*, ever so subtly.

Many people began to tacitly assume that human meaning is objective and transferable, because when they opened their mouths to talk about communication, that's what their language enabled them to say most easily. And their language made competing viewpoints very difficult, cumbersome, and time-consuming, both to think about and to express.

As the prevailing assumptions became more deeply embedded in the culture, other qualities of people began to change as well. There was a noticeable uplift in confidence, bordering on arrogance, that bouyed people's outlook on communicating with one another. People were able to feel secure that when they communicated, they simply shared their thoughts with others, and that others did the same with them. Part of this confidence grew from the heightened sense of control that people felt about communication, believing that the right words and actions could convey their intentions. Being in control felt good.

Both appreciation for self-control and faith in communication efficacy ran deep among people. So not surprisingly, communication "efficiency" became an important value and an end in itself among communicators. As such, *monologue* became the communication model and method of choice, with distinct roles for message senders and message receivers. Increasingly people began to see *dialogue* as the most superfluous and inefficient means of communication possible. To be sure, they believed dialogue was unnecessary for clarity, owing to the conviction that communication transfers meaning. But it became more than just unnecessary. Dialogue carried the added burden of being uncomfortable and discomfiting for most people, because it inevitably challenged their most cherished illusions about perfect communication and about their own self-control as communicators.

Without dialogue, each person in the land became ever more self-absorbed in all areas of behavior and communication, ignoring the needs of others. Monologue required it. Without dialogue, opportunities to collaborate with and to learn from others vanished. Without dialogue, there was no time or way to establish or maintain "community." Without dialogue, more and more people became "stuck," up to their knees, in just the world—just the *words*—of their own making.

The bedrock of the land had softened and turned to muck so gradually, so uneventfully, so comfortably, so silently, that scarcely anyone heard the distant laughter wafting from beyond the swamp.

THE LAST WORD

The Wizard of Con in this fable has two identities. The first is the conduit metaphor, and the second, the subtle deception—a "con"—that the conduit metaphor helps us perpetrate on ourselves. We're enticed by its promise of easy success in communicating, just like other "conned" victims so often pull themselves along toward easy money that looks too good to be true. But the result is the same in each case: the situation isn't what we were led—and led ourselves—to believe.

The conduit metaphorical view of communication is a habit of mind and of action, creeping like a swamp under and into the foundation of our lives. Like other habits, it can best be altered by diligent effort to replace it with another, more functional habit of mind and action. The confluences that feed the conduit metaphor in our lives—the English language, primarily, along with a host of physical artifacts—aren't going to dry up. The best we can do is to counter it with vigilance, new understandings of communication, and concerted efforts applying those understandings in every area of our lives where communication is relevant—meaning everywhere. Maybe communication isn't the single most important thing in the history and continuing existence of humanity, but it runs a photo-finish second to—and, allows us to talk about—whatever is. Communication *uses* us, shapes us, creates the world we know. We'd better learn how to *use* communication, and the time is now.

Near the beginning of this book, and numerous places throughout, the "communication-intensive" organization is mentioned. To survive and thrive in the dynamic organizational world of the future, organizations will need to be communication-intensive. A communication-intensive organization is an ideal that can only develop from the understanding and efforts of communication-intensive people. Being communication-intensive means having an appreciation for what "communication" is, for what it does and can do, for what its natural defining qualities are and aren't, for how it connects with so many different threads of our personal and professional roles—and most of all, for just how much and what kind of hard work is required to do it effectively. Equipped in that understanding of communication, we must live its consequences and implications. Only by doing the hard work of communication described in the chapters of this book—by examining our metaphors for communication, by being ever vigilant in the interests of accuracy, by investing our energies, our words, and our actions in dialogue and in relationships, by leading others while at the same time empowering them, by examining and communicating the assumptions and values that we want to express the cultures of our workplaces, by building diverse, open, and self-examining teams, by managing the changes of communications technologies, and managing the communication of change—only by doing *this* hard work are communication-intensive people and, therefore, communication-intensive organizations possible.

It can't be done alone. A solitary person subscribing to the ideas presented in this book, who "lives" and works among those of more conventional communication ideas and practices, will be but a small high and dry spot, bleached of all influence by communication complacency, laziness, and ignorance that extends right over the horizon in every direction. If you find yourself to be an island of this sort, perhaps this book can help you create other "islands," connected by bridges of dialogue you'll build from your own understanding of communication and consequent hard work. And if we persist, and if we're lucky, maybe there will be enough islands one day to harness the immense constructive power of communication, to undo the malevolent acts of the wizard and drain the swamp.

Bibliography

Aldag, R., & Stearns, T. (1991). *Management* (2nd ed.). Cincinnati: South-Western.

Argyris, C. (1990). *Overcoming organizational defenses: Facilitating organizational learning.* Boston: Allyn and Bacon.

Armstrong, D. (1992). *Managing by storying around: A new method of leadership.* New York: Doubleday Currency.

Axley, S. (1992, September-October). Delegate: Why we should, why we don't and how we can. *Industrial Management,* 16–19.

Axley, S. (1990, September-October). The practical qualities of effective leaders. *Industrial Management,* 29–31.

Axley, S. (1987a, July-August). Toward productive meetings: Advice from the firing line. *Industrial Management,* 19–20.

Axley, S. (1987b, June). Communication consultants and consulting: A survey of ABC members. *The Bulletin* of the Association for Business Communication, 8–15.

Axley, S. (1984). Managerial and organizational communication in terms of the conduit metaphor. *Academy of Management Review, 9,* 428–437.

Bateman, T., & Zeithaml, C. (1993). *Management: Function and strategy* (2nd ed.). Homewood, IL: Irwin.

Benne, K., & Sheats, P. (1948, Spring). Functional roles of group members. *The Journal of Social Issues,* 41–49.

Bennis, W. (1989). *On becoming a leader.* Reading, MA: Addison-Wesley, 1989.

Bishop, J. (1994, November 23). Studies conclude Doctors' manner, not ability, results in more lawsuits. *The Wall Street Journal,* p. B6.

Bragg, J., & Andrews, I. (1973). Participative decision making: An experimental study in a hospital. *Journal of Applied Behavioral Science, 9,* 727–735.

Brown, R. (1977). *A poetic for sociology.* Cambridge, England: Cambridge University Press.

Burke, K. (1978). Rhetoric, poetics, and philosophy. In D. Burks (Ed.), *Rhetoric, philosophy, and literature* (pp. 15–33). West Lafayette, IN: Purdue University Press.

Burke, K. (1973). The rhetorical situation. In L. Thayer (Ed.), *Communication: Ethical and moral issues* (pp. 263–275). London: Gordon and Breach Science Publishers.

Burke, K. (1966). *Language as symbolic action*. Berkeley, CA: University of California Press.

Burke, K. (1954). *Permanence and change*. Los Altos, CA: Hermes Publications.

Burke, K. (1945). *A grammar of motives*. Berkeley, CA: University of California Press.

Byrne, J. (1993, December 20). The horizontal corporation. *Business Week*, 76–81.

Cantril, H. (1982). *The invasion from Mars: A study in the psychology of panic*. Princeton, NJ: Princeton University Press.

Covey, S. (1989). *The 7 habits of highly effective people*. New York: Fireside.

Covin, T., & Kilmann, R. (1990). Participant perceptions of positive and negative influences on large-scale change. *Group & Organization Studies, 15*, 233–248.

Cummings, T., & Worley, C. (1993). *Organization development and change* (5th ed.). St. Paul: West Publishing Company.

Dayal, I., & Thomas, J. (1968). Operation KPE: Developing a new organization. *The Journal of Applied Behavioral Science, 4*, 473–505.

Denison, D. (1984, Autumn). Bringing corporate culture to the bottom line. *Organizational Dynamics*, 5–22.

DePree, M. (1992). *Leadership jazz*. New York: Doubleday Currency.

Downs, C., Clampitt, P., & Pfeiffer, A. (1988). Communication and organizational outcomes. In G. Goldbaber and G. Barnett (Eds.), *Handbook of organizational communication* (pp. 171–211). Norwood, NJ: Ablex Publishing Corporation.

Fernandez, J. (1972). Persuasions and performances: Of the beast in everybody...and the metaphors of everyman. *Daedalus, 101*, 39–60.

Fisher, A. (1993, August 23). Sexual harassment: What to do. *Fortune*, 84–88.

Geertz, C. (1973). *The interpretation of cultures*. New York: Basic Books.

Gibb, J. (1961) Defensive communication. *Journal of Communication, 11*, 141–148.

Glenn, E., & Pood, E. (1989, January). Listening self-inventory. *Supervisory Management*, 12–15.

Greiner, L. (1973, March-April). What managers think of participative leadership. *Harvard Business Review*, 111–117.

Hackman, J., & Oldham, G. (1980). *Work redesign*. Reading, MA: Addison-Wesley.

Hammer, M., & Champy, J. (1993). *Reengineering the corporation: A manifesto for business revolution*. New York: HarperBusiness.

Haney, W. (1986). *Communication and interpersonal relations: Text and cases*. (5th ed.). Homewood, IL: Irwin.

Hastings, A. (1970). Metaphor in rhetoric. *Western Speech, 34*, 181–193.

Hellriegel, D., & Slocum, J. (1992). *Management* (6th ed.). Reading, MA: Addison-Wesley.

Hitler, A. (1942). *Mein Kampf*. Translated by Ralph Mannheim. Boston: Houghton Mifflin.

Hofstede, G. (1984). The cultural relativity of the quality of life concept. *Academy of Management Review, 9*, 389–398.

Katzenbach, J., & Smith, D. (1993). *The wisdom of teams: Creating the high-performance organization*. Boston: Harvard Business School Press.

Kirkpatrick, D. (1993, December 27). Groupware goes boom. *Fortune*, 99–106.

Koch, H. (1970). *The panic broadcast: Portrait of an event*. Boston: Little, Brown & Co.

Lakoff, G., & Johnson, M. (1980). *Metaphors we live by.* Chicago: University of Chicago Press.

Lawler, E. (1986). *High involvement management.* San Francisco: Jossey-Bass.

Likert, R. (1961). *New patterns of management.* New York: McGraw-Hill.

Locke, E., & Schweiger, D. (1979). Participation in decision making: One more look. In B. Staw (Ed.), *Research in organizational behavior,* Vol. 1 (pp. 265–339). JAI Press: Greenwich, CT.

Marshak, R. (1993, Summer). Managing the metaphors of change. *Organizational Dynamics,* 44–56.

McCall, M., & Lombardo, M. (1983). What makes a top executive? *Psychology Today, 26,* 28–31.

McFarland, L., Senn, L., & Childress, J. (1993). *21st century leadership.* Los Angeles: The Leadership Press.

McGregor, D. (1960). *The human side of enterprise.* New York: McGraw-Hill.

Miles, R. (1975). *Theories of management: Implications for organizational behavior and development.* New York: McGraw-Hill.

Mitchell, R. (1979). *Less than words can say.* Boston: Little, Brown.

Mitchell, R., & Oneal, M. (1994, August 1). Managing by values. *Business Week,* 46–52.

Morgan, G. (1986). *Images of organization.* Beverly Hills, CA: Sage Publications.

O'Rourke, P. (1991). *Parliament of whores.* New York: The Atlantic Monthly Press.

Ott, J. (1989). *The organizational culture perspective.* Chicago: The Dorsey Press.

Palmer, A. (1993, June 28). An easygoing boss—and a master motivator. *Business Week,* 84.

Pearce, J. (1971). *The crack in the cosmic egg.* New York: Pocket Books.

Peters, T., & Waterman, R. (1982). *In search of excellence.* New York: Harper & Row.

Plunkett, L., & Fournier, R. (1991). *Participative management: Implementing empowerment.* New York: Wiley.

Redding, W. C. (1972). *Communication within the organization: An interpretive review of theory and research.* New York: Industrial Communication Council.

Reddy, M. (1979). The conduit metaphor—A case of frame conflict in our language about language. In A. Ortony (Ed.), *Metaphor and thought* (pp. 284–324). Cambridge, England: Cambridge University Press.

Rheingold, H. (1993). *The virtual community: Homesteading on the electronic frontier.* Reading, MA: Addison-Wesley.

Ricks, D. (1983). *Big business blunders: Mistakes in multinational marketing.* Homewood, IL: Dow Jones-Irwin.

Sashkin, M. (1984, Spring). Participative management is an ethical imperative. *Organizational Dynamics,* 5–22.

Schein, E. (1992). *Organizational culture and leadership* (2nd ed.). San Francisco: Jossey-Bass.

Schön, D. (1979). Generative metaphor: A perspective on problem-setting in social policy. In A. Ortony (Ed.), *Metaphor and thought* (pp. 254–283). Cambridge, England: Cambridge University Press.

Senge, P. (1990). *The fifth discipline.* New York: Doubleday Currency.

Senge, P., Roberts, C., Ross, R., Smith, B., & Kleiner, A. (1994). *The fifth discipline fieldbook.* New York: Doubleday Currency.

Smeltzer, L. (1991). An analysis of strategies for announcing organization-wide change.

Group & Organization Studies, 16, 5–24.

Steinbeck, J. (1941) *The log from the Sea of Cortez*. Middlesex, England: Penguin Books.

Walton, M. (1986). *The Deming management method*. New York: Perigree Books.

Walton, R. (1987). *Managing conflict: Interpersonal dialogue and third-party roles* (2nd ed.). Reading, MA: Addison-Wesley.

Watzlawick, P., Beavin, J., & Jackson, D. (1967). *Pragmatics of human communication*. New York: W. W. Norton & Company.

Weick, K. (1979). *The social psychology of organizing* (2nd ed.). Reading, MA: Addison-Wesley.

Wellins, R., Byham, W., & Wilson, J. (1991). *Empowered teams: Creating self-directed work groups that improve quality, productivity, and participation*. San Francisco: Jossey-Bass.

Whetten, D., & Cameron, K. (1991). *Developing management skills* (2nd ed.). New York: HarperCollins.

Whorf, B. (1941). The relation of habitual thought and behavior to language. In Leslie Spier, A. Irving Hallowell, & Stanley S. Newman (Eds.), *Language, Culture, and Personality: Essays in Memory of Edward Sapir* (pp. 75–93). Menasha, WI: Sapir Memorial Fund.

Yukl, G. (1989). *Leadership in organizations* (2nd ed.). Englewood Cliffs, NJ: Prentice-Hall.

Index

About the Author

STEPHEN R. AXLEY is Professor of Management in the College of Business and Technology at Western Illinois University. He has served as a consultant and trainer to more than sixty organizations in the private and public sectors, including several Fortune 500 firms and numerous agencies of three state governments. He has received numerous awards for outstanding classroom teaching of undergraduate and graduate students.

ISBN 0-89930-913-5

HARDCOVER BAR CODE

DATE DUE

Brodart Co.   Cat. # 55 137 001   Printed in USA